PENGUIN HANDBOOKS

The Penguin Guide to Su

Tony Lynes was born in 1929 and 1951. He studied social administration at the London School of Economics from 1956 to 1958. Since then he has researched and written on many aspects of social security. He was the first full-time secretary of the Child Poverty Action Group from 1966 to 1969 and an adviser to the Secretary of State for Social Services from 1974 to 1979. He received the 1984 Rosemary Delbridge Award for a one-man campaign which led to thousands of former claimants getting back payments of money wrongly deducted from their supplementary benefit.

Tony Lynes

THE PENGUIN GUIDE TO
Supplementary Benefits

*What you can claim
how to claim it
and how to appeal*

*Fifth Edition
with a Foreword by Lord Scarman*

Penguin Books

Penguin Books Ltd, Harmondsworth, Middlesex, England
Penguin Books, 40 West 23rd Street, New York, New York 10010, U.S.A.
Penguin Books Australia Ltd, Ringwood, Victoria, Australia
Penguin Books Canada Ltd, 2801 John Street, Markham, Ontario, Canada L3R 1B4
Penguin Books (N.Z.) Ltd, 182–190 Wairau Road, Auckland 10, New Zealand

First published 1972
Second edition 1974
Third edition 1975
Fourth edition 1981
Reprinted 1982
Fifth edition 1985

Made and printed in Great Britain by
Richard Clay (The Chaucer Press) Ltd, Bungay, Suffolk
Filmset in Monophoto Plantin

Contents

CONTENTS

6

9

CHAPTER 9
PAYMENTS TO THIRD PARTIES

Foreword to the 1981 Edition

BY THE RT. HON. LORD SCARMAN,
LORD OF APPEAL IN ORDINARY

The Penguin Guide to Supplementary Benefits is more than a guide. It is a modern classic. The lucidity of its exposition springs from the author's clarity of thought and his comprehensive knowledge of the subject. The fourth edition is timely. In 1980 Parliament introduced major changes in the legal structure of supplementary benefits. The Supplementary Benefits Commission has gone. The departmental officials, who acted for it in the local offices and made the initial decisions, have become 'benefit officers' responsible for their own decisions. They no longer exercise the wide, and, as it seemed to many, inexplicable discretions which before 1980 troubled claimants, advisers and observers of the system. Discretion has largely, though not totally, been replaced by detailed obligations imposed by Regulations. A high price has to be paid for converting discretion into legal rules: it is the price of complexity. No claimant can hope, unaided, to understand the Regulations. It is this gap in understanding which Tony Lynes's fourth edition of the *Guide* successfully bridges. He explains in clear, simple English the rights of claimants and the way in which they should tackle the job of obtaining them. It is not a law book (thank heavens!) but it will be very useful to lawyers and others who advise people in need.

The 1980 reforms are of very great importance. They are a logical development of the great principle that social security is not charity but a right. They recognize that all benefits payable to those in need, whether contributory or not, are interrelated rights to be administered in accordance with a body of consistent legal principle. The establishment of Social Security Commissioners, to whom appeals will go from Supplementary Benefit Appeal Tribunals, is more than a change of name and some additional functions for the National Insurance Commissioners. It is the establishment of a new legal order embracing all state benefits, whatever their source, available as a matter of right for those in need.

We have travelled a long way from Beveridge. He saw national insurance as the substantial protection of those in need. National assistance (now supplementary benefit) he saw merely as a safety net for those who could not claim insured benefits. The theory remains: but the reality is now otherwise. Supplementary benefit has become the very bedrock of social security. It exists so that every member of society may have his requirements met as of right. True it is that all a claimant's resources, including the benefits of national insurance, will be brought into the calculation of amount: but the right to receive enough by way of benefit to meet the requirements not merely of subsistence but of civilized living is basic. Supplementary benefit exists to satisfy that right.

Fortunately, there is nothing in Tony Lynes's book half as difficult to follow as this Foreword. That is as it should be. The author never overlooks his purpose – that of explaining in simple language a very complicated business. This book should find a place in every household in the Kingdom. It should not be necessary to go to a lawyer in order to claim benefit, save in the exceptional case: and, if you have this book at home, it will not be necessary. Of course, one hopes that a day will come when legal aid is available at tribunal hearings. But neither legal aid, nor even legal advice (which is already available), should ordinarily be needed. The law is inevitably complex, but most cases can be met without getting entangled in the law's complexities. Tony Lynes's *Guide* will see you through the maze – not always, but almost always. And, where it does not, it tells you where to go for help.

May 1981   Scarman

Foreword to the 1985 Edition

I welcome the fifth edition of Tony Lynes's 'classic'. There has been no change of principle in the law of supplementary benefits since the publication of the fourth edition. The process of bringing all social security benefits within the same legal framework has continued. The 'benefit officers' who decided supplementary benefit claims and the 'insurance officers' who performed the same function for national insurance benefits have been replaced by 'adjudication officers', with responsibilities covering the whole range of benefits. The Supplementary Benefit Appeal Tribunals have, similarly, been amalgamated with the National Insurance Tribunals to form a single body of Social Security Appeal Tribunals, whose independence is underlined by the appointment of Judge Byrt as the first President of Social Security Appeal Tribunals and the transfer of responsibility for administering the tribunal system from the Department of Health and Social Security to the Lord Chancellor's Office.

Subject to these changes, what I said in my foreword to the fourth edition applies with equal force to the present edition. We do, however, have more experience of the 1980 reforms than we had then. Despite the complexity of the regulations, claimants in their thousands have exercised their new right of appeal to the Social Security Commissioners – an indication that at least a minority of claimants are better informed, or better advised, than they were. Could this be a result of Tony Lynes's book? I think our author is entitled to some of the credit. The wider the book's distribution, the more effective the citizen is likely to be in establishing his entitlement to benefit.

January 1985   Scarman

Preface

The most important part of this book is the index. Much care has gone into making it as complete as possible. Without it, you may find that you have missed vital points affecting your rights or those of the person you are advising. So *please use it*.

Readers who are unfamiliar with the supplementary benefit scheme will also find it helpful to work through the examples in Appendix 1, which illustrate some of the main features of the scheme and show how the weekly benefit entitlement is calculated. Note, however, that the examples do not include any 'single payments' for exceptional needs, which are the subject of Chapter 7.

It is impossible to guarantee that any guide of this sort will be completely up to date, even on the day of publication. The supplementary benefit regulations are subject to frequent amendment and are constantly being reinterpreted by the Social Security Commissioners. This edition is based on the law as it stood in November 1984. New proposals for the treatment of people living in board and lodging accommodation, including private or voluntary hostels and residential homes, were published in November 1984. The proposals are summarized on page 64, but will probably be altered before coming into effect in April 1985. Other changes, resulting from the review of the scheme carried out in 1984, will probably be implemented in November 1985.

The most important regular change for most claimants is the annual 'up-rating' of benefit rates. The rates quoted in the following pages are those introduced in November 1984 and the examples given in the text and in Appendix 1 are based on those rates. The main rates are likely to be increased towards the end of November in each year by roughly the amount needed to compensate for the effect of inflation in the year up to the preceding May. The new rates are normally announced in June.

Acknowledgements

It is impossible to mention all those who have helped with successive editions of this book since it was first published in 1972, but I must acknowledge the continuing assistance I have received from officials at the Department of Health and Social Security and from the Child Poverty Action Group, whose annual publications, *National Welfare Benefits Handbook* and *Rights Guide to Non-means-tested Social Security Benefits*, are an indispensable aid to all who work in this field. For help with the present edition I would also like to thank Nick Raynsford and his colleagues at SHAC for their patient instruction in the mysteries of housing benefit, and the staff of the Peckham Citizens Advice Bureau for the opportunity of gaining some up-to-date practical experience of the working of the supplementary benefit scheme.

January 1985   Tony Lynes

Introduction

Supplementary benefit is the main safety net of the British social security system. Together with housing benefits, it goes a long way towards ensuring that nobody need fall below a minimum level of income which is intended to cover basic needs. At best, it is a low minimum – which makes it all the more important that people who qualify for supplementary benefit should not only claim it (many do not) but should receive their full entitlement.

This book is designed to help anyone who is either entitled to or already receiving supplementary benefit. It is also intended to help those who, in whatever capacity, advise claimants on their rights and help them to get what they are entitled to. Some of these advisers are qualified lawyers but most are not. So this is not a legal textbook – but it does aim to set out, in plain language, the legal rules of the scheme, as well as dealing with practical matters such as how to claim benefit, how to appeal, and what to do at an appeal hearing. Readers with no legal training should not be put off by the references to the regulations at the end of each chapter. For most purposes they can be ignored, but where disputes arise, and especially where the case has to be argued before an appeal tribunal, it is important to be able to point to the relevant provisions of the law.

This is not a guide to benefits for people in work. The supplementary benefit scheme normally excludes anyone in full-time employment. The housing benefit scheme provides benefits for people both in and out of work, but different rules apply to the two groups. The nearest equivalent to supplementary benefit for people in full-time work is the family income supplement (FIS), payable only to families with children. Chapter 15 provides a brief summary of these and other benefits for low-paid workers and some indications of where to look for more detailed information.

Social Security in Britain

Before describing the supplementary benefit scheme in detail, it may be helpful to give a brief summary of the broader framework of social security benefits of which it is a part.

The main form of state provision for those whose earnings are interrupted or terminated, and for their families, is the national insurance scheme, which provides benefits in return for contributions paid by insured persons and their employers. These *contributory* benefits are summarized in Table 1.

TABLE I: CONTRIBUTORY BENEFITS

Unemployment benefit	Flat-rate benefit payable after three days and continuing for up to a year.
Sickness benefit	Flat-rate benefit payable after three days for as long as incapacity for work continues or until replaced by invalidity pension; but not for any period covered by statutory sick pay (paid by employers for the first eight weeks of sickness, to be extended to 28 weeks from April 1986).
Invalidity benefit	(a) Flat-rate invalidity pension replacing sickness benefit after twenty-eight weeks of sickness and payable for as long as incapacity for work continues; (b) Invalidity allowance, varying with age at which incapacity began, provided this was more than five years before retirement pension age; (c) Additional earnings-related pension, based on earnings from 6 April 1978.
Maternity allowance	Flat-rate benefit for eighteen weeks, starting eleven weeks before baby is due, if the mother has worked and paid full contributions.
Retirement pension	(a) Basic pension paid on retirement at or after age 60 for women, 65 for men (may be reduced if earnings exceed £70 a week, but not after age 65 for women, 70 for men); (b) Graduated pension, based on earnings-related contributions between 6 April 1961 and 5 April 1975; (c) Additional earnings-related pension, based on earnings from 6 April 1978; (d) Increments earned by deferring retirement; (e) Addition for pensioners over 80.

Widow's benefits	(a) Flat-rate widow's allowance payable for first twenty-six weeks of widowhood;
	(b) Widowed mother's allowance payable when widow's allowance ceases, for as long as the widow has a son or daughter under 19 living with her;
	(c) Widow's pension payable *either* when widow's allowance ceases, if widow was over 40 on husband's death and is not entitled to widowed mother's allowance, *or* when widowed mother's allowance ceases if then over 40 (widow's pension is reduced if the widow is under 50 when husband dies or widowed mother's allowance ceases);
	(d) Earnings-related addition to widowed mother's allowance or widow's pension based on husband's earnings from 6 April 1978.
Child's special allowance	Payable to a divorced woman on her former husband's death, for a child towards whose maintenance he was contributing or liable to contribute.
Death grant	Lump sum payable on death.

Since all these benefits are subject to contribution conditions, some people do not get them because they have not paid (or been credited with) the right amount or 'class' of contributions. For instance, a man who has not contributed as either an employed or a self-employed person will not qualify for sickness benefit; and if he has contributed but has less than fifty times the minimum weekly contribution paid or credited in the last contribution year, he may qualify but his benefit will be reduced. A married woman who opted to pay the reduced married woman's contribution in the past and is still doing so does not earn a right to any of these benefits (for married women contributing for the first time the option no longer exists, and those still paying reduced contributions can change over to full contributions at any time).

A number of other benefits do not depend on contributions. These *non-contributory* benefits are summarized in Table 2. The table excludes benefits which are subject to a means test. It also excludes the industrial injuries and war pensions schemes, referred to below.

The disablement benefits shown in Table 2 – attendance allowance, mobility allowance and severe disablement allowance – are paid regardless of the cause of disability, but there is a separate and more generous *industrial injuries* scheme for employees suffering from the effects of accidents at work and industrial diseases. It provides a

TABLE 2: NON-CONTRIBUTORY BENEFITS

Child benefit	£6.85 per week for each child under 16 (or under 19 but still at school), payable whether the parents are in work or not. An extra 'one-parent benefit' of £4.25 per week is paid for the first child in a one-parent family. Child benefit is paid to whoever has responsibility for the child – not necessarily the parents.
Maternity grant	Lump sum payable either before or up to three months after the birth of a child.
Severe disablement allowance	Flat-rate benefit at a lower rate for people of working age, not entitled to invalidity benefit, who have been incapable of work for at least 28 weeks and are severely disabled, or were receiving a non-contributory invalidity pension in November 1984.
Attendance allowance	Flat-rate allowance for severely disabled people needing attention or supervision including children aged 2 or over. The disablement can be physical or mental.
Non-contributory retirement pension	Flat-rate pension at a lower rate than the basic retirement pension, for those over 80 who would not otherwise get this amount of pension.
Guardian's allowance	Payable to a person providing a home for a child whose parents are both dead. Can sometimes be paid on the death of only one parent where the parents are divorced; where the child is illegitimate and the mother is dead; or where the surviving parent cannot be traced or is serving a long prison sentence.
Invalid care allowance	Benefit for a person of working age, other than a married woman, caring for a severely disabled person who is getting attendance allowance. The allowance can continue after pension age.
Mobility allowance	Allowance for physically disabled adults under 65 and children aged 5 or over, unable or virtually unable to walk. On reaching age 65, a person already getting the allowance can continue to receive it.

disablement benefit based on the degree of disablement and supplemented by various additional allowances including a 'special hardship' allowance for loss of earning power. In cases of relatively slight disability, disablement benefit may be paid in a lump sum rather than as a weekly pension. A widow whose husband died as a result of an industrial accident or disease gets a more generous pension, and in some circumstances a pension or gratuity can be paid to a widower or other relative.

The *war pensions* scheme provides similar disablement pensions and death benefits. Although new awards are comparatively few, there are still many people drawing war pensions awarded in the past.

Many of the benefits in Tables 1 and 2 can be increased by allowances for a wife or husband and children. For example, an unemployed man receiving £28.45 per week unemployment benefit for himself is entitled to an addition of £17.55 for his wife, provided that her net earnings, if any, are not more than £17.55 after deducting national insurance contributions, fares and other work expenses. If the wife is unemployed, she can claim the same addition for her husband provided that his net earnings are not more than £17.55.

Retirement and invalidity pensions and widows' benefits, all regarded as long-term benefits, are paid at higher rates. The basic rate of retirement pension, widow's pension and widowed mother's allowance is £35.80 per week. The addition for the wife of a retirement pensioner (there is no similar allowance for a pensioner's husband) is £21.50; but if she is over 60 she gets the £21.50 as her own pension, unless she is entitled to a bigger pension on her own contribution record. The addition for a 'dependent' wife under 60 is reduced if her net earnings are more than £45 a week.

Child benefit is paid in addition to any other benefits the parents may be receiving, but a person receiving one of the long-term benefits gets an additional allowance of £7.65 for each child. But widows and other single parents getting this addition are either debarred from receiving the £4.25 one-parent benefit or, if they do receive it, have their other benefits reduced by the same amount.

Until 1980 there were two basic rates for the main weekly contributory benefits – one for the long-term benefits and one for the short-term (sickness benefit, unemployment benefit and maternity allowance). In 1980, the Government reduced by 5 per cent those benefits which were not then taxable, with a half-promise that the cuts would be restored once the benefits became taxable. As a result, sickness benefit and maternity allowance, which are still not taxed, are slightly lower than unemployment benefit; and, for the same reason, the basic invalidity benefit rate is slightly lower than the basic retirement pension, but this cut is to be restored in November 1985.

The Supplementary Benefit Scheme

The benefits listed in Tables 1 and 2 provide for a wide variety of circumstances which might otherwise cause financial hardship. Why, then, is it necessary to have yet another scheme from which, at the end of 1983, benefits were being paid to 4.3 million people to meet their own needs and those of 2.9 million wives and children – altogether 7.2 million people?

There are two reasons. The first is that where national insurance and similar benefits are available they are often inadequate, even when added to the claimant's other resources. This is most obviously true of the non-contributory benefits, such as severe disablement allowance, which are generally paid at much lower rates than those earned by contributions. But it is also true of the main national insurance benefits which, in very many cases, are below the levels of income provided by the supplementary benefit scheme. One of the main functions of supplementary benefit, therefore, is to top up the benefits payable under the national insurance scheme. In these cases it is truly 'supplementary'. But the supplementary benefit scheme also provides an income for a very large number of people – much larger than a few years ago, as a result of high unemployment – who are not entitled to national insurance benefits and are in many cases wholly or mainly dependent on supplementary benefit for their weekly income. In addition to unemployed people who have exhausted their entitlement to unemployment benefit, they include single parents, people looking after sick relatives, strikers and a variety of other people who do not satisfy the conditions for payment of insurance benefits.

The Adjudication Officer

Before November 1980, the responsibility for making decisions on individual claims for supplementary benefit lay with the Supplementary Benefits Commission, a body appointed for this purpose by the Secretary of State for Social Services. In practice these decisions were made on behalf of the Commission by officials of the Department of Health and Social Security, working in local social security offices. But the Commission was legally responsible for each decision and it issued detailed guidance to local office staff on the ways in which different types of cases were to be dealt with and, in particular, how the Commission's discretionary powers were to be used.

In November 1980, all this changed. The Supplementary Benefits

Commission was wound up. The officials who had acted as its agents in the local offices became 'benefit officers', appointed individually by the Secretary of State and directly responsible for their own decisions. Most of the Commission's discretionary powers – including the power to make weekly additions for 'exceptional circumstances' and lump sum payments for 'exceptional needs' – were replaced by legally binding regulations, on which the benefit officers had to base their decisions. To ensure that they used their powers with reasonable consistency and fairness, and in accordance with the law, a Chief Supplementary Benefit Officer was appointed, to issue general guidance as the Commission had done in the past and to advise on individual cases when necessary.

The roles of the benefit officers and the Chief Benefit Officer were copied from the system of adjudication that already existed under the national insurance scheme. Decisions on claims for insurance benefits, and also for the non-contributory benefits listed in Table 2, were made by 'insurance officers' under the guidance of the Chief Insurance Officer. In April 1984, the two systems were amalgamated. Benefit officers and insurance officers were all renamed *adjudication officers* – the term that is used throughout this book – and the functions of the two chief officers were transferred to a Chief Adjudication Officer, appointed by the Secretary of State, whose duties are:

(a) To advise adjudication officers on the performance of their functions;

(b) To keep under review the operation of the adjudication officer system and matters connected with it;

(c) To report annually to the Secretary of State (who must publish the report) on the standards of adjudication.

The guidance issued to adjudication officers on how to carry out their decision-making functions under the Supplementary Benefits Act now comes from the Chief Adjudication Officer, and is at present incorporated in the two loose-leaf volumes of the *S Manual*. But the individual adjudication officers, as independent authorities under the Act, remain responsible for ensuring that their decisions are in accordance with the law.

A claimant who is dissatisfied with a decision made by an adjudication officer has a right of appeal to a Social Security Appeal Tribunal, and a further right of appeal on a question of law to a Social Security Commissioner. The appeals system is described more fully in Chapter 16.

The Legal Framework

The Supplementary Benefits Act 1976, extensively amended by the Social Security Act 1980, provides the main legal framework of the supplementary benefit scheme. Most of the detailed rules of the scheme are to be found in regulations made by the Secretary of State for Social Services under the 1976 Act and approved by Parliament. Since the introduction of a right of appeal to a Commissioner in 1980, there has been a rapid growth of case law in this field, as Commissioners' decisions must be followed in subsequent cases, both by adjudication officers and by appeal tribunals. There has also been a much smaller number of High Court and Appeal Court decisions relating to supplementary benefit in recent years. The law of supplementary benefits comprises all these elements: Acts, regulations and case law.

Publications

For most purposes, this book should provide sufficient information about both the law and the Chief Adjudication Officer's guidance. Anyone involved in an appeal to a local tribunal or to a Social Security Commissioner may, however, want to find out exactly what the Act and regulations say or to look up the relevant Commissioners' decisions. They may also want to look up the Chief Adjudication Officer's guidance in the *S Manual*, though that guidance is addressed only to adjudication officers and is in no way binding on either the appeal tribunals or the Commissioners.

For the Acts and regulations, as amended, there are two reasonably accessible sources. One is a loose-leaf volume published by HM Stationery Office, *The Law Relating to Supplementary Benefits and Family Income Supplements*, often referred to as the 'Yellow Book'. It contains the full text of the relevant Acts and regulations and is kept more or less up to date by supplements issued from time to time. The price of the book itself depends on how many supplements to the current edition have to be bought with it; in November 1984 it was £60.65. Far better value for money is *CPAG's Supplementary Benefit and Family Income Supplement: the Legislation*, by John Mesher (published by Sweet and Maxwell, 2nd edition, 1985, price £13.00). As well as the Supplementary Benefits Act itself and the regulations, it provides a helpful commentary and numerous references to decisions of the Commissioners and the courts.

Only a selection of Commissioners' decisions is published. These are known as 'reported decisions' and are those which command the assent of a majority of Commissioners and are thought to 'contribute to an orderly development of the law'. Information about some of the unreported decisions can be found in various publications, including the *Welfare Rights Bulletin* published by the Child Poverty Action Group, but the decisions themselves are not published. Adjudication officers normally rely only on the reported decisions, but unreported decisions are equally binding on both adjudication officers and appeal tribunals, and it may sometimes be helpful for claimants to know about them. Most of the references to Commissioners' decisions in this book are to reported decisions, but a few unreported decisions are also mentioned. The reported decisions can be distinguished by their reference numbers which start with the prefix R(SB), while unreported decisions have reference numbers which begin with the letters CSB, CSSB or CWSB (see, for examples of both, references 52–60 on page 50).

The *S Manual* includes not only the Chief Adjudication Officer's guidance on the law, its interpretation and the use of such discretionary powers as adjudication officers still possess, but also a mass of procedural instructions to DHSS officials, for which the Chief Adjudication Officer is not responsible. It is published by the DHSS, not by HM Stationery Office, and the price includes a year's supply of amendments (currently £32.50 from DHSS Leaflets, PO Box 21, Stanmore, Middx HA7 1AY).

The only official guide to the scheme intended mainly for use by the public is the *Supplementary Benefits Handbook*. Readers of this book will find in it nearly all the information given in the official *Handbook*, often in more detail, but it is sometimes useful to be able to quote from an official publication. The *Handbook* is published by HM Stationery Office and the current (1984) edition costs £2.50. New editions are issued every year or two.

It is the policy of the Department of Health and Social Security to make all these official publications – the *Handbook*, the 'Yellow Book', reported Commissioners' decisions and the *S Manual* – available for consultation by members of the public at local social security offices. The precise arrangements are left to the manager of the office to decide. Local reference libraries should also hold copies of at least some of these volumes, but probably not all. Citizens Advice Bureaux all have the *Handbook* and the 'Yellow Book' and some also have the *S Manual*, but these are mainly for use by the staff of the Bureau, not by members of the public.

Information Leaflets

For those who want only simple, basic information about the scheme, perhaps to pass on to somebody who may be entitled to benefit, a number of leaflets are obtainable free from any social security office and from other sources including Citizens Advice Bureaux. Some provide general information, in particular leaflets SB 8 and SB 9 which are normally issued to people when they first claim supplementary benefit (SB 9 for unemployed claimants, SB 8 for others) and are intended to help them check the calculation of their benefit. Other leaflets deal with particular aspects of the scheme, such as help with heating costs (SB 17), weekly payments for special needs (SB 19), lump sum payments for special needs (SB 16), the treatment of capital resources (SB 18), unmarried couples living as husband and wife (SB 7) and trade disputes (SB 2). Local social security offices are expected to meet requests for up to five of any of the leaflets. Larger quantities can be ordered, free, from DHSS Leaflets, PO Box 21, Stanmore, Middx HA7 1AY.

The 'Passport' Benefits

Anyone receiving supplementary benefit is automatically entitled to certain other benefits and exemptions both for himself or herself and for other members of the 'assessment unit' (wife or husband and dependent children). Because supplementary benefit acts as a 'passport' to these benefits, they are sometimes known as 'passport benefits'. They include:

Exemption from prescription charges.

Free dental treatment and glasses (but only under the national health service).

Refund of fares for attending hospital for treatment under the national health service.

Free milk (a pint a day or baby milk) and vitamins for an expectant mother and/or a child under five.

Free school meals.

Free legal advice, subject to a capital limit (for details see page 282).

28

Chapter 1

Getting Supplementary Benefit

The Right to Benefit

The basic right to supplementary benefit is laid down in section 1 of the Supplementary Benefits Act 1976. Section 1, as amended, states that, subject to the provisions of the Act, 'every person in Great Britain of or over the age of 16 whose resources are insufficient to meet his requirements shall be entitled to benefit' in the form of a *supplementary pension* or a *supplementary allowance*. If the claimant is a single person over pension age (65 for men, 60 for women) or, in the case of a married couple, either the husband or the wife is over 65, they get a supplementary pension; if not, a supplementary allowance. In most cases the same rules apply to supplementary pensions and supplementary allowances. Throughout this book, therefore, the term 'supplementary benefit' is used for both kinds of benefit.

Supplementary benefit is normally paid weekly (or fortnightly if the claimant is unemployed) and is intended to provide for the requirements of the 'assessment unit' (see page 51) for the week, after taking into account any other resources they may have. In addition, a claimant may be entitled to 'single payments' from time to time under section 3 of the Act, to meet 'exceptional needs'. These are dealt with in Chapter 7 and they include a wide range of items, some of which are hardly 'exceptional', such as babies' nappies, blankets and sheets.

Finally, section 4 of the Supplementary Benefits Act provides for the payment of benefit 'in urgent cases', subject to special rules – see Chapter 8.

In most cases, there is a clear legal right to benefit, provided that the claimant's capital is not over £3,000 (excluding the value of his home) and that any income from other sources is less than the amount allowed for the weekly needs of the claimant or couple and their dependent children. But some people, mentioned below, are not entitled to supplementary benefit, however low their income may be, or can only get urgent need payments which they may have to repay. Others, such as

29

strikers and those regarded as voluntarily unemployed, have their benefit reduced below the normal level.

A person under 60 who is unemployed and not prevented from doing paid work by illness, the care of children or other domestic circumstances will usually have to be available for work as a condition of receiving supplementary benefit (except on grounds of urgent need – see Chapter 8).

People Who Cannot Claim

Full-time workers

People in full-time paid work cannot receive supplementary benefit,[1]* with the following exceptions:

(a) In an 'urgent case' (see Chapter 8);[2]

(b) During the first fifteen days after starting or restarting work (see page 267);[3]

(c) Disabled people who are self-employed and whose earning power, because of their disability, is substantially lower than that of other people in the same occupation ('substantially' is not defined but adjudication officers are told to regard a loss of earning power of 25 per cent or more as substantial);[4]

(d) A person who is 'engaged in minding children in the home and performs normal household duties';[5]

(e) Anyone on a government training scheme who is receiving a training allowance.[6]

Under (d), a full-time child-minder, looking after other people's children in her own home, can receive supplementary benefit. Adjudication officers are told that this also applies to 'a lone parent employed as a housekeeper who, as well as performing normal household duties, looks after her own and her employer's children (if any), provided that she is normally resident in her employer's home and regards it as her own'.[7] But it seems that the child-minder, whether living in her own or her employer's home, is only entitled to benefit if she has a child of her own, since she would otherwise be required to be available for employment.

Whether benefit is actually payable in any of these cases will depend on whether the person's earnings and other resources are enough to cover their needs. Note, in particular, that if the earnings are unduly

* References are printed at the end of each chapter.

low for the work done a higher figure may be assumed in calculating entitlement to supplementary benefit (see page 121).

In the case of a married couple, the fact that one partner is in full-time work need not prevent the other from claiming benefit if their combined resources are not sufficient to meet their requirements (the rules for deciding which of them can claim are explained below – pages 36–40).

A person in full-time work who is not eligible for supplementary benefit but who has a low income and at least one child may qualify for a family income supplement (FIS). The circumstances in which persons in full-time work may receive supplementary benefit or FIS are explained more fully in Chapter 15.

People recently in full-time work

Anyone under pension age (or over pension age but not yet retired) who claims supplementary benefit (except on retirement) after a period in full-time work will be treated as if still in work, and therefore not entitled to supplementary benefit, for a period of the same duration as the periods covered by the final payment or payments of wages or salary – including holiday pay or payment in lieu of notice.[8] The payments are treated as having been made on the day on which they were due,[9] unless for some reason they are not then available[10] – for example, because the employer has gone into liquidation.

Example: Jane Doe stopped work on Wednesday, 1 August. She received 4 days' wages and 8 days' holiday pay on the Friday, 3 August – 12 days' pay in all. She is therefore treated as being still in full-time work for 12 working days from Friday, 3 August, to Monday, 20 August (she worked a 5-day week when in employment). Supplementary benefit is payable from Tuesday, 21 August.

In the case of a monthly-paid employee, the payment will be treated as having been made on the normal monthly pay-day and the claimant will be treated as in full-time work for the appropriate number of days counting from then.

If the last earnings include bonus or commission for a different period from the wages or salary, the claimant is treated as in full-time work for a further period based on normal earnings spread over a 5-day week.[11] For example, if normal weekly earnings are £100 and the last payment consists of a week's wages plus £180 commission for an earlier period, the combined payment is treated as earnings for two weeks and four days.

The normal effect of these rules is that somebody who is paid weekly does not qualify for supplementary benefit for the first week after stopping work, while a monthly paid worker does not qualify for the first month. The period of disqualification is longer if the last wage or salary payment is for more than a week or a month, as the case may be. The disqualification period, however, cannot begin before the week in which the wages or salary is payable.[12] If that is after the date of stopping work, the claimant may be entitled to benefit in the interim, which may be as long as three or four weeks in the case of a monthly paid worker. Such entitlement would be unusual, because the previous wage or salary payment would normally cover that period (for example, if a full month's pay was received at the end of the previous month, it will be treated as available to meet the current month's living expenses). If the previous payment was for less than a full week or month, however, or if when spread over the appropriate period it leaves the claimant with an income below supplementary benefit level, benefit may be payable.

A similar but simpler rule applies to anybody who before claiming supplementary benefit was self-employed. He or she is treated as being still in full-time work and not entitled to benefit for the first fourteen days after stopping work, regardless of the amount of recent earnings or the date on which they were received.[13]

Strikers and people laid off because of a strike or lock-out

A man directly involved, however unwillingly, in a strike or lock-out cannot receive benefit for himself, except in very limited circumstances on grounds of urgent need, but he can claim for his wife and children, subject to a special deduction. Similarly, a woman involved in a strike may be able to claim for her husband and children but not for herself. A single striker, therefore, is not usually entitled to benefit. See Chapter 13.

Young people staying on at school

A young person over 16 but under 19 and still receiving full-time non-advanced education at a school or other recognized educational establishment cannot normally claim supplementary benefit, but child benefit remains payable to the parents. A full-time non-advanced course is one that is recognized as such for child benefit purposes.[14] Courses leading

32

to GCE A-levels (SCE 'Highers' in Scotland) or Ordinary National Certificate or Diploma count as non-advanced; those leading to a degree, Higher National Diploma or teaching qualification do not.[15] A non-advanced course can be at a school, sixth-form college, college of further education or, if special arrangements are made by the local authority, in hospital or at home. A course is treated as 'full-time' for child benefit purposes (and therefore for supplementary benefit) if it occupies more than 12 hours a week, excluding homework. (For the treatment of claimants taking *advanced* or *part-time* courses, see pages 255–9).

The simple test to be applied in most cases is whether child benefit is payable: if it is, the young person cannot claim supplementary benefit. But there are some exceptions. A young person over 16 who is still at school is not barred from receiving supplementary benefit if he or she is:

(a) responsible for a child of his or her own living in the same household. This means that a schoolgirl mother aged 16 or over can claim; but not if her parents are bringing up the child as a member of their own family, since they are then regarded as responsible for the child.

(b) severely handicapped, mentally or physically, and for this reason would be unlikely to obtain employment within twelve months if he or she were not at school.

(c) without parents and with no one acting in their place.

(d) estranged from his or her parents and living apart from them.

(e) taking a part-time course, subject to certain conditions (see pages 258–9), and prepared to give it up if a suitable job is available.[16]

If the pupil's parents are receiving child benefit for him or her, this will cease when supplementary benefit commences. In the case of a handicapped young person, the possibility of claiming a severe disablement allowance (see page 22) should also be considered; it will not affect subsequent entitlement to the long-term rate of supplementary benefit (see page 53).

On reaching the age of 19, young people still in full-time education are no longer treated as their parents' dependants for supplementary benefit purposes; but they are normally not entitled to benefit in their own right because they are not available for employment (see below, AVAILABILITY FOR WORK). If they qualify under one of the headings (a) to (d) above, however, the availability condition is waived until their twentieth birthday.[17] They can therefore stay on at school for an extra year and continue to receive benefit. For the treatment of other students over 19, see pages 256–7.

School-leavers

A young person leaving school cannot claim supplementary benefit immediately unless he or she is already 19 or over. School-leavers under 19 have to wait until whichever of the following dates is nearest:

The first Monday in January.
The Monday following Easter Monday.
The first Monday in September.
The Monday before their nineteenth birthday.

Until then, their parents can continue to draw child benefit for them, unless they are in full-time work or training, and to treat them as dependants for the purpose of any other benefit claim.[18]

Students

Most full-time students cannot claim supplementary benefit during term time, but there are some exceptions. The rules regarding both full-time and part-time students are explained in Chapter 14 (pages 255–9).

Availability for Work

A person under 60 who is unemployed and not prevented from doing paid work by illness, the care of children or other circumstances will usually have to be available for employment as a condition of receiving supplementary benefit [19] (except on grounds of urgent need – see Chapter 8). Normally this means being available for at least thirty hours a week of paid work of a kind that the person can reasonably be expected to do. People who are disabled and cannot work thirty hours a week have to be available for the number of hours they are usually capable of working.[20]

Claimants who, though under 60, are *not* required to be available for work are listed in regulation 6 of the Conditions of Entitlement Regulations. They fall into three broad categories – the sick and disabled; those with domestic responsibilities; and others for whom the requirement is inappropriate:

1. Sick and disabled

(a) People who are incapable of work through sickness or disablement – subject to medical evidence.

(b) Blind people who cannot do any work for which eyesight is essential and who for the last twelve months have not been used to working outside their home.

(c) Physically or mentally disabled people who have no prospects of employment and who in the last twelve months have worked on average less than four hours a week, have been available for employment for at least thirty-nine weeks, and have made reasonable efforts to find work and not refused any suitable employment.

(d) Severely handicapped school pupils and disabled students (see categories (j) and (k) on page 36).

(e) People who, because of sickness or disablement, cannot work full-time, but are doing part-time work for the number of hours per week that they are usually capable of working.

(f) Self-employed disabled people who, though working full-time, are not disqualified for supplementary benefit (see pages 268–9).

2. Domestic responsibilities

(a) Single parents with a child under 16 living with them – including single foster-parents where the foster-child has been with them for at least six months.

(b) Anyone caring for a sick husband, wife or child where the illness is temporary and no other arrangement can be made.

(c) Anyone 'regularly and substantially' engaged in caring for a severely disabled person who is either receiving an attendance allowance or would qualify for an 'additional requirement' for attendance needs (i.e. is awaiting the result of a claim for attendance allowance or intends to claim after the six months qualifying period – see page 76); but the requirement to be available for employment will not be waived for more than six months if other arrangements can be made for the care of the disabled person.

(d) A father, mother, brother, sister, aunt, uncle or grandparent looking after a child because the parent who normally does so is absent or ill – but if the person is not the child's father or mother, he or she must be living in the household of one of the parents.

3. Others

(a) An expectant mother within eleven weeks of the expected date of confinement, or within fifteen weeks if there are no suitable job vacancies – or at any time when she is unable to work because of her pregnancy.

(b) A woman aged 50 or over (or, less usually, a man aged 55 or over) who has been neither employed nor required to be available for employment during the past ten years and now has no employment prospects and lacks the training or experience to get back into employment.

35

(c) People receiving government training allowances, e.g. on a TOPS course or under the Youth Training Scheme.

(d) People receiving allowances under the Job Release scheme.

(e) Anyone who has to attend a court for three days or more, either as a party to the proceedings or as a JP, juror or witness.

(f) Open University students attending a residential course.

(g) A prisoner on remand or awaiting trial or sentence.

(h) A newly discharged prisoner who has not received a discharge grant (the availability requirement is waived for up to 7 days if it would be unreasonable to impose it).

(i) A refugee taking an English-language course so that he can get a job. The course must be more than 15 hours a week and have started within 12 months of his arrival in Great Britain. The availability requirement is waived for up to six months, extended to nine months if further tuition is needed.

(j) School pupils who are entitled to benefit in the exceptional circumstances mentioned under headings (a) to (d) on page 33.

(k) Students entitled to benefit during term time in the exceptional circumstances mentioned on page 256, including disabled students.

(l) People who already have a job and are getting supplementary benefit during the first fifteen days after starting work (see page 267).

(m) People affected by a trade dispute or claiming benefit during the fifteen days after returning to work (see Chapter 13).

(n) People receiving urgent need payments (this exemption is not, in fact, mentioned in regulation 6 but in the Urgent Cases Regulations – see page 183).

If the case does not fit into any of categories (a) to (m) but is 'analogous' to one of them, the benefit officer must waive the availability requirement if he thinks it would be unreasonable.[21]

Anyone under 60 who does not fall into one of the categories listed above and whose situation is not 'analogous' will be required to be available for employment. Provided that this requirement is satisfied, it will not normally make any difference to the amount of benefit payable in the short term. It may, however, affect entitlement to the higher long-term benefit rates if the claimant remains on benefit for a year or more, and a claimant previously getting benefit at the long-term rate will lose that advantage on becoming subject to the availability requirement. In a doubtful case, therefore, it may be worth appealing against the requirement.

Married Couples – Deciding Who Should Claim

A married couple, or a couple who are living as husband and wife though not legally married, are treated as a single unit for supplementary benefit purposes. Either the husband or the wife may be entitled to claim supplementary benefit, but they cannot both receive it at the same time so long as they are living together. Whoever makes the claim, benefit is assessed on their joint needs, taking into account their combined income and savings.[22]

In some cases the couple can choose which of them should make the claim. In other cases only one of them can do so.

Claimants under pension age

If the couple are already getting a family income supplement (FIS) and only one of them was in full-time work when FIS commenced, he or she must be the supplementary benefit claimant, at least until the FIS payments come to an end (they are normally made for 52 weeks) or, if the wife is the claimant and gives up full-time work because she is pregnant, until fifteen weeks before the birth is expected.[23]

In any other case, the claimant, whether the husband or the wife, must show that he or she was in one or more of the situations listed below for all or nearly all the six-month period preceding the claim (gaps of up to 21 days are ignored) or that neither of them can satisfy this condition. The situations are:

(a) Working for at least 8 hours a week, or off work because of a trade dispute at the place of work.

(b) Unemployed and available for work (either signing on at the unemployment benefit office or registered at a job centre or careers office), or an unemployed man over 60 no longer required to sign on.

(c) Unable to work because of sickness for which either a cash benefit was paid or contribution credits given.

(d) Getting an invalid care allowance (see page 22).

(e) On supplementary benefit and not required to be available for employment because of domestic responsibilities (a single parent, or caring for a child because of a parent's illness or absence or for a sick or disabled adult or child – see page 35, paragraphs 2(a) to (d)).

(f) Not entitled to supplementary benefit because either at school or a student.

(g) On a government training or similar course, including the Youth Training Scheme.

(h) Abroad or in prison.

It is not necessary to have been in the same situation for the whole six-month period. A claimant might, for example, have been working part of the time and unemployed the rest of the time.[24]

Claimants over pension age

If either the wife or the husband has reached pension age (60 for a woman, 65 for a man), she/he can be the claimant if *either* the conditions applicable to claimants under pension age are satisfied *or* she or he is getting a retirement pension based on her/his own contributions or has retired from full-time work not more than five years before pension age.[25]

Where there is a choice

When a claim is made by a husband or wife, the social security office checks that he or she is eligible to claim and asks whether the other partner has agreed to him or her making the claim. If they are both eligible but they either do not agree or cannot decide who should claim, officers are told to ensure that they are given leaflet N I 248 which explains the alternatives, and if necessary to interview them. If, after all this, they still cannot make an agreed decision, the decision is made by the social security office acting on behalf of the Secretary of State for Social Services. There is no right of appeal against this decision. Officials are instructed to base it on such factors as which partner 'has the strongest connection with the employment field', which of them pays the bills and which of them is getting other benefits such as unemployment benefit; but if there is a financial advantage in one of them claiming, he or she should normally be chosen as the claimant.[26]

In most cases, the amount of benefit payable will be the same whichever partner claims it. The main practical difference is that the claimant, unless over 60 or excused for other reasons (see pages 34–6), will be required to sign on at the unemployment benefit office and be available for work, while the non-claiming partner will not. In some cases, however, the choice of claimant may affect entitlement to the higher long-term rates of benefit, which are payable to claimants under 60 who have received supplementary benefit or long-term incapacity benefits for a year without having been required to be available for work (see pages 53–4). Where there is a choice, therefore, if one partner would have to be available for work and the other would not, it is generally better for the one who would not to make the claim.

If a claim is delayed because the couple need guidance on who should make it, this should be accepted as 'good cause' for the late claim (see page 43) and it should be backdated to the date on which the couple first notified their intention of claiming.[27] If one partner's claim has been turned down and the other partner makes a claim for the same period as soon as is 'reasonably practicable' after the refusal, the second claim *must* be backdated to the date of the first.[28]

Switching claimants

A couple can change their choice of claimant in any of these circumstances:

(a) If at least 52 weeks have passed since the start of the claim or since the last change of claimant, whichever is later.

(b) If the non-claiming partner did not satisfy the conditions for being a claimant set out on pages 37–8 when the claim was first made, but now does.

(c) If the claimant is required to be available for work and the non-claiming partner would not be (as explained above, it is generally better for the partner who is not required to be available for work to be the claimant).

(d) If there is a change in the family's circumstances which, in the adjudication officer's opinion, makes it reasonable to allow them to switch claimants – but if one of them is or would be required to be available for work, the change must be of a kind that affects their ability to satisfy that condition (for example, where a child previously living elsewhere joins the family).

(e) If they have been getting FIS and either the FIS payments have come to an end or the wife is the claimant and has given up full-time work to have a baby (in which case the change of claimant cannot take place more than fifteen weeks before the baby is due).[29]

Notification of the wish to switch claimants must be given in writing to the social security office, which will require confirmation that this is what both partners want. If they disagree, the social security office will decide, on behalf of the Secretary of State, whether the switch should be allowed.[30]

If the conditions for switching claimants were satisfied at an earlier date, and the couple so request, the change must be backdated, provided that throughout the intervening period there was good cause for the delay in making the change.[31] Ignorance of the complex rules on this subject or the fact that the couple did not fully understand the implications of one partner or the other being the claimant can be accepted as good cause for the delay.

If the non-claiming partner is eligible to claim but the conditions for switching claimants are not satisfied, it is possible to get round the rules by the claimant informing the social security office that he/she is ceasing to claim. A new claim can then be made by the other partner.[32] But this will seldom be advisable and should not be done without first ensuring that the change cannot be made otherwise and that the other partner will in fact be entitled to benefit.

How to Claim

Supplementary benefit must be claimed in writing. The normal method of claiming, except for unemployed people, is to get form SB 1 from the post office, which will also supply on request an envelope addressed to the local social security office – it does not need a stamp. All that need be written on the form is the claimant's name, address and date of birth. Retirement pensioners can use the form included in their pension order book. But there is no need to use an official form – a letter to the social security office will do. A claim by telephone can also be accepted provided that it is confirmed in writing, but the social security office may decide that the starting date of the claim should be the day on which written confirmation is received rather than the date of the telephone call.[33] A claim should normally be signed by the claimant in person. If, for example, he/she is too ill, someone else can make the claim but the claimant will be asked to confirm it in writing. If a person is incapable of dealing with his or her own claim, somebody else can be appointed to do so (see pages 208–9).

Anyone claiming because they are unemployed should get form B 1 from the unemployment benefit office. This is a longer form which asks for far more information about the claimant's circumstances – information which other claimants have to give in the course of an interview with a social security official. Using the longer form normally means that there is no need for an interview, but anyone who has difficulty in completing the form can get help with it at the social security office. Any special needs which may affect the amount of benefit (see Chapter 3) should be entered on the form. The claim is treated as having been made on the day on which the claimant applies for form B 1 at the unemployment benefit office, but if the completed form is not received at the social security office within twenty-one days the claim can be treated as having been withdrawn, unless there was a good reason for the delay.[34] The form should therefore be sent in as soon as possible, partially completed if necessary.

The Department of Health and Social Security is planning to introduce longer claim forms of this kind for all claimants, not just those who are unemployed. Meanwhile, claimants who apply on the simple SB 1 claim form are usually interviewed either at home or at the social security office (fares to the office are partially refunded in some cases – see pages 174–5). People over pension age who do not want to be visited at home will always be seen at the social security office if they make their wishes known. The main object of the interview is to obtain the information needed to calculate the benefit payable, if any. Social security offices aim to make home visits, where necessary, within a week of receiving the claim – sooner if the claimant is known to be in urgent need. The date from which benefit starts depends on when the claim was made, not on the date of the interview, so delays in visiting claimants should not cause any loss of benefit.

Claimants are required by the regulations to provide any certificates, documents, information and evidence that are needed to decide the claim, and to keep any reasonable appointment made for that purpose.[35] If a claimant fails to attend for an interview at the social security office, is not at home when advance notice of a visit has been given, or does not return a form with the information requested within twenty-one days, the claim may be treated as withdrawn unless a reasonable explanation of the failure is given.[36]

The Adjudication Officer's Decision

A claim for benefit, or any question arising in connection with a claim, must be dealt with by the social security office by submitting it 'forthwith' to an adjudication officer for decision,[37] and the adjudication officer must then, so far as practicable, make a decision within fourteen days. Alternatively, he has the power to refer the claim or question to an appeal tribunal instead of deciding it himself.[38]

When the adjudication officer has made a decision, the claimant must be informed of it in writing, unless the decision is implemented by a cash payment or it is a decision that benefit is no longer payable and it is reasonable not to give written notice (for example where the claimant already knows the reason). The claimant must also be informed of the right of appeal and the right to ask for a statement of reasons for the decision within twenty-eight days. If the decision is that supplementary benefit is payable, or would be payable but for the claimant's other income, a 'notice of assessment' must also be sent, if practicable, showing in broad outline how the benefit is or would be calculated.[39] The form used for this purpose, A 14 N, is a carbon copy of part of the assessment form, but much of the detail is omitted (much clearer printed notices of assessment will be provided when computers are installed in local offices for this purpose). The claimant should also have received a leaflet explaining supplementary benefit (SB 9 for unemployed claimants, SB 8 for others), which may help in making sense of the assessment. A more detailed explanation of the assessment will be supplied on request, usually on another form, A 124. Claimants should not hesitate to ask for this. The officials' instructions say, 'Ensure that form A 124 is completed so that it can be easily understood by members of the public. Do not use abbreviations or jargon.'[40]

Pay Days

Each claimant is given a regular pay day, and payment of benefit normally starts on the pay day following the claim, or on the day of the claim if it is the pay day.[41] Claimants who are also receiving a national insurance benefit generally have their supplementary benefit paid on the same day of the week. Those who are unemployed or sick but are not entitled to an insurance benefit get supplementary benefit on the day when the insurance benefit would have been paid. Pay day for most other claimants is Monday.[42]

Unemployed claimants who do not qualify for benefit until after the period covered by their final earnings (see pages 31–2) can get a first payment of benefit on the first day that they qualify, even if it is not their normal pay day.[43] This first payment will only be enough to cover their needs for the number of days remaining until the first pay day.

A claimant in immediate need of money may be entitled to an urgent need payment to tide him/her over the period up to the first pay day. Unlike most urgent need payments, it does not have to be repaid later (see page 191).

Late Claims

Benefit cannot normally be paid for a period before the claim reached the social security office. But there are some important exceptions:[44]

(a) A claim must be backdated if the claimant shows that, throughout the period in question, there was 'good cause' for the delay in claiming. A similar rule has applied to late claims for national insurance benefits for many years, and the national insurance case law on this subject has been held to be applicable to the backdating of supplementary benefit claims.[45] A claimant's ignorance of his/her rights is not, in itself, good cause for delay; but if it is due to failure to make enquiries which he/she could not reasonably have been expected to make, it may be accepted as good cause. Wrong information given by a social security official or somebody else on whom it was reasonable for the claimant to rely might also be good cause for not claiming. Illness or mental handicap can be good cause. In the case of mental handicap, if the person is unable to act on his/her own behalf, this is, in itself, good cause for failure to claim benefit during any period when no one else had been formally appointed to act for him/her (see pages 208–9, 'Appointees'). This is the case even if an unsuccessful claim was made on the person's behalf at an earlier date by a person who at that time had not been so appointed.[46]

(b) If the claimant has made a claim for some other social security benefit (including FIS) or a war disablement pension, and claims supplementary benefit as soon as is reasonably practicable after hearing the result of the other claim, the supplementary benefit claim is backdated to the date of the other claim. For example, if a claim for unemployment benefit fails and a claim for supplementary benefit is then made, it will be treated as having been made at the time of the unemployment benefit claim. Even if the first claim is successful, the claimant can still ask for the supplementary benefit claim to be backdated if supplementary benefit would have been payable in addition to the other benefit.

(c) If supplementary benefit entitlement was interrupted by a period in hospital and a new claim is made within 21 days of discharge from hospital, it is backdated to the day of discharge.

(d) If a claimant moves into a centre for alcoholics or drug addicts or a voluntary hostel for purposes similar to those of a resettlement unit, his claim for board and lodging payments is backdated to the day he arrived provided that he claims within three days.

(e) In the case of a married couple, if one partner has claimed unsuccessfully and the other then makes a claim as soon as is reasonably practicable, it will be treated as having been made at the time of the first claim (see page 39).

Even if one of these conditions is satisfied, the claim will not necessarily be backdated. It is up to the claimant to raise the question of backdating; otherwise, the adjudication officer may be under no obligation to consider this possibility.[47]

Preventing Double Payments

It often happens that supplementary benefit is payable – or is paid at a higher rate than it otherwise would be – because of delays in the receipt of other payments to which the claimant is entitled. When those payments are eventually received, the amount of supplementary benefit paid as a result of the delay can be recouped, either by deduction from the payment in question or by calling on the claimant to repay the money. The precise arrangements depend on the type of payment involved.

The most common situation in which this occurs is where some other social security benefit is due but is not paid in time to be taken into account in calculating the supplementary benefit entitlement. When the other benefit is paid, it can be 'abated' (i.e. reduced) by the amount of supplementary benefit that would not otherwise have been paid. This arrangement applies to the whole range of weekly social security benefits and pensions, including child benefit and FIS, and also to war pensions, Job Release allowances, training allowances from the Manpower Services Commission and social security benefits from other EEC countries. It also applies where supplementary benefit has been paid (or paid at a higher rate) because, for example, a separated husband is entitled to additions to a national insurance benefit for his wife which are paid late, with the result that he cannot make the maintenance payments for which he is liable. When the husband receives the additions, the amount of supplementary benefit paid to his wife because of the delay can be deducted from them.[48]

The power to recover money from the claimant, rather than by deduction from other benefit payments, is much wider. It applies in any case where, if a payment had been made on the first day of the period to which it relates (or to which it is 'fairly attributable'), less supplementary benefit would have been paid. This power can be used in the type of case mentioned above, where payment of another benefit is delayed: if a double payment is not prevented by means of a deduction from the other benefit, the claimant can be asked to repay the money instead. But it can also be used where the double payment results from delays in maintenance payments or in the payment of wages. For example, if a separated wife receives supplementary benefit because maintenance payments from her husband have not arrived on time, she can be required to repay that amount of benefit out of the maintenance payments when she receives them.[49]

In all these cases, it is for the adjudication officer to decide the amount of the double payment. This should normally be a straightforward calculation, but in case of dispute there is a right of appeal against his decision.[50] Once the amount has been fixed, however, it is for the Secretary of State to decide whether it should be recouped or not, and there is no appeal against that decision (in practice the decision will normally be taken by the local social security office, which can be asked to reconsider it if it seems unfair or harsh). It will anyway be unnecessary to resort to these methods of recovery if the amount involved is small and double payment can be prevented by treating it as a resource in the week in which it is received and reducing the supplementary benefit for that week.

Overpayments of Benefit

If supplementary benefit is overpaid as a result of the claimant or somebody else misrepresenting or failing to disclose a material fact, whether there was any fraudulent intention or not, the amount overpaid can be recovered by the Secretary of State from that person. It is for the adjudication officer to decide – subject to the right of appeal – whether there has been an overpayment and, if so, the amount recoverable.[51] Once that decision has been made, it is for the Secretary of State to decide whether, at what rate and by what means the money should be recovered, and there is no right of appeal against that decision.

It is important to note that there is no legal obligation to repay the money unless the overpayment resulted from the person concerned misrepresenting or failing to disclose a material fact. A person who has innocently received benefit as a result of a mistake by the social security office cannot be required to repay it. But if he or she ought to have realized that benefit was being overpaid but did nothing to prevent it – for example, where a change of circumstances has been reported to the local office but benefit continues at the same rate – the overpayment may be recoverable.[52]

Misrepresentation will result in the overpayment being recoverable even if it was entirely innocent and the person concerned did not even know the true facts. In this respect the supplementary benefit rules are harsher than those relating to national insurance benefits, under which an overpayment is not recoverable if the claimant can show that he/she exercised 'due care and diligence'.

Failure to disclose, on the other hand, implies that the person *knew* the material fact and could reasonably have been expected to report it. It is important to note that, although a claimant is required to report changes of circumstances in writing, all that is necessary to avoid recovery of an overpayment is that the facts have been disclosed, whether in writing or not.[53] Disclosure must normally have been made to the supplementary benefit office or an official from that office. In a number of Commissioners' decisions it has been held that disclosure of a fact to another section of the Department of Health and Social Security is not sufficient. Even the fact that another social security benefit has been awarded to the claimant or the claimant's wife or husband must be reported to the supplementary benefit office; it is never safe to assume that one part of the Department knows what other parts are doing. Reporting that a benefit has been claimed is not enough; the actual payment of the benefit must be reported.[54]

In some circumstances, reporting a material fact to someone other than an official at the supplementary benefit office *may* be sufficient. An unemployed claimant might reasonably assume that reporting a change of circumstances to the unemployment benefit office was all that was required. The Department of Health and Social Security does not accept this, arguing that the unemployment benefit office (i.e. the Department of Employment) does not act as their agent for this purpose. Recent Commissioners' decisions, however, have suggested that this view may be wrong and that, even if the unemployment benefit office is not the agent of the DHSS, the claimant will have fulfilled his obligation if he gives the information in circumstances in which it can reasonably be expected to be passed on to the supplementary benefit office. Similarly, in a case where a disabled claimant, on admission to hospital, had asked the hospital social worker to report the fact to the supplementary benefit office and the social worker had delayed doing so, it was decided that there had been no failure to disclose by the claimant, though it is possible that in such a case the social worker or her employer could be required to repay the overpaid benefit.[55]

An overpayment is recoverable only if made 'in consequence of' misrepresentation or failure to disclose a material fact. This means that any overpayment that occurred before the misrepresentation, or before the duty of disclosure commenced, is not recoverable. It also means that, once the true facts have been reported, any further overpayment will not be recoverable. It may, therefore, be important to establish the exact dates on which the relevant events occurred.

It is not always easy to say precisely how much benefit was overpaid, since this may involve estimating how much *would* have been paid if all the facts had been known. If it can be shown that additional benefit could have been awarded had the facts now disclosed been known at the outset, that additional benefit must be deducted from the overpayment in calculating the amount recoverable – but only to the extent that the claimant would qualify for the additional benefit without the need to ascertain additional facts or to make a fresh claim.[56]. Difficult questions can arise where, if the facts had been known, benefit might have been paid to some other person. This will not normally affect the amount of benefit recoverable, but it may do if, in the period in question, the two people were living in the same household and the claimant's needs would have been taken into account in the benefit payable to the other person.[57]

A further difficulty may arise where the overpayment results from undeclared or under-declared capital resources. Commissioners' decisions have suggested, and it has recently been confirmed by the Court of Appeal, that allowance should be made in such cases for the fact that, if the benefit had not been paid, part of the capital would have been used to meet the claimant's living expenses.[58] This is known as the 'diminishing capital concept'. For example, if the total capital is £4,000, the claimant would have been entitled to benefit once it was reduced below £3,000 (see page 130). The question to be decided is how long it would have taken to reach that situation, since it is for that period only that benefit has been overpaid. It seems reasonable to assume, for this purpose, that the capital would have been reduced each week by the amount of the overpaid benefit.

The burden of proof of overpayment and of the amount recoverable lies on the adjudication officer. A mere assertion by the adjudication officer that there is no record of an oral statement which the claimant claims to have made has been held by a Commissioner to be 'plainly insufficient to discharge the requisite burden of proof'. It must be shown that there are instructions and administrative arrangements to ensure that such a statement is recorded and attached to the file, and even then 'the weight of such evidence might be affected by how far it could be shown to have been in practice carried out, and to what extent not'.[59] A claimant who has reported a fact orally, therefore, should not agree to the recovery of an overpayment simply because the local office cannot find a record of the oral report.

The facts may be particularly difficult to prove in the not uncommon case where the existence of capital is revealed after the claimant's death. If there is clear evidence that the capital existed throughout the period in question, there is no problem. Difficulties arise where, for example, the claimant invested a sum of money during that period and it is not clear where the money came from or how long it had been in the claimant's possession. It is the duty of the executor or administrator of the claimant's estate to make all reasonable enquiries as to the origin of the money. If this is not done, the adjudication officer will be justified in assuming that the claimant had the money from the date of claiming supplementary benefit – just as he would be justified in so assuming if the claimant were still alive and refused to explain the origin of the money. But if, despite all reasonable enquiries, the origin of the money and the date of its acquisition remain unknown, it must be assumed to have been acquired on the date when it was invested, and only benefit paid after that date will be recoverable.[60]

Once the amount of benefit overpaid and recoverable has been settled, the Secretary of State can proceed to recover the money from the person responsible for the misrepresentation or failure to disclose (not necessarily the claimant). The money can be recovered either directly or by deduction from subsequent benefit payments. The benefits from which deductions can be made for this purpose include nearly all national insurance benefits, supplementary benefit and FIS – but not child benefit, maternity grant or death grant.[61]

The maximum deduction from current weekly payments of supplementary benefit for this purpose is £4.35 a week plus half of certain amounts of 'disregarded' income (items 34, 35 and 40 in Table 3 on page 118). If supplementary benefit is payable at the higher 'long-term' rate or the overpayment resulted from fraud, the maximum deduction is increased by £1.60 a week to £5.95 plus half the disregarded income. These maximum deductions are increased annually in line with the benefit rates. If deductions are also required for housing and fuel bills (see Chapter 9), they take priority so far as the basic maximum of £4.35 is concerned; but overpayments take priority for any money recovered out of disregarded income, and the additional £1.60 deduction can only be made for recovery of an overpayment.[62]

A person who has savings or other capital will normally be asked to repay the money in a lump sum. If it has to be repaid out of income and the person is not on supplementary benefit, the rate of repayment demanded will not be such as to reduce the income below the level to which it would be reduced if he or she were on supplementary benefit.

If an appeal is lodged against the adjudication officer's decision that there has been a recoverable overpayment, a question arises as to whether recovery should proceed while the appeal is pending. There is nothing to prevent the Secretary of State from starting the process of recovery by deduction from benefit payments or asking for direct repayment without waiting for the appeal decision. If the appeal tribunal or the Commissioner decides that the money was not recoverable, any deductions already made will have to be repaid. If money has been repaid voluntarily, however, it cannot be reclaimed if the tribunal or the Commissioner decides that, although there was an overpayment, it is not recoverable. In a case of this sort the Commissioner expressed his concern about the fact that the claimant had been asked to repay the money and had been doing so at £2 a week. This, the Commissioner said, was improper, as it pre-judged the decision of the tribunal or of the Commissioner.[63] The practical moral is clear: do not make voluntary repayments while an appeal is pending.

REFERENCES

1. SB Act, s. 6(1).
2. Urgent Cases Regs. 3(2)(c).
3. Conditions of Entitlement Regs. 9(2)(a).
4. Conditions of Entitlement Regs. 9(2)(b); *S Manual*, para. 1593(1).
5. Conditions of Entitlement Regs. 9(2)(c).
6. Conditions of Entitlement Regs. 9(2)(d).
7. *S Manual*, para. 1593(2).
8. Conditions of Entitlement Regs. 9(1)(b); Resources Regs. 10(3)(c); *Chief Supplementary Benefits Officer v. Cunningham* (Appendix to Commissioners' decision R (SB) 23/84).
9. Resources Regs. 9(2)(b).
10. Resources Regs. 4(2)(a).
11. Conditions of Entitlement Regs. 9(3)(a).
12. Resources Regs. 9(2)(b).
13. Conditions of Entitlement Regs. 9(1)(c).
14. SB Act, s. 6(2) and (3); Conditions of Entitlement Regs. 10(1)(a).
15. Child Benefit (General) Regs. 1(2).
16. Conditions of Entitlement Regs. 11.
17. Conditions of Entitlement Regs. 6(jj).
18. Conditions of Entitlement Regs. 10.
19. SB Act, s. 5; Conditions of Entitlement Regs. 6(p).

20. Conditions of Entitlement Regs. 4.
21. Conditions of Entitlement Regs. 6.
22. SB Act, schedule 1, para. 3(1).
23. Aggregation Regs. 1A(1)(*a*) and (3).
24. Aggregation Regs. 1A(1)(*b*) and (2)(*a*).
25. Aggregation Regs. 1A(1)(*b*).
26. Aggregation Regs. 1A(2)(*b*); Circular S/142, Appendix 2.
27. Circular S/142, Appendix 2.
28. Claims and Payments Regs. 5(2)(*aa*).
29. Aggregation Regs. 1A(3) and (4).
30. Aggregation Regs. 1A(5).
31. Aggregation Regs. 1A(6).
32. Circular S/142, Appendix 3.
33. Claims and Payments Regs. 3.
34. Claims and Payments Regs. 5A.
35. Claims and Payments Regs. 4.
36. Claims and Payments Regs. 5A.
37. Adjudication Regs., schedule 4, para. 1.
38. Adjudication Regs. 67.
39. Adjudication Regs. 68.
40. *S Manual*, para. 14558.
41. Determination of Questions Regs. 7(1)(*a*).
42. Determination of Questions Regs. 7(2).
43. Determination of Questions Regs. 7(1)(*a*).
44. Claims and Payments Regs. 5.
45. Commissioner's decision R (SB) 6/83.
46. R (SB) 9/84.
47. R (SB) 9/84.
48. SB Act, s. 12(1) and (2); Duplication and Overpayment Regs. 3 and 5.
49. SB Act, s. 12(1A); Duplication and Overpayment Regs. 4.
50. SB Act, s. 12(4).
51. SB Act, s. 20.
52. R (SB) 54/83.
53. R (SB) 40/84.
54. CSB 360/83; CSSB 38/83.
55. R (SB) 54/83; CSB 178/83; CSSB 188/82.
56. CSB 93/84.
57. CSB 1146/82.
58. CSB 53/81; *Chief Supplementary Benefit Officer v. Leary*, T.L.R. 19 October 1984.
59. CSB 347/83.
60. R (SB) 34/83.
61. Duplication and Overpayment Regs. 6.
62. Duplication and Overpayment Regs. 7; Claims and Payments Regs. 18(3).
63. CSB 649/83.

Chapter 2

Normal Requirements

The normal way of working out how much supplementary benefit is payable is quite simple, but there are a number of special rules for particular types of case. In the normal case, the benefit payable is the amount by which the claimant's resources fall short of his requirements;[1] and the method of calculating requirements and resources is laid down in schedule 1 of the Supplementary Benefits Act and the Requirements and Resources Regulations. Schedule 1 distinguishes three types of requirements that may have to be included in the calculation:

Normal requirements.
Additional requirements.
Housing requirements.[2]

The rules for calculating normal requirements are explained in this chapter. Additional and housing requirements are dealt with in the three following chapters. Some examples showing how these components are combined to arrive at the claimant's total requirements are given in Appendix 1.

The Assessment Unit

An 'assessment unit' is either a single person or a family group whose requirements and resources are added together ('aggregated' in the language of the Act) for the purpose of calculating entitlement to supplementary benefit. A married couple living in the same household, or an unmarried couple living together as husband and wife, are treated as one assessment unit (see pages 36–40 for the rules about which of them can claim benefit). Their dependent children who are living with them are also included in the assessment unit. Similarly, a single parent and his or her dependent children are one assessment unit.[3]

If there are other people living in the household – whether as lodgers, visitors or members of the family (including children who are no longer treated as dependent) – their requirements and resources are not taken into account, but they may be assumed to be making a contribution towards the housing costs. (See pages 92–3 and 105–6.) They can claim benefit in their own right, as separate assessment units.

The Act defines a child as a person under the age of 16,[4] but an older child is treated as a dependant if he or she is under 19 (or was under 19 at the start of the school year) and receiving full-time non-advanced education at a college, school or comparable establishment.[5] A young person aged 16 or over who has left school and is looking for a job or for some reason is unable to work is entitled to claim benefit as a separate assessment unit after the first few weeks. This is particularly important for a family with a handicapped child over 16 who is unable to work. Young people in this situation are entitled to an income of their own, whether their parents are rich or poor. At the other end of the scale, an old person living with grown-up children or other relatives can claim benefit, even if the relatives are able and willing to support him or her – though in practice a pensioner living with close relatives and drawing a retirement pension at the standard rate (£35.80 from November 1984) will not qualify for a supplementary pension unless he or she has special needs.

The Scale Rates

Supplementary benefit is intended to provide an income that people can live on – not just enough to keep them alive but an income related to the normal standards of the community as a whole. The amounts considered necessary to meet the normal requirements of the claimant and other members of the assessment unit, excluding the cost of housing, are laid down in schedule 1 of the Act (paragraph 2) and in the Requirements Regulations. These amounts, sometimes referred to as the *supplementary benefit scale rates*, are set out in Appendix 2. The scale rates apply to people living alone or as members of private households, but not to boarders or those living in old people's homes and hostels (see page 57).

Regulation 4 of the Requirements Regulations lists the items regarded as covered by the scale rates:

The category of normal requirements shall relate to all items of normal expenditure on day-to-day living, other than [housing], including in particular food, household fuel, the purchase, cleaning, repair and replacement of clothing and footwear, normal travel costs, weekly laundry costs, miscellaneous household expenses such as toilet articles, cleaning materials, window-cleaning and the replacement of small household goods (for example crockery, cutlery, cooking utensils, light bulbs) and leisure and amenity items such as television licence and rental, newspapers, confectionery and tobacco.

Claimants are not obliged to spend money on all the items mentioned; not are they prevented from spending it on items that are not mentioned. For example, although the list includes tobacco, it does not include beer and other alcoholic drinks. Television rental is mentioned but not the cost of buying a television set. Other items not mentioned include holidays and outings, pet foods, books, evening classes and the cost of a telephone. Yet these are all things that some people will want to spend part of their benefit on, possibly going short of what other people would consider more essential items like food and clothing. If they choose to do so, that is their right and they do not have to account to anybody for the way in which their money is spent.

The Secretary of State for Social Services can amend the scale rates by laying regulations before Parliament at any time.[6] In practice, in recent years, the scale rates have been increased at the same time as the main national insurance benefits, in November of each year.

The Long-term Rates

The normal requirements of those aged 60 or over and other long-term recipients (except the unemployed – see below) are assessed at the long-term rates shown in Appendix 2, which are considerably higher than the 'ordinary' rates applicable to other claimants. A married couple qualifies for the long-term rates if either the husband or the wife is 60 or over.

Claimants who do not qualify for the long-term rates on grounds of age can qualify if they have been getting supplementary benefit or an invalidity benefit for the last 52 weeks and have not been required to be available for work during that period. But the 52 weeks qualifying period can include one or more periods of up to 8 weeks each during which these conditions were not satisfied. The invalidity benefits which count for this purpose include invalidity pension, non-contributory invalidity pension, severe disablement allowance, and the unemployability supplement payable under the industrial injuries and war pension schemes.[7]

The effect of these rules is that an unemployed claimant, who is required to be available for work, will not qualify for the long-term rates so long as he or she is under 60, however long unemployment may last. This discrimination against the unemployed is generally agreed to be unfair and may eventually be abolished, but there is no sign of this happening at present.

There are special rules to help people qualify for the long-term rates in certain circumstances:

(a) If there is a change of claimant because the person who was claiming benefit dies or leaves the household, the new claimant, if under 60, may not have to draw benefit for 52 weeks to qualify for the long-term rate. In the case of a married couple, if the benefit was previously being paid at the long-term rate and the remaining partner claims within 8 weeks and is not required to be available for work, he or she will get the long-term rate straight away. If the partner who has died or left had not yet become entitled to the long-term rate, any period during which he or she had been receiving benefit without being required to be available for work counts towards the qualifying period for the remaining partner. Similarly, where there are children in the family and an older brother or sister who was previously treated as a dependant becomes responsible for them through the death or absence of the parent, he or she can take over the parent's entitlement to, or qualifying weeks for, the long-term rate.[8]

(b) Where a claimant who has been required to attend at the un-employment benefit office only once a quarter is no longer required to be available for work because, as a result of disablement, he has no prospects of finding a job, the period of quarterly attendance counts towards the 52 weeks' qualifying period for the long-term rate.[9]

(c) If a person under 60 receiving benefit at the long-term rate ceases to receive it for more than 8 weeks while in hospital, benefit can be paid again at the long-term rate at the end of the stay in hospital, provided that the break in entitlement is not longer than 78 weeks, of which all but 13 weeks must have been spent in hospital.[10]

In the case of a married couple, entitlement to the long-term rate may depend on which partner claims benefit, where both are under 60 and only one would be required to be available for work. They can, if necessary, switch claimants for the purpose of qualifying for the long-term rate (see pages 39–40).

Householders

The scale rates for a single person, in Appendix 2, are higher in the case of a householder than for a non-householder. For a couple, whether married or living together as husband and wife, the same rates apply whether the claimant is a householder or not.

To be treated as a householder, a single person must normally be solely responsible for meeting the housing costs – rent or mortgage payments, rates, etc. – of the accommodation he or she occupies, which may be a self-contained house or flat, a room or rooms with or without shared use of other parts of the house, or a caravan, mobile home or houseboat. It is not necessary for a tenant to have a written agreement or a rent book, provided that there is a legally enforceable liability to pay. A person who is paying no rent or other housing costs is treated as a householder if he or she alone has 'major control over household expenditure'. Someone occupying accommodation as a licensee, with or without a written agreement, can also be a householder, subject to the same test – sole responsibility for housing costs or major control over household expenditure.[11]

There is one exception to the rule that a householder must be the person legally liable to meet the housing costs. Where the person who is legally liable is not meeting those costs, and the claimant has to do so in order to continue to live in the home, he or she can be treated as the householder if the adjudication officer is satisfied that this is reason-able.[12] This means that where, for example, the tenancy agreement or mortgage is in a husband's name and he leaves the home, the wife can be treated as the householder.

Provided that the accommodation is more or less self-contained, these rules can be applied without difficulty in most cases. Difficulties arise where accommodation is shared. The regulations provide that a person is not to be treated as responsible for housing costs for which he or she is liable to 'a member of the same household'.[13] If rent is paid to somebody in the same house for the use of part of it, therefore, the person paying it will not be treated as a householder unless he or she is living as (or as part of) a separate household from the person to whom it is payable, although living under the same roof. Similarly, a claimant with no housing costs will not be treated as a householder unless he or she is 'the member of the household with major control over household expenditure'. This will be the case only if he or she is living as or in a separate household from the person responsible for the housing costs.

Whether there is a separate household, for the purposes of the preceding paragraph, is a question of fact which depends on the living arrangements in the particular case. The regulations do not define a 'household' but Commissioners' decisions have thrown some light on the matter. The kind of situation which commonly arises and in which there is no doubt that the claimant has a separate household is illustrated by a case in which a single woman shared a flat with three other people, one of whom was the tenant of the whole flat. She had exclusive use of a bedroom and shared use of the kitchen, bathroom and lounge. She paid £62 a month for rent and also a proportion of the fuel and telephone bills, but bought her own food and 'within the limits of her sub-tenancy agreement . . . was able to live independently in the accommodation occupied by her'. The Commissioner decided that the only reasonable conclusion that could be reached on the facts of the case was that she maintained a separate household and was not a member of anyone else's.[14]

Cooking and eating arrangements are often a good guide to whether a separate household exists: people who share meals are likely to be regarded as a single household. But a Commissioner decided in another case that a single man living in a small flat with three friends was a separate household, despite the fact that not only the cost of electricity, gas, telephone and cleaning but also the cost of food was divided equally. The determining factor in this case was the fact that the claimant had been granted a lease of his own room in the house.[15]

A householder who is temporarily away from home continues to be treated as a householder for the first 13 weeks' absence. But this does not apply in the case of a student on a full-time advanced course who goes away during the vacations.[16]

Joint Householders

As explained above, to qualify for the householder scale rate, the claimant must be the *only* person in the household with responsibility for the housing costs or major control over household expenditure. If the only reason for failing the householder test is that such responsibility or control is shared with another member of the household, the claimant can be treated as a joint householder: for example, where two or more friends rent a house or flat jointly and live as a single household. This applies even if, under the terms of the tenancy, the claimant is not legally liable for the housing costs, provided that the adjudication officer considers it reasonable and none of the people with whom the costs are shared is a close relative (parent, child, brother or sister) of the claimant. Even when sharing with a close relative, however, a claimant can be treated as a joint householder if legally liable for his or her share of the housing costs.[17]

A joint householder qualifies for the 'non-householder' scale rate plus his or her share of the difference between the householder and non-householder rates. Example F in Appendix 1 shows how the requirements of a joint householder in rented accommodation are calculated. The same principles apply where the accommodation is jointly owned, or where licensees share accommodation.

Non-householder or Boarder?

The way in which the normal requirements of single claimants who are not householders are assessed depends on which of a number of categories they fall into. There are special rules for each of the following:

	See pages
Boarders	59–64
Residents in Part III accommodation	249–53
Hospital patients	244–9
Persons in resettlement units	253
Persons attending residential re-establishment courses	231–2
Members of religious orders	253
Prisoners	253–5

In all other cases, the non-householder scale rates set out in Appendix 2 apply.[18] The distinction between a non-householder and a boarder is important, because the benefit entitlement of a boarder is normally based on the actual charge for board and lodging, or a reasonable commercial charge for lodgings (but see page 64: *New rules for boarders*). A boarder is defined in the regulations as a person who is not in one of the other special categories listed above and who *either* pays an inclusive charge for accommodation and at least some meals prepared and consumed on the premises *or* is living in a hotel, guesthouse, hostel, lodging-house or similar establishment, or in a reception centre for refugees; but the definition excludes 'any person whose accommodation and meals (if any) are provided by a close relative or other than on a commercial basis', people away on holiday who have been away for 13 weeks or less (their benefit is calculated as if they were still at home), and young people in the care of a local authority whose accommodation is provided and paid for by the authority (they get the non-householder rate).[19]

The non-householder category, therefore, mainly comprises people who do not qualify for treatment as householders (i.e. are not responsible for housing costs or, if the accommodation is free, do not have major control over household expenditure) and live in accommodation provided either by a close relative or on a non-commercial basis. 'Close relative' means a parent, child, step-parent, step-child, brother or sister.[20] So a son or daughter who has left school but is still living with his or her parents is a non-householder, not a boarder. Similarly, an elderly person living in the home of a single son or daughter is a non-householder. 'In-laws', however, do not count as close relatives and, in a case where a claimant was living with his sister and brother-in-law, a Commissioner concluded that for the 'close relative' exclusion to apply 'the provision must be predominantly if not exclusively made by and at the expense (in money or effort) of the close relative' (in this case, the sister). He also pointed out that the exclusion applied only where accommodation *and* meals (if any) were provided by a close relative or other than on a commercial basis. Thus, even if only the accommodation were to be regarded as provided by the brother-in-law, while the sister provided meals, the 'close relative' exclusion would not apply and the claimant could be treated as a boarder.[21] Similar considerations would arise in the case of a person living with a married son or daughter; or in any other case where board and lodging are provided jointly by a close relative and some other person who is not a close relative.

Even if the accommodation and meals are not provided by a close relative, however, the claimant will be treated as a boarder only if they are provided 'on a commercial basis'. The regulations do not define 'a commercial basis'. If the claimant's relationship to the householder is close, even if it does not fall within the definition of a close relative, the adjudication officer may assume that the arrangement is not commercial. The most obvious test is whether the charge being made is roughly in line with charges for commercial lodgings of similar standard. The guidance issued by the Chief Adjudication Officer, however, indicates that a charge below the market rate can be accepted as commercial:

Interpret 'commercial basis' broadly, not just that a profit has to be made. If the intention is to cover the cost of food plus a reasonable amount for the accommodation, regard the arrangement as commercial. For example, a charity or individual may charge sufficient to make ends meet but not necessarily to make a profit.[22]

Non-householders

Once it has been decided that the claimant is to be treated as a non-householder and not as a boarder, the amount actually paid for board and lodging makes no difference to the assessment of normal requirements, the non-householder rate being applied automatically, with a fixed addition of £3.30 a week as a contribution to housing costs if the claimant is aged 21 or over. Some claimants, who have been getting supplementary benefit at the non-householder rate since March 1983 or earlier, are still getting small additional amounts under earlier provisions which no longer apply.[23]

Boarders (*see page 64 for proposed new rules from April 1985*)

For supplementary benefit purposes a boarder is, as explained above, a person who either pays an inclusive charge for lodging and at least some meals or is living in a hotel, hostel, lodging-house or similar establishment, or in a reception centre for refugees. But people in the other special categories listed on page 57 are not treated as boarders; nor are those accommodated by a 'close relative' or on a non-commercial basis. Boarders, therefore, include both lodgers in the usual sense of the word and people living in various kinds of hostels and other residential accommodation, including privately run homes for old people and nursing homes.

A boarder's 'normal requirements' consist of an amount for *board and lodging* plus an allowance for *any meals not included* in the weekly board and lodging charge and an additional allowance for *personal expenses*. The amount allowed for board and lodging is usually the actual amount paid by the claimant, but it is subject to a *maximum*, which in turn is based on a *local limit*. The way in which both the maximum for the individual claimant and the local limit are arrived at is explained below (pages 60–63).

The *minimum* normal requirements of a boarder must not be less than the non-householder rate plus, for those aged 21 or over, the £3.30 non-householder's contribution to housing costs. The minimum amounts at November 1984 rates are shown on the next page. For a couple, the minimum level of normal requirements is £48.85, or £60.40 for a 'long-term' claimant (the married-couple scale rates plus the £3.30 housing contribution). If there are dependent children, minimum normal requirements, for a single person or

	Minimum normal requirements for a single boarder	
Age	*Ordinary rate*	*Long-term rate*
21 or over	£25.75	£31.85
18–20	£22.45	£28.55
16–17	£17.30	£21.90

(See pages 53–4 for the qualifying conditions for the long-term rate.)

a couple, are increased by the children's scale rates (see Appendix 2).[24]

If the weekly board and lodging charge does not cover all meals, a standard amount (£1.10 for breakfast and £1.55 for a midday or evening meal) is allowed for *each meal that is not included* – but these amounts can be reduced or disallowed if the meals are normally obtained at a reduced price or free. If they are obtainable on the premises the actual cost is allowed instead.[25]

Where board and lodging are provided free or at a reduced charge in return for services, the amount allowable for board and lodging is £4 a week (£8 for a couple where both provide services) if no charge at all is made for full board and lodging, and 'such amounts as may be reasonable in the circumstances' if there is a reduced charge or less than full board and lodging is provided. The minimum rates mentioned above do not apply.[26]

The allowance for *personal expenses*, for a single person, is £9.25 per week, or £10.30 for a claimant who would qualify for the long-term scale rate if not a boarder. For a married couple the allowance is twice as much – £18.50 or £20.60. If there are children who have not left school, the personal expenses allowance is increased by £3.10 for a child under 11, £4.75 for a child aged 11–15, £5.55 if aged 16–17, and £9.25 if 18 or over.[27] In the typical case of a single boarder, therefore, normal requirements are calculated by taking the actual board and lodging charge and adding £9.25 per week, or £10.30 for a claimant who is over 60 or has been receiving supplementary benefit or an invalidity benefit for a year or more without having to be available for employment.

The maximum allowance for board and lodging
(see page 64 for new rules)

Although in most cases the weekly charge for board and lodging (including the additions for meals not provided) is allowed in full, if it is above a maximum figure only the maximum is allowed (for exceptions to this rule, see pages 63–4). The maximum is not a fixed amount but depends on the circumstances of the case, the type of accommodation and the area. The regulations distinguish three types of accommodation: (*i*) nursing homes; (*ii*) residential homes for the elderly, mentally disordered and physically handicapped; and (*iii*) 'any other type of accommodation', which includes ordinary commercial lodgings but also centres for the rehabilitation of alcoholics or drug addicts and accommodation in a private household arranged by a local authority for somebody suffering from a mental disorder. (For further details of the treatment of claimants in nursing homes and residential homes, see pages 249–52.)

The adjudication officer is required to estimate the reasonable weekly charge for full board and lodging available in the area and of a standard suitable for claimants in whichever of the three types of accommodation the claimant is living (for a claimant staying in a rehabilitation centre for alcoholics or drug addicts, or a mentally disordered person for whom accommodation in a private household has been arranged by a local authority, the estimate must be for accommodation of type (*iii*) – ordinary board and lodging accommodation). If board and lodging charges in the area are 'unusually high', the adjudication officer can take instead the reasonable cost of accommodation in an adjoining area.[28]

The figure arrived at in this way is the maximum amount allowable for board and lodging in the case of a single claimant under pension age who does not suffer from any physical or mental disability. But the maximum is increased by £16.15 a week for a claimant who is over pension age (60 for a woman, 65 for a man) or 'infirm by reason of physical or mental disability' and not receiving an attendance or constant attendance allowance (see below). This does not mean that boarders who are elderly or infirm automatically get £16.15 extra benefit. It is only where the board and lodging charge (including any additions for meals not provided) is above the normal limit that the increase has any effect. Otherwise, the amount allowed for board and lodging is the actual weekly charge, regardless of the claimant's age or physical or mental state.[29]

The £16.15 increase in the maximum board and lodging charge applies also to people for whose accommodation the local authority (or, for a person staying in a nursing home, the health authority) has the power to make financial provision, or to provide the accommodation itself, but has refused to exercise that power. This includes people staying in homes and hostels for mothers and babies or for people who are or have been suffering from mental disorder or are mentally handicapped.

In the case of a married couple, the maximum amount allowed for board and lodging is the same as for two single persons. The £32.30 increase in the maximum applies if either partner is 65 or over (the regulations *appear* to mean that the higher maximum applies where a wife aged 60 or over is the claimant, even if both partners are under 65, but this was apparently not the intention). A child aged 11 or over counts as another adult for the purpose of calculating the maximum board and lodging charge for the family as a whole. For a younger child, the maximum is increased by 1½ times the child's scale rate (£14.40 from November 1984).[30]

If a boarder is receiving an attendance allowance, or a constant attendance allowance under the industrial injuries or war pension schemes, a board and lodging charge above the normal maximum will be allowed in the calculation of normal requirements only to the extent that the excess charge is not covered by the attendance allowance. In the case of a constant attendance allowance, any amount by which it exceeds the higher rate of attendance allowance (£28.60 a week from November 1984) is ignored for this purpose.[31]

The 'local limit' (see page 64 for new rules)

Although the responsibility for estimating a reasonable board and lodging charge for the area rests on the adjudication officer dealing with the particular case, in practice the same figure is used for all cases in the same area, varying only as between the three types of accommodation: nursing homes, residential homes and ordinary board and lodging ('any other type'). If there is any doubt as to whether a given charge will be allowed in full, this 'local limit' can be ascertained from the social security office (officers have been told to give this information in reply to enquiries).[32] It should be noted, however, that the local limit is not binding on an appeal tribunal, which must make its own decision as to what is a reasonable charge in the area. If the adjudication officer refuses to allow the full weekly charge, therefore, it may be worth appealing. If the local limit seems unreasonably low, written representations should be made to the local social security office with a view to getting it raised.

Officers are instructed to fix the local limit for ordinary board and lodging by finding out the charges made in the area for single rooms with full board in private houses, guest-houses, small hotels and hostels, including rehabilitation centres for alcoholics and drug addicts, but excluding accommodation which is 'exceptionally costly because it is of a standard considerably higher than the average person would expect to occupy permanently'. They are then to take the *highest* charge as the local limit, unless it is 'totally out of line with the charges being made by other establishments', in which case the next highest figure is to be used. But if the only accommodation available in the area is 'unreasonably expensive because, for example, it is luxurious', the limit set by a neighbouring social security office is to be used.[33]

The procedure for setting the local limit for residential homes (registered under section 1 of the Residential Homes Act 1980 or section 61 of the Social Work (Scotland) Act 1968) is similar. Information is obtained about the charges for single rooms in local homes, excluding any which 'seem exceptionally costly because they are providing luxurious accommodation or facilities'. The local limit is set at the level of 'the *highest* amount charged by a home which seems to be providing a suitable standard for the needs of the occupants' or, if this is totally out of line with other homes, the next highest figure which is not unreasonably expensive. Again, if all the local homes are unreasonably expensive, the limit set by a neighbouring office is to be used.[34]

Board and lodging charges above the maximum

If the board and lodging charge, including any additions for meals not provided, is above the maximum, it can still be allowed in full for up to 13 weeks, provided that the claimant has lived in the accommodation for more than twelve months, could afford the charges when he or she moved in, and cannot pay the charge above the maximum out of income otherwise disregarded (see pages 118–19). But this concession is allowed only where it is reasonable in order to allow time to find alternative accommodation. In deciding whether it is reasonable, the adjudication officer must have regard to the availability of and level of charges for board and lodging and the circumstances of the assessment unit – in particular the age and state of health of its members, the claimant's employment prospects and the effect of a change of school on the children's education. In practice, the claimant's age and state of health are likely to be the main factors, but any other factors, whether mentioned in the regulation or not, can be taken into account.[35]

The 13 weeks' period of grace does not apply to a claimant accommodated by a local authority because of homelessness.

New rules for boarders

Proposals for revised rules, to be introduced in April 1985, were published by the DHSS in November 1984.[36] They are summarized below, though at the time of writing it is not known whether they will be adopted in precisely this form.

Board and lodging limits (see pages 62–3). The limits will not be fixed by adjudication officers but by regulations against which there is no appeal (as a temporary measure they were frozen at the levels at which they stood on 5 September 1984, or reduced to those levels if they had been raised between September and November). Instead of local limits, there will be a national limit for each type of accommodation: homes for the elderly, for the mentally ill, for drug and alcohol misusers, for the mentally handicapped, for the physically handicapped, unregistered hostels (e.g. for homeless people, ex-offenders and battered wives), and ordinary board and lodging accommodation. For nursing homes, the normal limits will be increased by the higher rate of attendance allowance (£28.60 a week). Where existing local limits are lower, they will not be raised by more than 5 per cent. The £16.15 increase in the limits for certain claimants (see page 61) will apply only to elderly or infirm people in ordinary board and lodging accommodation.

Transitional protection. Claimants living in homes and hostels when the new rules commence will continue to receive existing rates of payment (for hostels, only if these are reasonable) for varying lengths of time.

Attendance allowance. Where this allowance is paid to people in private and voluntary homes, it will no longer be disregarded (see page 118). There will be transitional protection where the charges made by the home are above the new limit.

Personal expenses allowance. A single rate, probably £8.20, will apply both to boarders (instead of £9.25 or £10.30 – see page 60) and those in Part III residential accommodation (instead of £7.15 – see pages 249–51), with protection for existing claimants getting the boarders' rates.

16- to 17-year-olds. If they claim benefit as boarders in their 'normal local office area' or an adjacent area, they will be paid as 'non-householders' (see page 59) unless there are special reasons why they need board and lodging accommodation.

Unemployed people outside their 'normal local office area'. After a short period of payment for board and lodging they will be treated as 'non-householders'; but there will be protection for some older people who are used to living in board and lodging accommodation.

REFERENCES

1. SB Act, schedule 1, para. 1(1).
2. SB Act, schedule 1, para. 2(1).
3. Requirements Regs. 2(1).
4. SB Act, s. 34.
5. Aggregation Regs. 3.
6. SB Act, schedule 1, para. 2(1) and (4).
7. SB Act, schedule 1, para. 2(3); Requirements Regs. 7(1-3).
8. Requirements Regs. 7(5).
9. Requirements Regs. 7(3)(*b*).
10. Requirements Regs. 7(4)(*a*).
11. Requirements Regs. 5(6).
12. Requirements Regs. 14(3)(*a*)(ii).
13. Requirements Regs. 14(3)(*a*)(i).
14. CSSB 57/83.
15. R(SB) 13/82.
16. Requirements Regs. 5(6)(*c*).
17. Requirements Regs. 6(2) and 14(3)(*a*)(iv).
18. Requirements Regs. 6(1).
19. Requirements Regs. 9(13) and (14).
20. Requirements Regs. 2(1).
21. CSB 1025/82.
22. *S Manual*, para. 3302.
23. Requirements Regs. 23(3).
24. Requirements Regs. 9(5).
25. Requirements Regs. 9(4).
26. Requirements Regs. 9(11).
27. Requirements Regs. 9(12).
28. Requirements Regs. 9(6).
29. Requirements Regs. 9(7).
30. Requirements Regs. 9(6) and (7).
31. Requirements Regs. 9(8).
32. Circular S/143, para. 25.
33. *Ibid.*, para. 5(3).
34. *Ibid.*, para. 5(1) and (2).
35. Requirements Regs. 9(10).
36. *Supplementary benefit board and lodging payments: Proposals for change.*

Chapter 3

'Additional Requirements'

Chapter 2 described how the amount of money a claimant is assumed to need for his normal requirements, other than housing, is calculated. The scale rates are assumed to be enough to cover basic needs where there are no special circumstances. But the regulations also provide for a wide range of 'additional requirements'. They are part of the claimant's legal entitlement, provided that the conditions laid down in the regulations are satisfied.

In some cases where claimants have special needs which they cannot be expected to meet out of the amounts allowed for normal requirements, it is more appropriate to make a lump sum payment rather than a regular addition to the weekly benefit. The circumstances in which single payments of this kind are made are described in Chapter 7.

The additional requirements for which provision is made on a weekly basis are:

Age (claimant or wife aged 80 or over)
Blindness
Heating
Diet
Laundry
Baths
Domestic assistance
Attendance needs
Clothing (special needs)
Hire purchase of furniture and household equipment
Storage of furniture
Fares for visiting hospital patients, etc.
Boarding-out fees prior to adoption

In some cases the precise amount to be allowed is laid down in the regulations. In others it depends on the actual or estimated expenditure incurred. The rules for each category are explained below.

If the claimant's normal requirements are assessed at the long-term rates (see pages 53–4), £1 per week of the amount allowed for normal requirements is assumed to be available to pay for any additional requirements of adults, other than the first two listed above.[1] Thus, if a 'long-term' claimant is over 80 or blind, the small additions payable on these grounds are allowed in full; but if a long-term claimant needs extra heating, a special diet, domestic assistance, or any of the other items in the list except the last one (boarding-out fees), the total additional requirements for those items are reduced by £1. The £1 offset does *not* apply where the additional requirement is to meet the needs of a child (including a young person over 16 still treated as a dependant – see page 52) for heating, diet, baths, attendance, laundry, clothing or fares for the parents to visit the child.[2]

Where an additional requirement arises from medical causes (see, for example, the conditions for heating, diet and laundry additions, explained below), it will usually be helpful to get a note from the doctor or ask him to contact the social security office, but this is not essential if the adjudication officer accepts that the facts are as stated.

Addition for Over-80s

An extra 25p per week is allowed for each person aged 80 or over.[3] Thus, if a married couple are both over 80, their requirements are increased by 50p. A similar age addition is payable with the national insurance retirement pension. When a pensioner reaches the age of 80, therefore, the 25p will normally be added to the retirement pension, leaving the supplementary pension unchanged.

Blindness

An additional requirement of £1.25 a week is allowed if the claimant, the claimant's wife or husband or a child aged 16 or over but still treated as a dependant (see page 52) is blind or regained his or her eyesight at any time in the last six months when supplementary benefit was in payment. Where there is more than one blind person, £1.25 a week is allowed for each of them.

If a blind person aged 18 or over (or under 18 with a child) is a 'non-householder' (see pages 57–9) a further addition is allowed, of the amount needed to bring the non-householder scale rate up to the rate for a householder. The amount depends on whether the person qualifies for the long-term scale rate or not. At November 1984 rates, it is £7.15 a week on the long-term scale, £5.60 otherwise.[4]

The definition of blindness for supplementary benefit purposes is the same as that for registration of blind persons: 'so blind as to be unable to perform any work for which eyesight is essential'. But it is not necessary to be registered in order to claim the additional requirement for a blind person. If a blind person recovers his or her eyesight, the additions for blindness are not withdrawn until six months later.[5]

Heating

Special rules apply where a fixed charge for heating is paid to the landlord (see below, pages 70–72). In other cases where a need for extra expenditure on heating is recognized, the additional requirement is usually at one of two rates: £2.10 or £5.20 (from November 1984). Other amounts may be allowed in certain circumstances, explained below.

The *lower rate* of heating addition, £2.10, applies in any of the following cases:

(a) The claimant is a householder and *either*
  (i) the claimant or the claimant's wife or husband is 65 or over, but under 85, *or*
  (ii) there is a child under five.[6]

The addition continues for up to thirteen weeks during the temporary absence of the elderly person or child.[7]

(b) A member of the 'assessment unit' (the claimant or the claimant's wife, husband or child) needs extra warmth because of *either* chronic ill health, due for example to bronchitis, rheumatism, arthritis or anaemia, *or* restricted mobility due to a physical cause, for example general frailty.[8] 'Chronic' ill health is to be given its ordinary meaning of 'long lasting', 'constantly present' or 'permanent'; it is the duration of the illness that matters, not its severity.[9] 'Restricted' mobility covers any significant restriction, provided that the person 'will derive benefit (but not at all necessarily *curative* benefit) from extra warmth, and so "needs" it'.[10]

(c) The claimant is a householder and 'having regard in particular to whether the rooms are draughty or damp or exceptionally large, the home is difficult to heat adequately'.[11] The words 'in particular' can cause difficulties. In one case the Commissioner decided that the use of these words, rather than 'for example', meant that the *only* relevant factors were whether the rooms were draughty, damp or exceptionally large, or 'matters closely analogous thereto', and that the effect on the heating of the home (in this case a mobile home) of the materials of which it was constructed was not 'closely analogous'. Another Commissioner, however, took the view that the words following 'in particular' were illustrative and '*not* a comprehensive exposition of the circumstances which may qualify'.[12] The guidance issued by the Chief Adjudication Officer seems closer to this view, since he merely says that a heating addition is to be allowed where the accommodation is difficult to heat adequately and that, when considering conditions *other than* that the rooms are draughty, damp or exceptionally large, officers should take account of the condition of the accommodation, not whether the claimant's fuel expenditure is unusually high.[13] This clearly implies that the poor insulating quality of the materials of which the home is built can be sufficient justification for a heating addition.

(d) The claimant is a householder and the home is centrally heated and has not more than four rooms, not counting a bathroom, lavatory or hall (if there are more than four rooms the addition is £4.20 instead of £2.10). The central heating must be a single system and the normal means of heating the living *or* dining areas. It can take the form of night storage heaters.[14]

The *higher rate* of heating addition, £5.20, applies in any of the following cases:

(e) The claimant is a householder and either the claimant or the claimant's wife or husband is aged 85 or over.[15]

(f) Any member of the assessment unit is a disabled person receiving mobility allowance or attendance (or constant attendance) allowance, or a war pensioner's mobility supplement, or with a car, invalid carriage or car maintenance allowance provided by the DHSS.[16]

(g) A member of the assessment unit *either* needs extra warmth because, through physical illness or disability, he or she is confined to the home or unable to leave it alone *or* needs extra warmth or a constant temperature because of a serious physical illness.[17]

(h) As in (c) above, but the home is *exceptionally* difficult to heat adequately, for example because it is very old or in a very exposed situation (as in (c), regard must be had 'in particular to whether the rooms are draughty or damp or exceptionally large').[18]

Estates with high heating costs

For people living on housing estates with heating systems which the Secretary of State for Social Services has recognized as having disproportionately high running costs, the central heating additions in (d) above are doubled: £4.20 a week for up to four rooms (not counting bathroom, lavatory and hall), £8.40 for more than four rooms.[19] If a particular estate with an expensive heating system has not been 'recognized', the local social security office should be asked to take up the matter with DHSS headquarters so that formal recognition can be obtained. The double rate of heating addition cannot be given until this has been done, though claimants living on the estate may, of course, be entitled to heating additions on other grounds meanwhile (including higher-rate additions on the grounds that the accommodation is 'exceptionally difficult to heat' – see (h) above – which can be backdated for up to 52 weeks – see page 275).[20]

Estates likely to be recognized as having disproportionately costly heating systems are those with central heating fired by oil, on-peak electricity and 'certain non-standard tariffs for off-peak electricity', but not those on the 'economy 7' or normal 8-hour 'white meter' tariff.[21] There is no appeal against a refusal by the Secretary of State to recognize an estate but, once an estate has been recognized, the double-rate addition should be given automatically for anyone living on the estate from then on.

More than one heating addition

The normal rule is that a claimant can only get one heating addition. If the conditions for more than one addition are satisfied and they are at different rates, the highest one is paid.[22] But there are some exceptions:

(a) If there is an entitlement to a lower-rate addition under both (b) and (c) on page 68 (a need for extra warmth due to ill health or restricted mobility *and* the home is difficult to heat), a higher-rate addition (£5.20) is given instead.[23]

(b) If more than one person in the assessment unit is disabled and qualifies for a higher-rate addition under (f), the addition must be given for *each* person who qualifies.[24]

Fuel charge made by landlord

If the landlord makes a fixed charge for fuel as a condition of the tenancy, or charges a rent which includes the supply of fuel for heating, cooking, hot water, lighting or all of these, the fuel charge is taken into account by the local authority in calculating the housing benefit payable (see pages 101–2). If the charge covers *all the heating needs of the household*, including any extra heating needed for reasons of health, etc., none of the supplementary benefit heating additions described above are payable.[25] But there are special arrangements for the following cases where the landlord's fuel charge would otherwise not be covered by either housing benefit or supplementary benefit:

(a) In the case of a single person who for the time being is living as a boarder or in a residential home or re-establishment centre, or has been in hospital for more than eight weeks or away from home for more than thirteen weeks, the fuel deduction made by the local authority in calculating the housing benefit is allowed as a heating addition to supplementary benefit.[26]

(b) If a person paying rent but not eligible for a rent rebate or allowance under the housing benefit scheme (e.g. a Crown tenant or co-owner) has to pay a separately identifiable charge for fuel which is more than the standard housing benefit fuel deductions (see page 101), the excess is allowed as a heating addition;[27] and if such a person is for the time being a boarder or in one of the other situations mentioned in (a) above, the full charge for fuel is allowed as a heating addition, not just the excess.[28]

If the charge covers *only part of the heating needs*, it does not affect entitlement to heating additions (a) to (h) on pages 68–9; but the double-rate addition for an estate with high heating costs does not apply where a fixed charge is made by the landlord, whether for full or partial heating.[29] As the normal heating additions are available where the charge made by the landlord covers only partial heating, but not where full heating is provided, it is important that the charge should not be assumed to be for full heating if it does not in fact cover all the heating needs. The guidance issued by the Chief Adjudication Officer points out, in particular, that heating which is adequate for one tenant may not be so for another who is in ill health or whose accommodation is difficult to heat; that a system controlled by the landlord may be intended to give full heating but may not be adequate for tenants with special heating needs; that some systems are only intended as background heating; and that the charge cannot be regarded as covering all necessary heating if other forms of heating are used because the system is turned off during certain hours or at certain times of the year.[30] Whether the charge covers full or only partial heating will also affect housing benefit (see pages 101–2); but even if the local authority treats it as covering full heating, that decision is not binding for supplementary benefit purposes and the adjudication officer or an appeal tribunal may take a different view. Moreover, the local authority is concerned only with the adequacy of the heating system for the accommodation and cannot take into account any special needs of the people living in it.

Joint householders

If a joint householder (see pages 56–7) qualifies for a heating addition on personal grounds (age, ill-health, restricted mobility or disablement), it is paid in full. But if the heating addition is related to the accommodation (hard to heat, central heating, high-cost estate heating, or a fuel charge made by the landlord), it is divided by the number of people in the household who share responsibility for the housing costs or major control over household expenditure.[31]

Diet

If a special diet is needed for medical reasons by any member of the assessment unit, an additional requirement is allowed, the amount of which depends on the nature of the illness and, in some cases, the extra cost involved, but is usually £1.55 per week. For the following conditions, the amount allowed is £3.60 per week (from November 1984):

Diabetes
Peptic (including stomach and duodenal) ulcer
Throat condition causing serious difficulty in swallowing
Ulcerative colitis
A form of tuberculosis for which the person is being treated with drugs
An illness requiring a diet analogous to that required for the illnesses listed above.[32]

The patient's doctor will be able to advise on whether any of these applies or whether the illness, though not listed above, requires an 'analogous' diet.

In the case of an illness not on the above list, requiring a special diet the extra cost of which is substantially more than £3.60 a week, the actual 'weekly cost of the diet' is allowed to the extent that the foods are not available on prescription.[33] Although the Commissioners have interpreted this as meaning that only the cost of those items in the diet that would not be in a normal diet is an additional requirement,[34] it is clear that the intention, reflected in the guidance issued to adjudication officers, was and still is that the *total* cost of the diet should be allowed as an additional requirement, not just the excess over the cost of a normal diet, despite the fact that a normal diet is already provided for in the scale rates.[35]

If the extra cost of the diet needed for an illness not listed above is not substantially more than £3.60, but there is *some* extra cost compared with a normal diet, an addition of £1.55 a week (from November 1984) is given. The £1.55 rate of diet addition applies also to anyone needing a diet involving extra cost because he or she is convalescing from a major illness or operation, and to a child needing a special diet because he or she is living with someone being treated for respiratory tuberculosis.[36]

For a person undergoing renal dialysis, a specially high rate of diet addition, £10.35 a week (from November 1984), is allowed.[37]

Only one diet addition can be given for any individual, at the highest rate for which he or she qualifies, but where more than one member of the family qualifies an addition can be given for each of them.[38]

Laundry

An additional requirement for laundry expenses can arise in two types of case:

(a) Where the laundry cannot be done at home, either because the claimant and any other adults in the household are ill, disabled or infirm or because there are no suitable washing or drying facilities (note that even where the washing facilities are suitable the drying facilities may not be, and this will provide sufficient grounds for a laundry addition);

(b) Where the quantity of laundry is substantially greater than would be normal for the person concerned, for example because of incontinence.

The additional requirement is the amount by which the estimated weekly laundry costs exceed 50p. In calculating the weekly laundry costs, the costs of any washing done at home (hot water, washing powder, etc.) should be taken into account, as well as laundry or launderette charges. Note, however, that in a 'long-term' case, only additional requirements over £1 are counted (see page 67). For example, if the laundry costs amount to £2.50 per week, the additional requirement will be £2; but in a long-term case, if there are no other additional requirements, £1 will be set off against the long-term scale rate, leaving only £1 to be included as an additional requirement for laundry.

If a claimant qualifies under (a) but a laundry or launderette is not available or, owing to sickness or disablement, cannot be used, the possibility of a single payment for a washing machine should be considered (see page 149). Once such a payment has been made, however, no additional requirement is allowed under (a) above unless the circumstances have changed.[39]

Baths

There is an additional requirement of 25p for each additional bath where a person needs more than one bath a week on medical grounds.[40] Thus, where a daily bath is required, the additional requirement will be six times 25p, or £1.50 per week.

Domestic Assistance

The full amount paid for domestic assistance counts as an additional requirement, subject to the £1 offset in a 'long-term' case (see page 67), provided that all the following conditions are satisfied:

(a) The charge is made for assistance with ordinary domestic tasks such as cleaning and cooking. Window cleaning and errands do not count – but child-minding does;[41]

(b) The assistance is essential because the claimant and the claimant's wife or husband, if any, 'are unable to carry out all those tasks by reason of old age, ill health, disability or heavy family responsibilities';

(c) The assistance is not provided by a local authority or by a close relative (parent, child, brother or sister) who incurs only 'minimal' expenses;

(d) The charge is reasonable or, where residential assistance is needed (for example, in a case of very severe disablement), it is not more than £44.90 per week (twice the non-householder scale rate of £22.45).[42]

The exclusion of charges made for local authority home helps is particularly important. In Scotland, local authorities are not allowed to charge people on supplementary benefit for home helps, but in England and Wales they can and often do, although this is discouraged by the Government. A person on supplementary benefit who needs help with domestic tasks may, therefore, prefer to make a private arrangement, the cost of which can be met as an additional requirement. In two Commissioners' decisions it has been suggested that an additional requirement for domestic help should not be allowed if the home help service available in the area could meet the person's needs,[43] but this is not what the regulations say. The guidance issued by the Chief Adjudication Officer makes it quite clear that claimants who seek advice must be told both of the existence of the home help service and of the possibility of an additional requirement for private help, and left to choose which arrangement to make; and if a claimant decides to give up having a local authority home help and make private arrangements, officers are told not to query the claimant's action but to consider allowing an additional requirement in the normal way. If the local authority decides that a home help is no longer needed, however, an additional requirement will not be allowed for private help unless there are good reasons for disagreeing with the authority's decision.[44]

In the case of domestic help provided by a close relative – parent or child (including a step-parent or step-child), brother or sister – an additional requirement is allowed only if the relative incurs expenses which are more than 'minimal'. This is interpreted as meaning that the relative *either* incurs travelling expenses of more than £1 a week *or* has had to give up work or work reduced hours in order to provide the assistance.[45] Whoever is providing the assistance, an additional requirement is allowed only if there is a definite charge. Where assistance is provided by a relative or friend, therefore, it is important to fix the charge before approaching the social security office for help with it.

Domestic assistance does not include services to a disabled person of a kind for which attendance allowance is payable (see below). If the service provided includes both attendance and help with domestic tasks, therefore, a decision will have to be made as to how much of the charge is for domestic assistance.[46]

The rule that the charge for non-residential assistance must be reasonable can be interpreted in two ways: either as meaning that if the charge is not reasonable no allowance can be made for it, or as meaning that an additional requirement can be allowed for the part of the charge that would be considered reasonable. The intention, reflected in the guidance to adjudication officers,[47] was that if the charge was not reasonable no additional requirement should be allowed. The Child Poverty Action Group's *National Welfare Benefits Handbook*, however, takes the opposite view,[48] which is also given some support in a case where the Commissioner said it was 'strongly arguable that the reasonable weekly charge should be payable in such circumstances.'[49]

Attendance Needs

An attendance allowance is payable under section 35 of the Social Security Act 1975, where a person, including a child aged 2 or over, is severely disabled, physically or mentally, and (in the words of the official leaflet) has 'needed a lot of looking after for at least six months'. Where these conditions are satisfied, or will be satisfied at the end of the six months qualifying period, but an attendance allowance is not yet in payment, the cost of attendance counts as an additional requirement for supplementary benefit purposes.[50] The main condition is that, in the opinion of the adjudication officer, the person concerned needs

(i) frequent attention in connection with his bodily functions; or
(ii) continual supervision in order to avoid substantial danger to himself or others, throughout the day or night;
and is likely to continue to do so for at least six months.

This is almost identical with the basic condition of entitlement to an attendance allowance, except that to qualify for an attendance allowance the person must already have been in this situation for six months.

The second condition is that *either* attendance allowance has not been claimed because the six months qualifying period has not been completed, but the adjudication officer is satisfied that a claim will be made within six months, *or* a claim has been made but not yet decided. The additional requirement ceases once the attendance allowance claim has been decided, whether the decision is in the claimant's favour or not, or after six months if no claim for attendance allowance has been made by then. But if the attendance allowance claim is turned down only on the grounds that the disabled person has not lived in the United Kingdom long enough to qualify, the additional requirement continues.

The amount of the additional requirement is the actual weekly cost of attendance, up to a maximum of £19.10 a week (from November 1984) – the *lower* of the two rates at which attendance allowance is paid (attendance allowance is paid at £28.60 a week where attention or supervision is needed both day and night).

Problems may arise both in deciding whether the main condition – a long-term need for attention or supervision throughout the day or night – is satisfied and in calculating the cost of attendance. On the first point, although the condition is virtually the same as for attendance allowance, the procedure for deciding whether it is satisfied is different. All claims for attendance allowance are submitted to the Attendance Allowance Board, which has to decide on the basis of a doctor's report whether the need for attendance is sufficient to qualify for the benefit. Whether an additional requirement is allowed for supplementary benefit purposes, on the other hand, depends on whether *in the opinion of the adjudication officer* the condition is satisfied. For this purpose, 'frequent attention' and 'continual supervision' are given the same meanings as they have for attendance allowance claims. Adjudication officers are told to 'regard

(1) "frequent attention" as meaning helping the disabled person, at least three times daily, with activities that any fit person would normally do for himself, e.g. dressing, eating or going to the lavatory. This does not include normal domestic duties;

(2) "continual supervision" as meaning watching over the disabled person because there is a likelihood of an incident involving substantial danger occurring frequently or at unpredictable intervals. The disabled person must be incapable of summoning help if such an incident occurs.

Where the disabled person is under 16, the attention or supervision must be more than would be required by a normal child of the same age or sex.'

But they are also told to accept without further enquiry a statement by the claimant's doctor that he considers the conditions to be satisfied.[51]

If the adjudication officer decides that there is no additional requirement and subsequently an attendance allowance is awarded, he should use his power to review the original decision and pay arrears (see page 275).[52]

Where an attendant is paid solely for providing personal attention and supervision for a disabled person, there should be no difficulty in ascertaining the weekly cost. If the attendant also provides other services, such as cleaning and cooking, it may be necessary to estimate the proportion of the total cost applicable to these services. Consideration should then be given to whether that proportion can be covered by an additional requirement for domestic assistance (see pages 74–5). If the attendant is a close relative whose services are provided free, there may still be an additional requirement in respect of any incidental expenses for which the attendant is reimbursed.

Note that while, for supplementary benefit purposes, there must be some actual cost in order to qualify for an additional requirement for attendance needs, an attendance allowance can be claimed after the six months qualifying period regardless of whether attendance is provided on a paid basis or not.

Note also that the attendant, if not the husband or wife of the disabled person, may have a separate entitlement to supplementary benefit.

Clothing and Footwear

Abnormal wear and tear

The regulations provide for an additional requirement where a person 'suffers from a physical or mental condition which has the consequence that his clothing or footwear wears out unusually quickly'. The amount of the additional requirement is 'the estimated extra cost, calculated on a weekly basis, of repairing or replacing the clothing or footwear'.[53]

In calculating the extra cost, it is necessary to make an estimate both of the actual expenditure on repairs and replacement of the relevant items of clothing or footwear over a period of time, and the normal cost of these items for a person not suffering from the condition in question. Only the difference is allowable. The clothing price lists given in Appendix 3 may be used as a guide to the cost of particular items, but where more durable clothing is needed the extra cost should be taken into account. If the benefit officer's estimate seems unreasonably low, it may be worth appealing.

If there is an immediate need for particular items of clothing or footwear, the possibility of entitlement to a single payment for these items should also be considered (see pages 162–8).

Special clothing or footwear

Where a person's stature or size or a physical disability make it necessary to buy items of clothing or footwear costing significantly more than the standard sizes or fittings, the extra cost, calculated on a weekly basis, is allowed as an additional requirement.[54] Officers are given detailed guidance on what can be regarded as standard sizes and fittings, based on the range of clothing obtainable from chain stores or mail order catalogues at a standard price or not more than 20 per cent above the standard price.[55] Where clothing of standard sizes has to be altered to make it wearable, the cost of alterations should be taken into account. But no allowance is made for special clothing or footwear obtainable under the National Health Service.

Hire Purchase of Furniture and Household Equipment

Where essential furniture or household equipment (defined as on page 146) is being bought under a hire-purchase agreement entered into before payment of supplementary benefit commenced, help with the outstanding instalments can be given either in the form of an additional requirement, increasing the weekly supplementary benefit entitlement normally by the amount (or weekly equivalent) of the instalments,[56] or by a single payment to enable the whole of the outstanding debt to be paid off. Which method is appropriate depends on whether supplementary benefit is likely to remain in payment for the remainder of the period of the hire-purchase agreement or not. A claimant who, in the opinion of the adjudication officer, is likely to remain on benefit throughout that period may be entitled to a single payment (see pages 155–6). If there are 'substantial grounds' for believing that during the term of the agreement payment of benefit will cease, he or she may be entitled to a weekly addition. If there appears to be a strong possibility that benefit will remain in payment, it is generally worth asking for a single payment rather than a weekly addition, since this will enable the whole of the remaining debt to be cleared, provided that it is not more than the full cost of similar items of reasonable quality. A single payment may not be the best solution, however, if the claimant has savings over £500, since the single payment will be reduced by the amount of savings over £500 (if the savings over £500 are enough to pay off the whole of the remaining instalments, there is no entitlement to either a single payment or a weekly addition). If the hire-purchase agreement was entered into after payment of supplementary benefit began, the instalments cannot be met by a weekly addition, only by a single payment.

Where a weekly addition is applicable, it will be of the amount needed to meet current instalments, excluding any arrears and any payments which can be postponed with the supplier's agreement or which are covered by an insurance clause in the hire-purchase agreement. Only payments for items of furniture or equipment which are mainly used by the claimant, the claimant's wife/husband and children will be included; not items used mainly by lodgers or non-dependent members of the household, including children who have left school. The question of cost or quality, however, does not arise. However expensive the items may be, the additional requirement will not be reduced on these grounds.[57]

The arrangements described above apply only to goods on hire purchase, not to furniture and equipment that already belong to the claimant and for which he is paying by instalments under a credit-sale agreement.

Storage of Furniture

Storage charges for 'essential household effects' belonging to and intended for use by the assessment unit can be treated as an additional requirement for up to twelve months where storage is necessary, the cost is reasonable and 'the person is using his best endeavours to obtain accommodation which will remove the necessity for storage'; but not if the claimant is a homeless person and the local authority can meet the storage charges under section 4 of the Housing (Homeless Persons) Act 1977.[58]

Visits to People in Hospital and Residential Accommodation

The cost of visiting somebody in hospital, a nursing home, or a home for elderly or disabled people can be met either by an additional requirement, if *regular* visits are made, or by a single payment in other cases. The provisions regarding single payments for this purpose are explained on pages 173–4. Single payments can also be made for the cost of an overnight stay if the return journey cannot be completed in a day, or accommodation for a longer period if this is necessary; and if the visitor cannot travel alone, a single payment can be made for the expenses of an escort. Where regular travelling expenses are met by an additional requirement, single payments can be made in addition for the cost of accommodation or an escort. The details given below should therefore be read in conjunction with the information about single payments on pages 173–4. Note also that the cost of visiting a critically ill relative who is *not* in hospital or residential accommodation can be met by an urgent need payment (see page 196).

An additional requirement for the cost of visiting arises only where the visitor's relationship to the person being visited (referred to as 'the patient' in the following paragraphs) is one of the following:

(a) a member of the household in which the patient lived before admission to the hospital or home (including a husband or wife);

(b) a 'close relative' – parent or step-parent, child or step-child, brother or sister;

(c) a more distant relative where the patient has no other relative who has visited recently and intends to continue visiting.

The costs that can be met are the second-class fare by whatever form of public transport is used (not necessarily the cheapest, but air travel is excluded) or the cost of petrol for private transport – but if public transport is available the cost of petrol will be met only up to the cost of public transport. A taxi will be paid for if public transport is not available or the visitor is physically disabled and unable to use it. If he or she is incapable of travelling alone, the fares of a companion are also allowed. There is no limit on the frequency of visits or the total cost for which provision can be made. The visits must, however, be within the United Kingdom.

The additional requirement is based on the average weekly cost. Where the patient and the visitor are still treated as members of the same assessment unit, however, the additional requirement for visiting may be reduced. This is because part of the benefit payable for the patient's own needs is assumed to be available for visiting expenses. The amounts deducted from the weekly cost of visiting in calculating the additional requirement depend partly on whether normal requirements have been assessed on the 'ordinary' scale or the long-term scale. From November 1984, the deductions are as follows:

	Ordinary scale	Long-term scale
Married couple – one member in hospital or home:		
Up to 8 weeks	£10.35	£14.25
More than 8 weeks	3.20	7.10
Single parent in hospital or home up to 8 weeks:		
Householder	20.90	28.55
Non-householder (see pages 58–9)	15.30	21.40
Dependent child in hospital or home up to 12 weeks:		
Under 11	2.45	2.45
11–15	7.20	7.20
16–17	10.15	10.15
18 or over	15.30	15.30

The amount allowed as an additional requirement is the weekly cost of visiting, less the appropriate deduction. In a case not listed above, e.g.

where a child has been in hospital more than twelve weeks, or in any case where the patient is no longer treated as a member of the assessment unit, no deduction is made and the visiting expenses are allowed in full.[59]

Boarding-out Fees Prior to Adoption

Where a child of the family is to be adopted, there may be a period during which the child, though still treated as a member of the household, is 'boarded out' with foster-parents and a boarding-out fee is payable. To the extent that the fee is not covered by the supplementary benefit scale rate for the child, it will be met (up to the amount of the boarding-out fee that the local authority would pay) by an additional requirement for the first eight weeks or for such longer period as the benefit officer may allow for completion of the adoption arrangements.[60]

REFERENCES

1. Requirements Regs. 11(2A).
2. Requirements Regs. 11(2B).
3. Requirements Regs., schedule 4, para. 9.
4. Requirements Regs., schedule 4, para. 12.
5. Requirements Regs. 2(1).
6. Requirements Regs., schedule 4, para. 8.
7. Requirements Regs. 12(2)(c)(ii).
8. Requirements Regs., schedule 4, para. 1(1).
9. CSB 702/82 and 339/83; R (SB) 41/84.
10. CSB 339/83.
11. Requirements Regs., schedule 4, para. 2(a).
12. CSB 1049/82 and 339/83.
13. S Manual, paras. 4161–3.
14. Requirements Regs., schedule 4, para. 3.
15. Requirements Regs., schedule 4, para. 8.
16. Requirements Regs., schedule 4, para. 7.
17. Requirements Regs., schedule 4, para. 1(2) and (3).
18. Requirements Regs., schedule 4, para. 2(b).
19. Requirements Regs., schedule 4, para. 6.
20. S Manual, para. 4298.
21. S Manual, para. 4294.
22. Requirements Regs. 12(2)(f).
23. Requirements Regs. 12(2)(d)(ii).
24. Requirements Regs. 12(2)(i).

25. Requirements Regs. 12(2)(*g*).
26. Requirements Regs., schedule 4, para. 5.
27. Requirements Regs., schedule 4, para. 4.
28. Requirements Regs. 12(3).
29. Requirements Regs. 12(2)(*g*).
30. *S Manual*, para. 4246.
31. Requirements Regs. 12(5)(*a*).
32. Requirements Regs., schedule 4, para. 14(*a*).
33. Requirements Regs., schedule 4, para. 14(*e*).
34. CSB 517/82 and 1148/82.
35. *S Manual*, para. 4737.
36. Requirements Regs., schedule 4, para. 14(*b*) and (*c*).
37. Requirements Regs., schedule 4, para. 14(*d*).
38. Requirements Regs. 13(2).
39. Requirements Regs., schedule 4, para. 18.
40. Requirements Regs., schedule 4, para. 11.
41. R (SB) 39/83.
42. Requirements Regs., schedule 4, para. 15.
43. CSB 629/82 and 1133/82.
44. *S Manual*, para. 4767.
45. *S Manual*, para. 4771.
46. CSB 201/83.
47. *S Manual*, para. 4781.
48. Janet Allbeson and John Douglas, *National Welfare Benefits Handbook*, 14th edition, p. 33.
49. CSB 201/83.
50. Requirements Regs., schedule 4, para. 10.
51. *S Manual*, paras. 4493–4.
52. *S Manual*, para. 4521.
53. Requirements Regs., schedule 4, para. 19.
54. Requirements Regs., schedule 4, para. 20.
55. *S Manual*, paras. 4914–15.
56. Requirements Regs., schedule 4, para. 16.
57. *S Manual*, para. 4791(1).
58. Requirements Regs., schedule 4, para. 21.
59. Requirements Regs., schedule 4, para. 17.
60. Requirements Regs., schedule 4, para. 13.

Chapter 4

Housing Costs –
Mainly for Owner-Occupiers

People on supplementary benefit get help with their housing costs from either or both of two sources. Money to pay rent and rates comes in the form of *housing benefit* paid by the local authority. Other housing costs are taken into account as *housing requirements* in calculating the weekly supplementary benefit payments. The local authority housing benefit scheme is not just for people on supplementary benefit but covers nearly everybody paying rent or rates and whose income is fairly low. For those *not* on supplementary benefit, however, housing benefit usually covers only part of the rent and/or rates, with the result that the income they have left after paying the balance of the rent and rates may be less than they would get on supplementary benefit. Some people in this situation can get a third type of benefit known as *housing benefit supplement*. This supplement is paid by the local authority as an addition to the housing benefit; but as it is paid under the supplementary benefit regulations, it gives entitlement to the additional benefits payable to people on supplementary benefit, including the single payments for exceptional needs described in Chapter 7.

This chapter deals with the housing requirements included in the weekly supplementary benefit payments. Housing benefit and housing benefit supplement are the subject of Chapter 5.

Housing Requirements

The housing requirements taken into account in calculating supplementary benefit are:

Costs of buying or renting the home

Mortgage interest (see pages 86–8).
Payments under a co-ownership scheme not eligible for housing benefit (see page 89).
Ground rent on a long lease (more than 21 years).

Rent paid by a Crown tenant.

Croft rent in Scotland.

Payments for a tent or tent site.

Maintenance and services

Interest on loans for repairs and improvements (see pages 89–91).

House maintenance and insurance (see page 91).

Service charges, e.g. for maintenance, insurance, management and cleaning of common areas, if not covered by housing benefit (see page 91).

Water and (except in Scotland) sewerage charges (see pages 91–2).

Charges for emptying cess-pits or septic tanks.

Materials for servicing a chemical toilet.

Miscellaneous

Payments 'analogous' to any of the above.[1]

No separate allowance is made for the housing costs of a *boarder*, which are assumed to be included in the board and lodging charge (though a boarder who is not on supplementary benefit may be entitled to housing benefit). For a *'non-householder'*, a fixed allowance is made for housing costs (see page 59).

Housing requirements are included in the supplementary benefit calculation only where the claimant or a member of the assessment unit is responsible for the expenditure. Being 'responsible' normally means being legally liable (but not to a member of the same household) for the item in question, whether under a written agreement or not. But the adjudication officer may, if he thinks it is reasonable, treat as responsible for the expenditure a person who, though not legally liable, has to keep up the payments in order to remain in the home – for instance, where the home is in the husband's name but the wife has to make the payments in his absence.[2] Where responsibility is shared, the claimant is treated as responsible for an appropriate share of the expenditure, provided that the adjudication officer is satisfied that this is reasonable and provided also that the responsibility is not shared with a parent, step-parent, child, step-child, brother or sister of the claimant.[3] Officers are told to calculate the 'appropriate' share by dividing the total cost by the number of persons treated as sharing it.[4] If this does not produce a fair result, however, the claimant should ask for the calculation to be done in a different way.

Where the payments taken into account as housing requirements cover the provision of heating, hot water, lighting or cooking fuel, a fixed deduction is made for these items in the same way as in the calculation of housing benefit (see page 101), a smaller deduction being made if only partial heating, etc., is provided.[5]

Housing requirements are taken into account on a weekly basis, whether the expenditure is actually made weekly or at other intervals. The weekly equivalent is calculated, where necessary, by dividing the amount payable for the year by 52. Where payments are waived for a specific purpose, e.g. while repairs are carried out, no adjustment is made in the benefit payable for the first eight weeks.[6]

Mortgage Payments

The housing requirements of a claimant who owns his or her home or is buying it will normally include water and sewerage charges, ground rent if any, an allowance for maintenance and insurance, and the interest on the mortgage – or on money borrowed without a mortgage for the purpose of buying or improving the home. But if a claimant, while on supplementary benefit, arranges to buy his or her existing home, the housing requirements, initially at least, will not be increased as a result (see pages 88–9).

Mortgage payments are usually made monthly and consist partly of interest on the capital sum borrowed and partly of repayments of the capital sum. Only the interest can be included in the claimant's housing requirements, not the capital repayments.[7] The reason for this is that it is considered wrong that public money should be used to help a private individual acquire a permanent asset (though the same objection does not seem to apply where the help takes the form of an improvement grant or the sale of a council house at less than its market value). The premiums on a life assurance policy taken out as a condition of the mortgage also do not count as housing requirements.[8]

For the interest to be included in the claimant's housing requirements, the purpose of the mortgage must normally have been either to acquire the home or, in certain circumstances (see pages 89–91), to pay for repairs or improvements. There are, however, two types of case where interest on a mortgage for other purposes can be included. The first is where the mortgage is in the name of the claimant's husband or wife (alone or jointly with the claimant) who has left the home and cannot or will not pay the interest, so that the claimant has to pay it in order to retain the home.[9] The second is where the money was borrowed for business purposes and the claimant intends to sell the home in order to discharge the business liabilities. The interest is then allowed for up to six months if this is essential to allow the sale to be made on reasonable terms.[10]

To find out how much of each mortgage payment is interest and how much is capital, it may be necessary to ask the lender (building society, local council, etc.) to supply the figures. The claimant can do this or authorize the social security office to approach the lender. Where, as is usually the case, tax relief has been deducted, it is the net interest paid by the claimant that is taken into account.[11] If there is a reduction in the amount of interest included in the mortgage payments, whether through a fall in interest rates or because the outstanding debt has been reduced, supplementary benefit entitlement is not affected provided that the mortgage payments are continuing at the same rate. The reduction is, however, taken into account the next time the benefit is adjusted for some other reason.[12]

The 'interest only' rule often seems unfair, especially where the total mortgage payments are less than the rent of similar accommodation. The rule, however, is laid down in the regulations and must be applied. In practice, hardship can usually be avoided by asking the lender to agree to only the interest being paid while the borrower is in receipt of supplementary benefit. Most lenders will agree, but sometimes there are difficulties, particularly if the payments are already in arrears; and, of course, deferment of capital repayments means it will take longer to pay off the mortgage. Moreover, some people may not want to make such a request, and there may be little point in doing so if supplementary benefit is likely to be paid for a short time only.

There are three other possible ways of getting round the 'interest only' rule. One is to sublet part of the home. The net proceeds of subletting (calculated as explained on page 103) are first set off against any housing benefit and the balance is regarded as available to meet the capital repayments on the mortgage and is ignored to the extent that it is needed for this purpose. But this concession is given only if (a) the claimant is not in a position to pay off the mortgage and still have more than £500 capital left, excluding the value of the home, and (b) any possible reduction or suspension of the capital repayments has been obtained.[13]

The second possibility is to take in a lodger. A fixed deduction will then be made from the housing requirements, but the actual payments made by the lodger will be ignored (see pages 92–3) and any 'profit' can go towards the mortgage payments. Similarly, any contribution to the mortgage payments made by a non-dependent member of the family – e.g. a child of working age – will not affect the claimant's benefit entitlement.

The third possible solution is to obtain an allowance from a charity, a relative (other than a 'liable relative' – see page 211) or some other source. Provided that the money is given voluntarily for the purpose of meeting the capital repayments and is used for that purpose, it will not affect the amount of benefit payable.[14]

Tenants Who Buy their Homes

If a tenant who already enjoys security of tenure as a council tenant or under the Rent Act buys his or her home, whether from a private landlord or under the arrangements for sale of council houses, the housing requirements after the purchase will be restricted to the 'eligible rent' on which housing benefit was calculated before the purchase (see page 100) plus water and sewerage charges. Thus, the total benefit will not be increased to meet any additional costs resulting from the purchase. The restriction does not apply if, when the person became liable to complete the purchase (normally the date of exchanging contracts), he or she was not in receipt of supplementary benefit; and it ceases to apply if at any time it becomes inappropriate because of a major change of circumstances which affects the claimant's ability to meet the housing costs.[15] The underlying principle is that, in taking on the increased commitment, a claimant should be prepared to meet the extra cost out of his or her existing income – but if subsequent events prevent this, the claimant will be treated in the same way as any other owner-occupier. In one Commissioner's decision it was suggested that if the claimant reasonably believed that his benefit would be increased, the discovery – too late – of his error might constitute a 'major change of circumstances' for this purpose.[16] Other more likely examples of major changes of circumstances justifying the lifting of the restriction, taken from the guidance issued to officers, are a reduction in earnings or other income, a substantial reduction of capital, the loss of income of a kind that is to some extent disregarded for supplementary benefit purposes, and the departure from the household of a non-dependent member who was in full-time work.[17]

If a claimant to whom the restriction applies ceases to receive supplementary benefit but claims again within eight weeks, the restriction will be imposed again. But if the interruption of benefit is more than eight weeks, the restriction will not apply when benefit recommences.[18]

Co-ownership

In a co-ownership housing society, each of the 'tenants' acquires an interest in the capital value of the properties held by the society. A member who leaves after a qualifying period may be entitled to a payment from the society in respect of his or her share. The weekly or monthly 'rent' enables the society to meet the mortgage repayments on the properties. In effect, therefore, a co-owner is in much the same position as an owner-occupier. The regulations, however, treat members of co-ownership societies more generously, by allowing the whole of the payments to be included in their housing requirements, even though they include a contribution towards the capital repayments as well as the mortgage interest.[19] A co-owner's housing requirements may also include water and sewerage charges, ground rent, management charges, and a fixed allowance for maintenance and insurance (see page 91).

Members of a housing co-operative who do not have a right to a share in the capital value of the property are treated in the same way as private tenants: their rent is not treated as a housing requirement for supplementary benefit purposes, but qualifies for a rent allowance from the local authority.[20]

Rental Purchase

This is a method of buying a house, found mainly in the north-west of England and generally confined to property of low value, often nearing the end of its life. It has more in common with hire purchase than with the purchase of a house by means of a mortgage, since ownership of the house does not change hands until the final instalment is paid. Payments under a rental purchase agreement are not allowed as housing requirements but qualify in full for a rent allowance from the local authority, even though part of the payments is for the capital value of the house.[21]

Interest on Loans for Repairs and Improvements

If money has been borrowed to pay for major repairs or improvements to the home, the interest on the loan can be included in the claimant's housing requirements. The loan may be secured by a mortgage, but the interest is allowed whether there is a mortgage or not.[22] The claimant need not own the property: for instance, a tenant might borrow money to improve the storage facilities of the home.

If the claimant has capital over £500 (excluding the value of the home) the excess is deducted from the loan before calculating the amount of interest allowable. For example if the outstanding loan is £1,000 and the claimant has £700 in the bank, £200 of this will be deducted from the £1,000 and interest on the remaining £800 only will be included in the housing requirements.[23]

The regulation sets out the purposes for which the money must have been borrowed if the interest is to count as a housing requirement. It must either have been for 'major repairs necessary to maintain the fabric of the home' or for one or more of the following improvements 'undertaken with a view to improving its fitness for occupation':

(a) installation of a fixed bath or shower, wash basin, sink or lavatory (including plumbing);
(b) damp-proofing;
(c) provision or improvement of ventilation and natural lighting;
(d) provision of electric lighting and sockets;
(e) provision or improvement of drainage facilities;
(f) improvements to the structural condition of the home;
(g) improvements to food storage, preparation and cooking facilities;
(h) provision of heating, including central heating;
(i) provision of storage facilities for fuel and refuse;
(j) improvements to the insulation of the home;
(k) 'other improvements which are reasonable in the circumstances'.[24]

The list, with its 'catch-all' final category, is comprehensive. Interest should be allowed on a loan for any reasonable improvement to the basic facilities or structure of the home, whether the sum involved is large or small and whether the improvements were carried out before or after payment of supplementary benefit commenced.

Where the loan is for repairs rather than improvements, the repairs must be both 'major' and 'necessary to maintain the fabric of the home'. Minor repairs must be financed in other ways – either out of the weekly 'maintenance and insurance' allowance for owner-occupiers and tenants who are responsible for repairs (see below) or by means of a single payment for a repair costing up to £325 which cannot be financed in any other way (see page 160).

If survey fees are incurred in connection with a loan for repairs or improvements, they can be met by means of a single payment (see page 157).

House Maintenance and Insurance

A weekly allowance for maintenance and insurance of the home is included in the housing requirements of a claimant who owns or is buying his or her home, or is a member of a co-ownership scheme, or a tenant who, under the lease or tenancy agreement, has to pay for all structural repairs or insurance. The allowance is £1.80 a week. If the insurance alone comes to more than this, however, the allowance can be increased to such amount as is reasonable having regard to any special circumstances such as a high fire risk. The increased allowance should be more than the cost of insurance, to allow something for repairs in addition.[25]

If repairs are needed which cannot be paid for out of what remains of the weekly allowance after paying for insurance, it should be possible to get a single payment for the cost of the repairs (see page 160). If the weekly allowance only covers the cost of insurance, single payments should be made for *all* essential minor repairs.

Service Charges

Charges for services such as maintenance, insurance, management or cleaning of common areas are included in the claimant's housing requirements if they are not covered by housing benefit – for example if the claimant has a long lease or is a member of a co-ownership scheme. Certain services are excluded, however – window-cleaning in the claimant's own accommodation, sports facilities, laundry, any facility which is 'not reasonably necessary for the proper enjoyment' of the accommodation having regard to the claimant's age and other circumstances and the type and location of the dwelling, and any service that comes within the definition of 'normal requirements', such as heating (see pages 52–3).[26]

Water and Sewerage Charges

If the claimant is responsible for the water and (except in Scotland) sewerage charges or they are included in the rent, they will be included in the housing requirements for supplementary benefit purposes but will not necessarily be paid as part of the weekly supplementary benefit.

If the claimant is a tenant of a local authority which collects water charges, the DHSS pays the charges direct to the local authority, provided that this leaves the claimant with some supplementary benefit. Similarly, if the claimant is a private tenant and pays the water charges to the landlord, either as part of an inclusive rent or as a separate item, the water charges are added to the housing benefit paid by the local authority, again provided that this leaves the claimant with some supplementary benefit.[27] In all other cases – people who pay water charges direct to the water authority or whose supplementary benefit entitlement is less than the water charges – the charges are included in the normal supplementary benefit assessment.

Income from Subletting

If part of the claimant's home is let to a tenant or sub-tenant, the proceeds, calculated as explained on page 103, are first deducted from the housing costs met by housing benefit. Any balance remaining, unless it is needed to meet the capital repayments on a mortgage (see page 87), is then deducted from any housing requirements (other than water charges) taken into account in the supplementary benefit calculation.[28] If there is still a balance remaining after that, it is treated as an income resource of which up to £4 can be disregarded (item 40(d) in the table on page 119) and the rest is deducted from the supplementary benefit payable for living expenses.[29] There will usually be some delay in finding out from the local authority how much of the proceeds of subletting is to be deducted from the supplementary benefit. Meanwhile, an interim deduction of £12 a week can be made for each sub-tenant if the claimant is an owner-occupier, or £8 a week otherwise; but the interim deduction must not reduce the supplementary benefit payable to less than 10p a week.[30]

Deductions for Boarders and Other Non-dependants

If there are people aged 16 or over living in the household, other than the claimant's wife or husband and dependent children or a person in one of the groups mentioned in the next paragraph, they are assumed to be making a contribution to the housing costs, which is taken into account in calculating the claimant's entitlement to *either* housing benefit *or* supplementary benefit.[31] If the claimant receives housing benefit for the rent, the non-dependant's assumed contribution is deducted from the housing benefit (see pages 105–6). If the claimant is an owner-occupier, or a tenant whose rent is included in the supplementary benefit calculation (e.g. a Crown tenant or long leaseholder), the non-dependant's contribution is deducted from the housing requirements. The amounts are the same: a standard deduction of £6.60, reduced to £2.35 for a non-dependant in any of the following categories:

(a) Under 18.
(b) Over pension age.
(c) On supplementary benefit.
(d) On unemployment benefit, sickness benefit (or sick pay) or maternity allowance for the past eight weeks (including 'waiting days' for which the benefit in question was not paid), and at present having no income other than these benefits and child benefit. Provided that the non-dependant signs a statement to this effect, the lower rate of deduction is backdated to the time when the conditions were first satisfied.

In the case of a non-dependent couple, only one deduction is made, and the lower rate applies if either of them satisfies one of the above conditions (e.g. has been on unemployment benefit for eight weeks). No additional deduction is made for a non-dependant's child.[32]

No deduction at all is made for a non-dependant in one of the following categories:

(a) Under 21 and on supplementary benefit.
(b) Under 18 and receiving a severe disablement allowance.
(c) A student at least partially maintained by the claimant.
(d) A Youth Training Scheme trainee.
(e) A non-paying visitor.
(f) Where the claimant is blind (or regained his or her eyesight in the last six months while on supplementary benefit) or the non-dependant is providing residential domestic help to a severely disabled member of the assessment unit.
(g) A boarder, if the claimant normally takes in three or more boarders (but part of the income received from them is treated as the claimant's earnings – see page 121).[33]

Mortgage Interest, etc. not Allowed in Full

If a claimant's full housing costs were automatically met by either supplementary benefit or housing benefit, there would be cases in which people would be allowed to remain in very expensive accommodation for long periods at public expense. Both the supplementary benefit and housing benefit regulations seek to prevent this without causing hardship where it would be unreasonable to expect claimants to move.

The housing requirements included in the supplementary benefit calculation (in practice this means mortgage interest and payments under a co-ownership scheme) can be reduced on the grounds that, and to the extent that, *either* the home, excluding any part which is sublet or used for boarders, is unnecessarily large, *or* it is in 'an unnecessarily expensive area'. But this does not apply if it would be unreasonable to expect the claimant to seek cheaper accommodation. In deciding whether it would be reasonable or not, the adjudication officer must have regard to the availability of suitable accommodation and the level of housing costs in the area, and to 'the circumstances of the assessment unit', including the age and state of health of its members, the claimant's employment prospects and the effect on a child's education if the move resulted in a change of school. Although these are the only factors mentioned in the regulation, other 'circumstances of the assessment unit' can also be taken into account – e.g. how long they have occupied their present home, whether it is particularly suitable for their needs, and how long they are likely to need supplementary benefit.

If the adjudication officer does decide that it is reasonable to expect the claimant to look for somewhere cheaper, the full housing requirements must still be met for the first six months on supplementary benefit if the claimant, or the claimant's wife or husband, was able to meet the financial commitments for the home when they were first entered into. In the case of a mortgage it can generally be assumed that this was the case, since otherwise they would not have been able to borrow the money (but note the rule regarding tenants who buy their homes while on supplementary benefit – see page 88). After the first six months, the housing costs must be met in full for a further six months if the claimant is doing his best to find cheaper accommodation.[34]

In practice, it will seldom make sense for an owner-occupier to sell up and move simply because only part of the mortgage interest is covered by the supplementary benefit payments. Subletting or taking in a boarder may be a more satisfactory solution, especially if the reason for the restriction is that the home is considered unnecessarily large.

Absence from Home

The amounts allowed for housing requirements must relate to the claimant's home, and the regulations define 'home' as the accommodation in Great Britain *normally* occupied by the assessment unit (the claimant and the claimant's wife, husband and dependent children, if any) and any other members of the same household.[35] The costs of the home (including rent and rates – see page 106) can still be met, therefore, even if they are temporarily absent from it. A single person who qualifies for the householder scale rate continues to be treated as a householder while away from home for up to thirteen weeks, unless he or she is a student absent from the term-time 'home' during normal vacations.[36] The housing requirements, however, can continue to be met after the claimant has ceased to be treated as a householder. The rule is that the housing requirements (other than for a student's term-time accommodation) *may* be met provided that the absence has not lasted, and is not likely to last, for substantially more than a year (in practice this is taken to mean up to fifteen months) and that it is reasonable that the accommodation should be retained. This discretionary power to meet housing costs during absence from home can be used where the claimant is admitted to hospital or Part III accommodation, or to a re-establishment centre, is staying with relatives, or has to move out temporarily while the home is being repaired or redecorated.[37]

Housing costs may also be met on a discretionary basis for up to a year where this is reasonable pending completion of the sale of the home. Thus, if and when it is decided that it is no longer reasonable for the claimant to retain his or her home because he or she is unlikely to return to it, up to another year can be allowed for the sale of the home, during which the outgoings – mortgage interest, etc. – will continue to be met. The claimant is expected to provide evidence of the efforts to dispose of the home and the situation is reviewed every three months.[38]

Two Homes

A claimant's housing costs cannot normally be met for more than one home at a time, whether by supplementary benefit or by housing benefit. But there are two exceptions: where a claimant unavoidably has to pay for two homes, the costs of both can be met for up to four weeks; and if the reason is that the claimant moved out of the first home for fear of domestic violence, the costs of both homes can be met for as long as is reasonable.[39] For the corresponding provision in the housing benefit scheme, see pages 106–7.

REFERENCES

1. Requirements Regs. 14(1) and 18(1).
2. Requirements Regs. 15(3).
3. Requirements Regs. 14(3).
4. *S Manual*, para. 5027.
5. Requirements Regs. 18(3).
6. Requirements Regs. 18(6).
7. Requirements Regs. 15(1).
8. R (SB) 46/83.
9. Requirements Regs. 15(3).
10. Requirements Regs. 15(4).
11. Requirements Regs. 15(1).
12. Requirements Regs. 15(2); Adjudication Regs. 87(3).
13. Requirements Regs. 22(2).
14. Resources Regs. 11(4)(*j*)(ii).
15. Requirements Regs. 20.
16. CSB 356/82.
17. *S Manual*, paras. 5151–2.
18. Requirements Regs. 20(2)(*c*).
19. Requirements Regs. 18(1)(*c*).
20. Housing Benefits Regs. 8(1) and (2)(*d*).
21. Housing Benefits Regs. 2(1) (definition of 'rent').
22. Requirements Regs. 17(1).
23. Requirements Regs. 17(2).
24. Requirements Regs. 17(3).
25. Requirements Regs. 16.
26. Claims and Payments Regs. 15A.
27. Requirements Regs. 18(1)(*e*).
28. Requirements Regs. 22(2).
29. Resources Regs. 11(5)(*d*).
30. Urgent Cases Regs. 19(3)–(5).
31. Requirements Regs. 22(3) and (5)(*d*).
32. Requirements Regs. 22(4), (6) and (7).
33. Requirements Regs. 22(5).
34. Requirements Regs. 21.
35. Requirements Regs. 2(1).

36. Requirements Regs. 5(6)(*c*).
37. Requirements Regs. 14(4)(*a*); *S Manual*, paras. 5117–18.
38. Requirements Regs. 14(4)(*b*); *S Manual*, paras. 5120–21.
39. Requirements Regs. 14(5)(*b*).

Chapter 5

Housing Costs – Rent and Rates

Most of this chapter is not about supplementary benefit but about the ways in which people on supplementary benefit get their rent and rates paid by the local authority under the housing benefit scheme. But it also deals with the very important question of entitlement to housing benefit supplement which, as explained at the beginning of Chapter 4, is a form of supplementary benefit although paid in conjunction with housing benefit by the local authority.

Certificated Housing Benefit

The basic principle is that anyone on supplementary benefit who is paying rent or rates for their home, except as a boarder, should receive housing benefit to cover the full amount of their rent and rates.[1] But in some cases the housing benefit covers only part of the rent and rates: where part of the accommodation is sublet, where there is a non-dependent member of the household (including a boarder), where the accommodation is considered unreasonably large or expensive, or where the rent includes the cost of fuel or charges for facilities such as personal laundry and window cleaning. There are also a few types of cases, already mentioned in Chapter 4, where provision for rent is made in the supplementary benefit scheme and not as housing benefit: long leaseholders (other than those buying part of their home under a shared ownership scheme), Crown tenants, co-owners, crofters and tent-dwellers.[2]

The payments made under the housing benefit scheme are of three kinds: *rate rebates*, *rent rebates* for council and New Town tenants, and *rent allowances* for private tenants. 'Rent', for this purpose, includes payments made by licensees as well as tenants, payments under a rental purchase agreement (see page 89), mooring fees for houseboats and site charges for caravans, provided that they are used as the claimant's home.[3] It can also include the rent of a separate garage (see page 100).

When supplementary benefit is awarded to a person who is responsible for housing expenditure – rent, rates or both – the Department of Health and Social Security issues a certificate to the local authority, informing them of the date from which supplementary benefit is payable and, if the dwelling is shared, the proportion of the rent and rates for which the person is responsible.[4] The local authority must then award housing benefit, starting from the same date,[5] to meet the whole of the person's 'eligible' rent and rates, less any deduction for non-dependants.[6] This is known as *certificated housing benefit*. The person may already have been getting housing benefit before supplementary benefit began. This is known as *standard housing benefit*. If so, it is immediately replaced by certificated housing benefit. Whether housing benefit was awarded previously or not, a person claiming supplementary benefit does not have to make a separate claim for housing benefit. It may be necessary to send the local council details of the housing costs and of any sub-tenants, but a form will be provided for this purpose – there is no need to ask for it.

A person is not treated as responsible for housing expenditure, and therefore eligible for certificated housing benefit, if the payments are made to a member of the same household[7] (but note that people living in the same house are not necessarily members of the same household – see pages 55–6). If responsibility is shared with other members of the household who are not close relatives (parents, step-parents, children, step-children, brothers or sisters), each of them may be eligible for housing benefit to cover his or her share.[8] A person with no legal liability for the rent or rates is treated as responsible for them if he or she has to pay them in order to remain in the home and the supplementary benefit adjudication officer accepts that it is reasonable to treat him or her as responsible (see page 55).[9]

Calculation of Certificated Housing Benefit

In a completely straightforward case, the claimant is entitled to a rent rebate or rent allowance of the full amount of rent he or she is paying, and a rate rebate of the full amount of general rates.[10] But a number of adjustments may have to be made, with the result that the rebate or allowance is less than the actual rent or rates. There are three main stages in the calculation. The first is to ascertain the *eligible rent* or *eligible rates*. The second is to consider whether the eligible rent or rates should be reduced because the accommodation is *'unsuitable'* (unreasonably large or expensive). The third stage is to make any necessary deductions for *non-dependants*, including boarders. The rebate or allowance is the amount remaining after these deductions.

Eligible Rent

The eligible rent, for the purpose of either a rent rebate (for a council tenant) or a rent allowance (for a private tenant) is the full rent calculated on a weekly basis, after deducting any of the following items:

    (a) Rates.
    (b) Water charges.
    (c) Fuel.
    (d) Certain service charges.
    (e) The proceeds of subletting.

Each of these deductions is explained more fully below.

If the rent of the accommodation is restricted by law to the 'fair rent' registered by a rent officer or the 'reasonable rent' fixed by a rent tribunal, the eligible rent, after making the above deductions, must not be more than this amount.[11]

If the rent is payable at intervals of more than a week, the weekly equivalent must be calculated. If there are rent-free periods in the course of a year, the rent for the whole year must be divided by 52 or 53 to arrive at the weekly rent for this purpose.[12]

Garages, gardens, etc.

Any building or land which is 'used for the purposes of the dwelling' is treated as part of it, and the rent paid for it is therefore treated as part of the 'eligible rent', if *either* it was acquired at the same time and the home, if rented, could not have been rented separately, *or* the claimant has made or is making all reasonable efforts to get rid of the liability.[13] Otherwise, the proportion of the rent which relates to these parts of the property is excluded in calculating the eligible rent.

Rates

If the rates are paid by the landlord, the rent will be assumed to include them and the amount 'fairly attributable' to rates will be deducted in calculating the eligible rent.[14] The claimant does not lose as a result, since the amount deducted will qualify for a rate rebate instead.

Water charges

A similar deduction is made for any water and sewerage charges covered by the rent.[15] Again, the claimant does not suffer, since these items are provided for in the supplementary benefit regulations, though for practical purposes they are treated, in most cases, as if they were covered by the housing benefit scheme (see page 92).

Fuel

If the rent covers the provision of fuel for heating, hot water, lighting, cooking, or any combination of these, other than lighting and heating of communal areas, a deduction is made in calculating the eligible rent, since normal fuel costs are assumed to be covered by the supplementary benefit scale rates. If the charge varies with the amount of fuel used, the actual charge is deducted from the rent. If it is part of an inclusive rent and not separately identifiable, the deduction is as follows, depending on the purposes for which fuel is supplied:

For heating (other than hot water)	£6.25
For hot water	0.75
For lighting	0.50
For cooking	0.75

For example, if the rent includes fuel for heating and hot water but the claimant has to pay separately for lighting and cooking fuel, the deduction will be £7. These amounts apply also where a fixed charge is made which *is* separately identifiable, unless the charge for any item is lower, in which case the actual charge is deducted.[16]

If the rent includes heating but the heating provided is not adequate for the dwelling, the local authority can make such smaller deduction as it considers reasonable in the circumstances.[17] Two questions arise in such cases: is the heating adequate and, if not, by how much should the normal deduction be reduced? A circular issued to local authorities by the Department of Health and Social Security offers guidance on both these points (guidance which the local authority is not bound to follow but normally will). In considering whether the heating is adequate, the local authority is not concerned with any special needs which the claimant or anyone else living in the accommodation may have, for example, because of ill health or age – these needs can be met, if necessary, as 'additional requirements' in the supplementary benefit assessment (see pages 68–9). What the local authority has to decide is whether the heating would be adequate if there were no such special needs. The DHSS circular suggests that a suitable standard for judging this might be that, when the outside temperature is just below freezing (minus 1° Centigrade), the heating system should be capable of achieving temperatures of 21° in living-rooms, 18° in 'circulation areas' and 15° in bedrooms (the Fahrenheit equivalents are 70°, 65° and 60°). If the heating is switched off for a period during the night or for less than twelve weeks during the summer, the circular suggests, this will not normally mean that it does not provide full heating. The circular also gives some examples of the amounts by which it would be appropriate to reduce the maximum deduction of £6.25 where the heating does not come up to this standard: 10 per cent if the heating is shut down for, say, 20 weeks in the summer; 10 to 20 per cent if the system cannot maintain an adequate temperature in the bedrooms; 20 to 40 per cent if the system is designed to provide a lower standard of heating.[18]

The type of case envisaged in the DHSS circular is that of a claimant living on a council estate with what is intended to be full central heating. The same standards should, however, be applied in the less common situation where a private tenant is paying a rent which includes the provision of heating.

Service charges

Services other than heating are generally treated in the same way for housing benefit purposes as for supplementary benefit (see page 91). Charges for services such as maintenance, insurance, management and cleaning of common areas can be included in the eligible rent provided that they are, or were originally, payable as a condition of the tenancy. But if the rent includes charges for window cleaning (other than in communal areas), sports facilities (other than a children's play area), laundry (except facilities to do one's own) and services which the local authority considers 'not reasonably necessary for the proper enjoyment of the dwelling', taking into account the claimant's age and other circumstances and the type and location of the dwelling, these charges, or the amount of rent 'fairly attributable' to them, must be deducted in calculating the eligible rent. The local authority also has a discretionary power to deduct such amount as it considers appropriate if it considers a charge made for any other service, except the use of furniture, to be excessive; but this power seems unnecessary since, in the case of a private tenant, there is an overriding power to reduce the eligible rent if it is unreasonably high (see page 104).[19]

Income from subletting

Any rent (adjusted as explained below) received from letting or subletting part of the home, other than to a boarder, is deducted in calculating the eligible rent.[20] If it is more than enough to cancel out the eligible rent altogether, or there is no eligible rent (e.g. if the claimant is an owner-occupier), the balance is deducted from the rate rebate that would otherwise be payable,[21] and if there is still a balance left over after that, it is taken into account in the supplementary benefit calculation (see pages 92 and 119 – item 40(d) in the table). It is generally more advantageous to the claimant if a person living in the home is treated as a boarder rather than a sub-tenant, since the actual payments made by boarders are ignored, only the fixed 'non-dependant' deductions being made (at most, £8.80 a week – see page 105). Provision of a token amount of food, however, will not convert a sub-tenant into a boarder. For this purpose, a boarder is someone making payments of which a 'substantial proportion' is for board.[22]

The amount to be deducted for the proceeds of subletting is the weekly rent paid by the sub-tenant, reduced by the amount considered by the local authority to be for rates, water charges, food (if any) and fuel for heating, hot water, lighting or cooking. A further reduction is made for services and furniture: £2.90 a week if furniture is provided by the claimant, £1.45 if not – and 35p a week if the letting includes a garage or outbuilding.[23]

Eligible Rates

Calculation of the eligible rates, on which the rate rebate is based, is more straightforward. Normally the total rates (general, not water rates) payable in respect of the home are 'eligible', whether paid direct by the claimant or by the landlord. If the claimant's household occupies only part of the premises, the other part being let to somebody else or sublet by the claimant, the eligible rates are the proportion that relates to the claimant's accommodation.[24] Similarly, if the accommodation is shared, the Department of Health and Social Security decides, and tells the local authority, what proportion of the rates the claimant is to be treated as responsible for.[25] If only part of the premises is residential accommodation, only the rates for that part are 'eligible'.[26] The rules regarding rates paid for garages, gardens, etc., are the same as in the calculation of eligible rent (see page 100). If the rates are not paid weekly, they must be converted into a weekly amount; and if they are paid with the rent, and rent-free weeks are allowed, the annual rates bill must be divided by either 52 or 53 to arrive at the weekly figure.[27]

'Unsuitable' Accommodation

Having calculated the eligible rent as explained above, the local authority, subject to certain safeguards, can substitute a lower figure, of whatever amount it considers appropriate, if *either* the home is larger than is reasonably required by the people living in it, including any non-dependants or sub-tenants, *or* the eligible rates or rent are unreasonably high compared with suitable alternative accommodation in the same local authority area, either because of the location of the home (i.e. it is in a particularly expensive area) or, if it is rented from a private landlord or housing association, for any other reason.[28]

Although the regulation which gives the local authority this power is headed *'Unsuitable accommodation'*, the accommodation may be entirely suitable from the claimant's point of view. The regulation therefore places some important restrictions on the ways in which the powers can be used. First, in deciding whether the eligible rates or rent are unreasonably high, other accommodation is not to be considered suitable unless it offers 'reasonably equivalent' security of tenure.[29] A DHSS circular dealing with this point adds, 'The accommodation should also only be regarded as suitable if it is of an adequate size and in a reasonable condition.'[30]

Secondly, the power to substitute a lower figure for the eligible rent is not to be used if it would be unreasonable to expect the claimant to look for somewhere cheaper. For this purpose, the local authority must have regard to the availability of suitable alternative accommodation, not necessarily in the same council area – and here, too, 'suitable' means with reasonably equivalent security of tenure. It must also have regard to the circumstances of the people concerned – not just the claimant, wife or husband and children, but any non-dependants, boarders or sub-tenants – in deciding whether it is reasonable to expect the claimant to seek cheaper accommodation. Among the circumstances to be taken into account, the regulation mentions, in particular, their age and state of health, how long they have been living there, the claimant's employment prospects, and the effect on the children's education if a move resulted in a change of school.[31]

Finally, if the authority concludes that it is reasonable to expect the claimant to move, no reduction is to be made in the eligible rent during his or her first six months in receipt of housing benefit if the claimant or a member of the household could afford the accommodation when they originally took it on.[32] If the six months expired before supplementary benefit commenced (e.g. where the claimant received 'standard' housing benefit while in work), this final safeguard will no longer apply.

These rules are very similar to those relating to 'unnecessarily' high mortgage interest (see pages 93–5). An important difference, however, is that while the adjudication officer *must* restrict the amount allowed for mortgage interest if it is unnecessarily high and none of the safeguards apply, the local authority *may* restrict the eligible rates or rent but is not obliged to do so. This difference should be borne in mind both by local authorities and by claimants who are considering whether to apply for a review of the authority's decision.

Deductions for Boarders and Other Non-dependants

The deductions made from the eligible rent in calculating the rent rebate or rent allowance, in a case where there is a boarder or other non-dependent member of the claimant's household, are virtually the same as the deductions from supplementary benefit where the claimant is an owner-occupier and there are non-dependants in the household. The standard deduction is £6.60 a week, but this is reduced to £2.35 in certain cases, while in other cases no deduction is made.[33] The circumstances in which each rate applies are explained on pages 92–3 and are not repeated here.

Similar deductions are made in calculating the rate rebate. The two rates of deduction are £2.20 and £0.95 per week and the rules for deciding whether the higher or lower rate or neither applies are exactly the same as for a rent rebate or allowance.[34]

The only significant difference between the supplementary benefit and housing benefit deductions for non-dependants is in cases where there are three or more boarders. If the claimant is an owner-occupier, no deduction is made from the housing requirements for supplementary benefit purposes, in view of the fact that part of the income received from the boarders is taken into account as earnings. In the housing benefit scheme, the normal deductions are made for each boarder, regardless of the number of boarders in the household. If there are three or more boarders, however, the amount taken into account as earnings for supplementary benefit purposes is reduced by the amounts deducted from the housing benefits by the local authority.[35]

For the lower rate of deductions to apply where a non-dependant has been on sickness or unemployment benefit or maternity allowance for eight weeks, the claimant must apply in writing to the local authority and submit a statement signed by the non-dependant, on the lines explained on page 93.[36] An owner-occupier will need to apply both to the social security office and to the local authority in order to get the lower rate of deduction applied for both supplementary benefit and rate rebate purposes.

Absence from Home

Housing benefit remains payable during a period of absence from home if the circumstances are such that housing costs would be met under the supplementary benefit scheme.[37] The supplementary benefit rules on this subject are explained on page 95; for example, the housing requirements of a hospital patient are met if the absence from home is not expected to last more than fifteen months, and housing benefit should therefore continue for the same period. More generally, temporary absence for up to thirteen weeks does not affect 'householder' status for supplementary benefit purposes (except in the case of a student absent from his term-time home during the vacations) and should not affect entitlement to housing benefit.

Deposits and Rent in Advance

If a claimant moving into private rented accommodation has to pay a deposit to the landlord or rent in advance, extra help may be available in the form of a single payment of supplementary benefit (see page 157). If a single payment is made for rent in advance, it will be deducted from the eligible rent in the following weeks, whether the claimant is still receiving supplementary benefit or not.[38]

Two Homes

Housing benefit cannot normally be paid for more than one home, though in some cases a single home may consist of two adjacent premises. If a claimant is moving or has just moved, however, benefit can be paid for both homes for up to four weeks if the overlap is unavoidable.[39] A similar provision in the supplementary benefit regulations enables the mortgage interest and other outgoings to be met if either the old or the new home is owned by the claimant (see pages 95–6).

If the move is due to fear of domestic violence, it does not have to be shown that the need to pay for two homes is unavoidable but only that it is reasonable for the costs of both homes to be provided for. The four-week limit does not apply; double payment can continue for as long as the local authority considers reasonable.[40]

Housing Benefit Supplement

'Certificated' housing benefit, as explained in the earlier part of this chapter, normally covers the full amount of eligible rent and rates, subject to any deduction for non-dependants. 'Standard' housing benefit, payable to people who are not on supplementary benefit, varies in amount depending on the claimant's income and household size and type, as well as on the amount of eligible rent and rates. In most cases, standard housing benefit does not cover the eligible rent and rates in full, the claimant being left to pay part of them out of his or her other income.

Housing benefit supplement is intended to deal with the situation where a claimant would be entitled to supplementary benefit but for the fact that his income is (by supplementary benefit standards) more than enough to meet his non-housing needs; but it is not enough to meet, in addition, the housing needs that are not covered by standard housing benefit. If nothing were done to remedy the situation, the claimant would be left with a net income below supplementary benefit level, after paying the rent and rates. Housing benefit supplement fills this gap. As the name implies, it is paid with standard housing benefit by the local authority, not by the social security office. In spite of this, it is in fact a form of supplementary benefit.[41] This has the important consequence that the claimant is entitled to the 'extras' that go with supplementary benefit: the single payments for exceptional needs described in Chapter 7, 'passport' exemption from health service charges, and free school meals. A period in receipt of housing benefit supplement also counts towards the twelve months' qualifying period which enables claimants under sixty, except the unemployed, to receive supplementary benefit at the higher long-term rates (see page 53). Even a small amount of housing benefit supplement is, therefore, well worth having.

To find out whether a person is entitled to housing benefit supplement involves two calculations (see example G in Appendix 1). The social security office has to work out the amount by which the claimant's income exceeds his requirements, excluding rent and rates (but including any 'additional' requirements for heating, diet, etc. – see Chapter 3). This is the 'excess income figure'. Secondly, the local authority has to work out how much the claimant will be expected to contribute towards his eligible rent and rates – i.e. the amount of rent and rates not covered by the standard housing benefit and any deductions for non-dependants. This is known as the 'net housing costs figure'. If the net housing costs are higher than the excess income, the claimant is entitled to a housing benefit supplement to fill the gap.[42] The supplement is normally paid as an addition to the standard rent rebate or allowance. In the case of an owner-occupier it is added to the rate rebate. If the rent rebate or allowance, including the supplement, would be more than the eligible rent, the excess is added to the rate rebate.[43]

The process of claiming benefits can start with a claim for either supplementary benefit or housing benefit – the amounts payable should be the same in either case. If the initial claim is for supplementary benefit and it is turned down on the grounds that the claimant's income is too high and for no other reason, the social security office should give the claimant a claim form for housing benefit, showing the 'excess income figure'. If the supplementary benefit claim fails for other reasons – e.g. the claimant is in full-time work, has capital over £3,000 or is on strike – there can be no entitlement to housing benefit supplement and, if the social security office issues a housing benefit claim form, it will not show the 'excess income figure'.

On receiving the claim form, the local authority will work out the standard housing benefit, the net housing costs and the housing benefit supplement, if any. The final decision as to entitlement to housing benefit supplement and the amount payable must be taken by the adjudication officer at the social security office, since it is payable under the supplementary benefit regulations. Until that decision has been made, the supplement should be paid on an interim basis,[44] starting from the date of the supplementary benefit claim. If the adjudication officer decides that a larger amount is due, arrears will be paid. If the adjudication officer reduces the supplement, any overpayment that has already occurred will not be recovered unless it was due to misrepresentation or failure to disclose a material fact (see page 45) – and in that case it is the social security office and not the local authority that has the power to demand repayment.

If the claimant starts by claiming housing benefit instead of supplementary benefit, the local authority will calculate the entitlement to standard housing benefit, if any, and should then consider whether the claimant might be entitled to supplementary benefit or housing benefit supplement. If the income after deducting the net housing costs does not seem to be much above supplementary benefit level, the claimant should be referred to the social security office. If a claim for supplementary benefit is made within one month of notification of the housing benefit award, it will be backdated to the day on which the housing benefit claim reached the local authority.[45]

The effect of these rules is that the starting date for whichever benefit is payable should be the same whether the claimant approaches the social security office first or the local authority first. The main disadvantage of starting with the local authority is that there is no certainty that the officials dealing with the housing benefit claim will inform the claimant of a possible entitlement to supplementary benefit or housing benefit supplement. There is thus less risk of underpayment if supplementary benefit is claimed first; and there is the further advantage that, if there is any entitlement to supplementary benefit (other than housing benefit supplement), certificated housing benefit will be paid without the need for a second claim.

Housing Benefit Appeals

The supplementary benefit appeals machinery is described in Chapter 16. Claimants have a right of appeal, first, to an independent local tribunal and then, on a point of law, to a Social Security Commissioner. Appeals relating to housing benefit supplement are dealt with in exactly the same way. However, a claimant who is dissatisfied with a decision relating to housing benefit, other than housing benefit supplement, has no similar right of appeal to an independent tribunal. Instead, there is a right to have the decision 'reviewed' by the local authority which made it, followed if necessary by a further review by a review board appointed by the authority and consisting of not less than three members of the authority.

The first stage in this formal review procedure is for the claimant to make written representations to the local authority about the decision on his or her claim within six weeks. The claimant also has a right to a written statement showing how the benefit is calculated or why no benefit is payable, and the reasons for any reduction of the eligible rates or rent on grounds of 'unsuitable accommodation' (see pages 104–5).

If a statement of this kind is requested, the time taken to supply it is added to the six weeks allowed for making representations about the decision.[46]

The authority must review the decision and inform the claimant in writing that it has been either altered or confirmed, giving reasons in either case.[47] The claimant then has 28 days, or longer if the authority agrees, to write 'requiring' a further review by the review board and stating the grounds on which it is required.[48] The review board must hold an oral hearing within six weeks, or as soon as is reasonably practicable. The claimant must have reasonable notice of the hearing. Travelling expenses for attending the hearing can be paid, at the local authority's discretion, to the claimant and one other person accompanying or representing the claimant.[49]

The procedure at the review board's hearing is to a large extent left to them to decide. If there are not three members present, the hearing can be conducted by two members with the claimant's consent. The claimant has a right to be present, except while the board is considering its decision, to be accompanied or represented by another person, to make written representations, to call witnesses and to question any other witnesses. The hearing, however, need not be at all formal: the board can 'receive representations and evidence from such persons present as they consider appropriate'. If the board cannot agree among themselves, they can decide by a majority vote. In the case of a tie, the chairman has a casting vote.[50] A copy of the review board's decision, including the reasons for the decision and the board's findings on material questions of fact, must be sent to the claimant within seven days or, if this is not practicable, as soon as possible.[51] There is no requirement that the claimant should be told whether the decision was unanimous.

There are two essential differences between the review board and a social security appeal tribunal. The first is that the review board, being appointed by the local authority whose decisions are under review and consisting of members of the authority, can hardly be regarded as an independent body. The second is that there is no second-tier appeal body, such as the Social Security Commissioners, to ensure that the review board is carrying out its functions in a proper manner and in accordance with the law. The only remedy if it fails to do so is an application to the High Court for judicial review. Nevertheless, the review board is under the same duty as any other tribunal to give the claimant a fair hearing and to give adequate reasons for its decision.

REFERENCES

1. Housing Benefits Regs. 9(1).
2. Housing Benefits Regs. 7(2) and 8(2).
3. Housing Benefits Regs. 2(1).
4. Housing Benefits Regs. 9(1) and (2).
5. Housing Benefits Regs. 25(1)(b).
6. Housing Benefits Regs. 21(1)(a).
7. Requirements Regs. 14(3)(a)(i).
8. Requirements Regs. 14(3)(a)(iv).
9. Requirements Regs. 14(3)(a)(ii).
10. Housing Benefits Regs. 21(1)(a).
11. Housing Benefits Regs. 16(2) and (5).
12. Housing Benefits Regs. 12A.
13. Housing Benefits Regs. 2(5)(a).
14. Housing Benefits Regs. 16(2)(a)(i).
15. Housing Benefits Regs. 16(2)(a)(ii).
16. Housing Benefits Regs. 16(2)(b) and schedule 3, paras. 2–6.
17. Housing Benefits Regs., schedule 3, para. 5.
18. Circular HB(83)5.
19. Housing Benefits Regs. 16(2)(c) and schedule 3, paras. 7–9.
20. Housing Benefits Regs. 16(2)(d).
21. Housing Benefits Regs. 21(2) and (3).
22. Housing Benefits Regs. 2(1) (definition of 'non-dependant').
23. Housing Benefits Regs., schedule 3, paras. 10–11.
24. Housing Benefits Regs. 15(2) and (3).
25. Housing Benefits Regs. 9(2)(a).
26. Housing Benefits Regs. 15(4).
27. Housing Benefits Regs. 12A.
28. Housing Benefits Regs. 17(1).
29. Housing Benefits Regs. 17(4).
30. Circular HB(84)1.
31. Housing Benefits Regs. 17(2).
32. Housing Benefits Regs. 17(3).
33. Housing Benefits Regs. 18(2).
34. Housing Benefits Regs. 18(1).
35. Resources Regs. 10(3)(e)(ii).
36. Housing Benefits Regs. 28A.
37. Housing Benefits Regs. 2(1) (definition of 'qualifying supplementary benefit').
38. Housing Benefits Regs. 16(4A).
39. Housing Benefits Regs. 5(2)(b).
40. Housing Benefits Regs. 5(2)(a).
41. Requirements Regs. 19(1).
42. Requirements Regs. 19(2).
43. Circular HB(82)2, para. 14.21.

44. Circular HB(82)2, para. 14.16.
45. Claims and Payments Regs. 5(2)(*bb*).
46. Housing Benefits Regs. 45(5) and 46.
47. Housing Benefits Regs. 46(1).
48. Housing Benefits Regs. 47.
49. Housing Benefits Regs. 48(1), (3) and (7).
50. Housing Benefits Regs. 48(2), (4), (5), (6) and (8).
51. Housing Benefits Regs. 49(3).

Chapter 6

Resources

Chapters 2, 3 and 4 described how a claimant's 'requirements' are calculated for supplementary benefit purposes. The next stage in working out the amount of benefit payable is to calculate the amount of 'resources' to be set against the total requirements. This chapter explains how that is done.

The basic principle is that, if money is available from other sources to meet the needs of the assessment unit (claimant, wife or husband, and dependent children), there is no need for supplementary benefit to duplicate these resources. A claimant may, however, have limited amounts of income or savings (known as 'disregards') without any loss of benefit. The rules about the treatment of income are summarized in Table 3 (see pages 117–19). Fuller details of some of the disregards are given on pages 120–29. Finally, the effect of savings and other capital resources on entitlement to supplementary benefit is explained. The main rules about capital resources are that the value of the claimant's house, if he owns it, and any other capital not exceeding £3,000, together with any income derived from it (with rare exceptions explained below), are ignored in calculating the weekly benefit entitlement, and that a claimant whose capital, excluding his home, amounts to more than £3,000 is not entitled to supplementary benefit. For more details about capital resources, see pages 129–33.

The Distinction between Capital and Income

A person's capital consists of the money, investments and other property that he *possesses*. His income is the amount he *receives* over a period of time. In most cases the distinction is clear, but sometimes money received by a claimant is treated as capital rather than as income. If it takes the form of a periodic payment, like wages or dividends, it is clearly income. A single lump sum payment, on the other hand, is usually treated as capital. Thus the national insurance death grant and maternity grant are both treated as capital payments. Similarly, a redundancy payment, if it takes the form of a lump sum, counts as capital, not as income. So does a bequest or the proceeds of an insurance policy.

The distinction is important for supplementary benefit, because most kinds of income affect the amount of benefit payable, while capital has no effect on the weekly benefit entitlement unless it is over £3,000 (entitlement to single payments is affected by capital over £500 – see page 142). It is therefore generally to the claimant's advantage if a sum of money received by him is treated as a capital payment rather than as income. Although the regulations do not define either capital or income, they contain a number of rules for the treatment of particular types of cases, which are explained in the following pages.

Deprivation of Resources

Claimants may be treated as possessing resources of which they have deprived themselves for the purpose of obtaining supplementary benefit, or getting more benefit.[1] These are known as *notional resources*. Thus, a claimant with capital resources over the £3,000 limit who deliberately gets rid of part of those resources in order to qualify for supplementary benefit may find that he or she is still not entitled to benefit. The adjudication officer must consider three questions: (i) Did the claimant deprive himself or herself of the resources in question? (ii) If so, was it for the purpose of obtaining supplementary benefit (or more benefit)? (iii) If so, would it be right to treat all or part of those resources as still possessed by the claimant, since the power to do so is discretionary?

'Deprivation' of resources usually means giving them away to somebody else. Spending money, whether on necessaries or inessentials, does not amount to deprivation. Nor is it deprivation if the resources are simply converted into a different form. Adjudication officers are therefore told that capital used in any of the following ways should *not* be taken into account as notional resources:

(a) to buy an annuity producing a current income (i.e. converting a capital resource into an income resource);

(b) to buy personal possessions such as a car, furniture, washing machine or television (but note that personal possessions bought to get round the £3,000 limit *may* be taken into account as actual resources – see below);

(c) to pay for a holiday;

(d) to improve the fabric of the home;
(e) to repay the mortgage;
(f) to buy a home;
(g) to live at the standard the claimant is used to.

Circumstances which, officers are told, could amount to deprivation include the transfer to someone else of a lump sum of money, an income resource or the title to a property which is not the claimant's home, investing money so that it cannot be realized, or putting it into a trust which cannot be revoked.[2]

The second question – whether the deprivation of resources was for the purpose of obtaining benefit – may be more difficult to decide, since it depends on the claimant's intentions. If the resources were disposed of a considerable time before supplementary benefit was claimed, this will normally suggest that it was done for some other purpose. Other points to be considered are whether there was a reasonable motive for disposing of the resources other than claiming supplementary benefit (e.g. to help a close relative in urgent need), and whether the claimant was aware that possession of the resources in question could affect his or her entitlement to benefit (if not, the purpose of disposing of them cannot have been to obtain supplementary benefit).

Finally, even if it is decided that the claimant disposed of the resources for the purpose of obtaining benefit, the adjudication officer has a duty to consider whether they should be taken into account as notional resources. The guidance issued to officers assumes that the resources *will* be taken into account,[3] but the regulations say only that they *may* be taken into account. It is particularly important to stress this point in an appeal against the adjudication officer's decision, since the appeal tribunal has the same discretionary power to ignore such resources if there are good grounds for doing so.

If resources which the claimant does not actually possess are taken into account as notional resources, a further decision has to be made as to the period of time for which the resources are to be taken into account. If, for example, the claimant has given away a sum of money in order to qualify for benefit, it must be assumed that, had the money not been given away, it would have had to be used for living expenses so that, eventually, the claimant's capital would have been reduced to £3,000 and benefit would have become payable. It would obviously be wrong to treat the resources as notionally available for a longer period than they would have been actually available. Officers are told to assume that the notional capital would be reduced each week by the amount of supplementary benefit that would have been payable if the capital had been ignored, rounded up to the nearest £10.[4] For example, if the claimant's total capital, including notional capital, is £4,000 and he would otherwise be entitled to supplementary benefit of £25 a week, he will be assumed to 'spend' the notional capital at the rate of £30 a week and it will take 34 weeks to reduce the total to £3,000. From then on, supplementary benefit will be payable. But there is nothing to prevent a claimant who has actual capital as well as notional capital from spending it at a faster rate and thus qualifying for benefit sooner.

Personal Possessions

Capital held in the form of personal possessions is normally disregarded entirely for supplementary benefit purposes. This includes not only strictly personal items but furniture, electrical equipment and a car. But there are some exceptions, which are mentioned here because they may result in a claimant's capital exceeding the £3,000 limit. Personal possessions must be taken into account (there is no discretion) if

(a) they are in the nature of an investment – valuable antiques, works of art or expensive jewellery might come into this category, but only if they were acquired as a way of investing money so that it is available for the future; or

(b) they were acquired for the purpose of obtaining supplementary benefit, by using capital resources which would otherwise have been taken into account (the same questions have to be asked as in a case of deprivation of resources – see above); or

(c) it would be unreasonable to disregard them, 'having regard to their nature, use, likely value and the standard of living of other persons in similar circumstances' – for example, a very expensive car or yacht.[5]

If personal possessions are to be taken into account, their present value must be estimated. This means the price at which they could be sold, after deducting any expenses that would be involved.

Resources Due or Available but Not Received

The adjudication officer may, if he thinks it reasonable, take into account any resource which would be available if applied for or which is due but has not yet been paid. This does not apply to social security benefits and similar payments, from which any supplementary benefit paid because they are delayed can be recovered in due course (see pages 44–5).[6] Officers are told to take into account sums of money due but not yet received only if in the circumstances it would be unreasonable to pay benefit in full – for example where payments are delayed because of a strike by pay clerks or post office workers.[7] But even if the money owing is not taken into account as a 'notional' resource, the debt itself is an actual resource to be taken into account at its market value (see page 132).

Income

The treatment of income from various sources is summarized in Table 3. Part A of the table shows the kinds of income taken into account in full; part B shows those wholly disregarded or treated as capital (which comes to the same thing); and part C shows those that are disregarded up to certain limits. Fuller details of the treatment of particular types of income are given in the pages following the table.

TABLE 3: TREATMENT OF INCOME RESOURCES

A. *Income taken into account in full* [8]
1. Child benefit and one-parent benefit.
2. Family income supplement.
3. National insurance benefits (except those mentioned under B and C), including non-contributory benefits; emergency payments in lieu of social security benefits; and some analogous payments to people not entitled to national insurance benefits.
4. Occupational pensions, retirement annuities and redundancy payments (but not treated as income if paid as a lump sum).
5. Employer's sick pay.
6. MSC training allowances (for living expenses only).
7. Job release allowance.
8. Enterprise allowance.
9. Prisoner's discharge grant.
10. Student grants (including assumed parental contributions), except as mentioned in 27, 36 and 38 below.
11. Benefits and grants analogous to any of the above under foreign schemes.
12. Maintenance payments by a liable relative.
13. Payments by an immigrant's sponsor.
14. Income from premises for sale or occupied by an aged or incapacitated relative (see page 132, item (j)).
15. Income from deposit with a housing association (see page 132, item (i)).

(*Note:* Income under 14 and 15 is taken into account only if the claimant's total capital, including the premises or deposit, is over £3,000.)

B. *Income wholly disregarded*[9] *or (items 20–22 and 33) treated as capital*[10]

16. Income from capital (except as mentioned in 14 and 15 above and 40(c) below).

17. Housing benefit.

18. Attendance allowance and constant attendance allowance (but see page 64).

19. Mobility allowance and war pensioners' mobility supplement.

    20. Maternity grant (the £25 lump sum, *not* the weekly maternity allowance).

21. Death grant.

22. Disablement gratuity.

23. Resettlement benefit (paid after a long stay in hospital).

24. Voluntary payments (except by a liable relative) for purposes not covered by supplementary benefit or housing benefit (holidays, mortgage capital repayments, etc.) or for 'leisure or amenity' items.

25. Occasional gifts in cash or kind, not exceeding £100 each.

26. Victoria Cross and George Cross annuities.

27. Grants to school pupils or students for the cost of living away from home.

28. Concessions in kind (e.g. concessionary coal and bus passes).

29. Earnings of dependent children, other than those who have left school and are working full-time.

30. Boarding-out allowances for up to three foster-children.

31. Board and lodging charge from up to two boarders and contributions to housing costs by non-dependent members of the household.

32. Certain payments to lifeboat men, part-time firemen, etc. (see page 123).

33. PAYE refunds, unless paid to a person returning to work after a trade dispute or suspended from work.

C. *Income partially disregarded*

The amounts disregarded are as follows:

34. £4 of the claimant's net weekly earnings and, for a single parent, half the next £16.

35. £4 of the wife's or husband's net weekly earnings.[11]

36. Any part of a student's grant paid for the extra costs of disablement or for a wife or children outside the UK,[12] and £2 a week of the grant if the student is disabled or has a child.[13]

37. Any part of an adoption allowance which exceeds the supplementary benefit 'requirements' of the adopted child.[14]

38. £7.50 a week of an education maintenance allowance (higher school bursary in Scotland) – or £9.50 if for a young person attending a college of further education.[15]

39. £100 of any occasional gift (unless treated as capital – see page 129).[16]

40. £4 a week of *other income* consisting of any of the following:

    (a) PAYE refunds to people returning to work after a trade dispute or suspended from work (see page 123).

(b) A disablement pension, war widow's pension or industrial death benefit.

(c) Income derived from a new home the claimant has bought and intends to occupy within six months of purchase.

(d) The 'profit' from subletting where the proceeds exceed the total housing costs (see page 92).

(e) Any other income not mentioned above, including voluntary payments by relatives, charities, etc. (other than those covered by items 12, 24, 25 and 39).[17]

The fact that certain income is 'disregarded' does not necessarily mean that it will not affect entitlement to supplementary benefit. Unless it is spent in the same week, it will increase the amount of capital held by the claimant, and this may mean either that benefit is no longer payable (if the total capital is over £3,000) or that entitlement to single payments for exceptional needs is affected (if it is over £500 – see page 142).

Where income of any kind is taken into account the adjudication officer has to decide from what date and for what period it should be taken into account. The regulations say that where a payment of income is 'in respect of a period' it is to be taken into account for a period of equal length. For example, two weeks' wages will be taken into account as income over a period of two weeks, while a half-yearly interest payment will be spread over half a year. A monthly payment must be multiplied by twelve and divided by 52 to arrive at the weekly equivalent. If the payment does not relate to a particular period of time, the adjudication officer has to decide what would be a fair period to assume.[18]

The starting date of the period for which the income is taken into account depends on whether it was payable before the first week for which benefit is paid. If it was, it is taken into account from the date on which it was payable. If it was payable after benefit commenced, it is taken into account from the beginning of a benefit week – either the week in which it was payable or the earliest practicable week after that.[19] The date when income is 'payable' is normally the date when it first becomes due, whether it is actually paid on that date or not; but it may be difficult to argue that it was not payable until *after* the date when it was paid. In the absence of evidence to the contrary it will be assumed that the payment was made on the date on which it was payable.[20] A special rule applies to a final payment of unemployment, sickness or invalidity benefits or of maternity allowance: it is to be treated as paid on the day after the period for which the preceding payment of the benefit would have been taken into account[21] – which is precisely what one would expect. More generally, where regular payments are received from a particular source, only one week's payment is to be taken into account for any week.[22]

If the claimant was in work immediately before claiming supplementary benefit, the final payments made by the employer may be treated as covering the claimant's needs for a longer period than under the rules explained above. This is because, where those payments include more than one item – e.g. final earnings, payments in lieu of notice and holiday pay – the periods to which they relate are added together in deciding how long the claimant must wait before becoming entitled to benefit (see page 31).

Earnings

The first £4 per week of a claimant's net earnings and the first £4 net earnings of the claimant's wife or husband are ignored. If the claimant is a single parent, half of the next £16 is also ignored.[23] A single parent earning £20 a week is thus allowed to keep £12 (£4 plus half of £16), the other £8 being deducted from the weekly benefit. In each case it is *net* earnings that count. This means what is left after paying income tax, national insurance contributions (including voluntary Class 3 contributions),[24] contributions to the employer's pension scheme, and any 'expenses reasonably incurred' in connection with the employment. Deductible expenses include fares to work and any other travelling expenses connected with the job (the cost of private transport or taxis is allowed where necessary); the cost of having children minded while a parent is working; and 15p towards the cost of each meal taken in working hours.[25] Other expenses not specifically mentioned in the regulations but which are accepted as 'reasonably incurred' include subscriptions to trade unions and professional bodies, the extra cost of working clothes and laundry, basic tools and, for an apprentice, fares to attend classes and the cost of books and tuition fees.[26]

A child's earnings, including those of a young person over 16 but still at school, are ignored entirely. Once a child has left school, however, if he or she starts full-time work while still treated as a dependant (see page 34) the earnings are taken into account in assessing the parent's benefit to the extent necessary to remove the child's needs from the assessment, like any other income of the child (see page 133).[27]

Earnings are defined as including payments in kind (except one free meal a day, which is ignored),[28] any bonus or commission except the first £10 of a Christmas bonus,[29] retaining fees, payments in lieu of notice, maternity pay, and holiday pay unless received more than four weeks after the job ended. A loan or 'sub' from the employer is treated as earnings.[30] Sick pay is *not* treated as earnings and is taken into account in full.[31]

If a person provides services either without pay or at a low rate of pay for somebody who could afford to pay for them, the adjudication officer has a discretionary power to take into account assumed earnings.[32] But this power is not used where the work is of a kind that would normally be done voluntarily, either for a charity or similar body or for somebody with a low income who is elderly, disabled, sick or a single parent.[33]

The following types of income are also treated as earnings, which means that they are subject to the earnings disregard of £4 a week (and half the next £16 for a single parent):

(a) Where accommodation is provided for three or more boarders (even if it is not all occupied), one-third of the payments received for board and lodging, *less* the 'non-dependant' deductions made from the claimant's housing benefit because of the boarders (see page 105).[34]

(b) Retaining fees paid by boarders.[35]

(c) One-third of any payments received for child-minding in the claimant's home.[36]

(d) Where payments are received for fostering four or more children under arrangements made by a local authority or under the Child Care Act 1980, half the amount by which the total payments exceed £34.60 a week per child[37] (twice the supplementary benefit scale rate for a 16–17-year-old) – payments for fostering less than four children being disregarded entirely[38] (but different rules apply to income from private fostering arrangements[39] which should, if possible, be discussed in advance with the social security office).

In the case of a married (or unmarried) couple, it can make a difference whether income from boarders or foster-children is treated as earnings of the wife or the husband – or both. If one of them has other earnings of which £4 are disregarded, it will be more advantageous to treat such income as that of the other partner, who will then also qualify for the £4 disregard. If neither of them has other earnings, they will be better off if the income is treated as their joint earnings so that £8 can be disregarded.

If a person's actual weekly earnings are 'not immediately ascertainable', the adjudication officer must calculate or estimate them 'as best he may, having regard to the information (if any) available to him and to what appear to him to be the probabilities of the case'.[40] Fluctuating earnings can be averaged over whatever period the adjudication officer considers reasonable.[41] Earnings from self-employment, in particular, may have to be estimated. Officers are given detailed guidance on how to do this.[42] Where business accounts for the preceding year are available, the profit or loss shown by them will normally be used as a basis for the estimate. Officers are told not to allow depreciation as a business expense but, instead, to deduct the actual amount spent on new or replacement capital assets such as machinery, vehicles and other equipment. This may be more advantageous to the claimant or it may not; but it is not in accordance with normal accounting practice and was declared wrong by a Commissioner (he seems to have taken the view that both depreciation and the actual cost of replacements were allowable expenses, which is perhaps over-generous).[43]

If a seasonal worker claims supplementary benefit, part of the seasonal earnings may be treated as available to meet his or her expenses during the off-season. If the total earnings during the last period of normal employment were more than *either* 2½ times the total supplementary benefit requirements (excluding housing requirements) of the assessment unit for the period *or* three times the ordinary scale rate for a single householder (£84.15) – whichever is greater – the excess is divided by the number of weeks in the off-season and treated as weekly earnings for that period.[44] If this rule leaves the claimant without sufficient available resources to meet basic needs, he or she may be entitled to urgent need payments (see page 193).

The same principle applies to a person whose work is of an intermittent nature and who had substantial earnings in the past three months. If the *gross* earnings (before deducting tax and national insurance contributions) for the thirteen weeks before claiming benefit, averaged over the number of weeks in that period for which supplementary benefit was not paid, were more than ten times the ordinary scale rate for a single householder (i.e., at November 1984 benefit rates, more than £280.50 a week), the excess is carried forward and treated as weekly earnings of that amount.[45] For example, if the total earnings for the previous thirteen weeks were £4,500 and supplementary benefit was not paid at any time during that period, the first £3,646.50 (thirteen times £280.50) would be disregarded and the remainder, £853.50, would be treated as income of £280.50 a week for the next three weeks (it would actually last more than three weeks at that rate, but fractions of a week are ignored), and supplementary benefit would not be payable until the fourth week. (Part of this period might anyway be excluded under the normal rules regarding the treatment of final earnings – see page 31.) Urgent need payments may be available where necessary to meet basic needs during the exclusion period (see page 193).

There are special provisions for encouraging certain kinds of voluntary or part-time service by disregarding earnings derived from them. These relate to lifeboat men, part-time firemen, auxiliary coastguards (except payments for watch duties) and training expense allowances and other payments of up to £4 a week to members of the Territorial Army and Volunteer Reserves.[46] The annual bounty paid to the territorial and reserve forces does not count as income, only as capital.[47]

The rules regarding the treatment of earnings of strikers and other people affected by trade disputes are explained on pages 236–7.

Tax refunds

A PAYE tax refund is normally treated as a capital payment and does not affect entitlement to supplementary benefit unless it raises the total capital resources above the £3,000 limit. The only exception is a PAYE tax refund to a claimant affected by or returning to work after a trade dispute or who, though still employed, has had his employment temporarily suspended. In these cases, the tax refund is treated as income.[48] In the case of a person participating in or directly interested in a trade dispute (see pages 234–5), the refund is taken into account in full. In other cases, it is one of the items included in item 40 in Table 3, the first £4 of which is disregarded.[49]

Refunds of income tax other than PAYE are taken into account as income [50] and treated in the same way as the income on which the tax was paid. Such refunds appear to qualify for the £4 weekly disregard as 'other income' (item 40(e)), but this is not allowed in practice.

Child benefit

Both child benefit of £6.85 per child and the one-parent benefit of £4.25 for the first child in a one-parent family are taken into account in full.[51] This is because the supplementary benefit scale rates for children, ranging from £9.60 for a child under 11 to £22.45 for a 'dependent' young person aged 18 or over, together with the amounts allowed for additional requirements, are intended to provide in full for the needs of the child. If child benefit were disregarded wholly or in part, those needs would be provided for twice over. In the case of a single parent with a child under 11, this rule may seem to operate unfairly, since the child benefit of £11.10 (including the £4.25 one-parent benefit) is more than the supplementary benefit rate of £9.60, and the difference of £1.50 a week is, in effect, deducted from the amount allowed for the parent's needs. The law, however, is clear and leaves no room for argument.

Family income supplement

Although, as explained in Chapter 15, FIS is a benefit for people in full-time work who are not eligible for supplementary benefit, it is normally awarded for a fifty-two-week period, during which it remains in payment at the same rate regardless of any change of circumstances. It may therefore happen that supplementary benefit is payable for part of that period – for example, if the claimant is sick or unemployed. If so, the FIS payments are taken into account in full in calculating the supplementary benefit payable.[52]

National insurance benefits

Most of the benefits listed in Tables 1 and 2 (pages 20–22) are intended, like supplementary benefit, to provide for the normal living expenses of claimants and their families. As with child benefit, therefore, these benefits have to be fully taken into account in the calculation of supplementary benefit,[53] to prevent double provision for the same needs. The exceptions are:

(a) Lump sum benefits such as maternity grant and death grant, treated as capital payments and thus disregarded except where they affect entitlement to certain single payments or raise the claimant's capital resources above the £3,000 limit.[54]

(b) Attendance and mobility allowance,[55] which are intended to meet the extra costs of disability for which the supplementary benefit scale rates do not provide.

(c) Disablement pensions paid under the industrial injuries and war pensions schemes, which are not intended to cover normal living expenses but to compensate for 'loss of faculty'. They qualify for the

£4 'other income' disregard (item 40 in Table 3), and the widows' pensions paid under these schemes are treated in the same way.[56]

Occupational pensions and redundancy payments

An occupational pension from an employer's pension scheme is normally taken into account in full as income; but if part of it represents compensation for injury, disease or death resulting from the employment, or is a discretionary payment from a hardship fund, that part is disregarded up to £4 a week under the 'other income' disregard.[57] Individual retirement annuities for which self-employed people can contribute and claim tax relief are taken into account in full as income.[58] Lump sum payments from occupational schemes, on the other hand, count as capital.

The same distinction applies to redundancy payments. Weekly or monthly payments count as income and are taken into account in full.[59] Lump sum payments count as capital.

Employer's sick pay

Sick pay from an employer is taken into account in full.[60] Although it may be indistinguishable from a normal payment of wages or salary, the £4 earnings disregard does not apply.

Student grants

A student grant payable for a full-time course is normally taken into account in full (after deducting any allowance for books, travelling expenses, etc.) as income for the period to which it relates.[61] If the grant is reduced by an assumed contribution from the student's parents, the parental contribution is also taken into account, whether it is actually paid or not. A student cannot, therefore, claim supplementary benefit on the grounds that his parents have failed to maintain him to the extent assumed by the education authority. But this does not apply if the student is disabled, married (or living with somebody as husband and wife) or has a dependent child; in these cases, parental contributions are taken into account only to the extent that they are in fact paid.[62] A student who is disabled or a parent also has £2 a week of the grant disregarded for supplementary benefit purposes. A disabled student is defined as one who 'by reason of a disability would, in comparison with other students, be unlikely to be able to obtain employment within a reasonable period of time'.[63] Any additional grant to cover expenses arising from disablement is also disregarded. If a member of the assessment unit is temporarily away from home on a course, any allowance paid to cover expenses while living away is disregarded. So is an allowance for the support of a wife or child outside the United Kingdom.[64]

Maintenance payments by a liable relative

Maintenance payments made to a claimant or to a claimant's wife, husband or child by a liable relative are normally taken into account in full as income,[65] unlike voluntary payments by other relatives of which up to £4 a week can be disregarded. A liable relative means a husband or ex-husband, wife or ex-wife, or the father or mother of a dependent child. A man is treated as the father of an illegitimate child not only where there is an affiliation order but also where 'by reason of payments which he is making' to or for the child it is reasonable to treat him as the father. An immigrant's sponsor is also a 'liable relative' for this purpose (see page 127).[66]

Maintenance payments to or for a child are taken fully into account, even if they exceed the child's own requirements, contrary to the normal practice of disregarding any excess of a child's income over his or her requirements (see page 133).[67] There is thus no advantage, for supplementary benefit (though there may be for income tax), in arranging for maintenance to be payable to the child rather than to the mother. Nor is there generally any advantage in a liable relative making payments to a third party instead of to the claimant – for example, by paying gas or electricity bills. Such payments are treated as the claimant's income unless it is unreasonable to do so.[68]

Lump sum payments from other sources are normally treated as capital, but special rules apply to a lump sum received from a liable relative (this does not include occasional gifts of up to £100 each, a sum paid as one partner's share of the assets on the breakdown of the marriage or a sum paid from the estate of a deceased liable relative).[69] If the lump sum is for arrears of maintenance, and supplementary benefit has been paid during the period to which the lump sum relates, the claimant will be asked to repay the amount of benefit that would not have been paid if maintenance had been paid regularly (see pages 44–5). Other lump sum payments from a liable relative are treated as income *unless* the liable relative is also making periodical maintenance payments of at least the amount needed to remove the need for supplementary benefit.[70] If no periodic payments are being made, the lump sum is treated as a weekly income of *either* £2 more than the supplementary benefit that would otherwise be payable *or* such higher amount as may be payable under a court order. No benefit is payable for the number of whole weeks the lump sum would last on that basis (but see below if it does not actually last that long). If the lump sum is paid only for the maintenance of a child, it is treated as income of the amount of the child's normal and additional requirements (or the amount payable for the child under a court order if that is greater) for the number of weeks it would last on that basis, and the claimant's benefit is reduced accordingly.[71]

If, when the lump sum is paid, the liable relative is also making periodical maintenance payments but they are less than the amount needed to remove the need for supplementary benefit, the lump sum is treated as a weekly income of the amount needed to bring the maintenance payments up to *either* £2 more than the amount of supplementary benefit that would be payable if there were no maintenance payments *or* such higher amount as may be payable under a court order.[72]

The assumed income from a lump sum payment may have to be recalculated from time to time – for example, on a change in the supplementary benefit rates or in the periodical payments made by the liable relative. It may also happen that the lump sum has been used up before the end of the period for which it was assumed to last. The regulations say that only such part of the lump sum as 'may at that time reasonably be considered to form part of the resources of the assessment unit' is to be taken into account.[73] Once it has been spent, therefore, it will no longer affect entitlement to benefit, unless it can be shown that the claimant deprived herself or himself of it in order to obtain benefit. In a case decided by a Commissioner, the claimant had received a lump sum of £6,000 but had used it to buy the home in which she was living. It was therefore no longer part of her resources and she was once more entitled to benefit.[74]

Payments by an immigrant's sponsor

Payments to an immigrant by a person who, on or after 23 May 1980, gave a written undertaking to be responsible for his or her maintenance are treated in the same way as maintenance payments by a liable relative (see above).[75]

Voluntary payments and gifts

Voluntary payments or gifts, whether from relatives, friends, a charity or some other source, may be either wholly or partially taken into account or entirely disregarded, depending on the circumstances. It is therefore advisable to ascertain in advance what effect a voluntary payment or gift is likely to have on the recipient's entitlement to supplementary benefit. A gift in the form of money paid to a third party for the claimant's benefit is normally treated as if it had been paid to the claimant.[76]

An occasional gift, whether in cash or in kind, will be disregarded provided that its value is not more than £100.[77] Payments which are both intended and actually used either for some item which is not covered by supplementary benefit or for 'a leisure or amenity item' are also disregarded, provided that they are not made by a 'liable relative'.[78] This enables a claimant to obtain help from other sources, without any loss of benefit, for a wide variety of purposes, including the following:

(a) Mortgage capital repayments.
(b) The unmet part of a rent or board and lodging charge (see pages 104–5 and 59–65).
(c) The cost of a holiday.
(d) Furniture or major items of household equipment.
(e) Purchase or rental of a television or radio set.
(f) Home decorating and insulation.
(g) Private medical treatment.
(h) School fees.
(i) Newspapers, cigarettes and sweets.

Payments for these purposes will be disregarded whether they are occasional gifts or regular allowances.

Voluntary payments which are not merely occasional gifts and are not specifically intended for items such as those mentioned in the previous paragraph are taken into account but, provided that they are not made by a liable relative, are included in the income qualifying for the £4 disregard[79] (item 40 in Table 3). A weekly allowance from a relative (other than a liable relative) or from a friend or a charity can therefore benefit the claimant to the extent of £4 a week. Above this level the whole of any excess will be deducted from the weekly supplementary benefit, unless the money is earmarked for items such as those listed above. Even the £4 disregard, however, cannot be taken for granted, because it may already have been absorbed by income from other sources such as a disablement pension. When arranging for regular voluntary payments to be made to a supplementary benefit claimant, therefore, it is advisable either to specify that they are for particular expenses of a kind that will enable them to be disregarded, or to check that they will be covered by the £4 disregard.

If a claimant receives an occasional gift worth more than £100, it will usually be proper to treat it as a capital payment, not as income.[80] The weekly supplementary benefit payments will not be affected unless the £3,000 capital limit is exceeded or the gift comes from a liable relative and has to be treated as a maintenance payment. If a gift over £100, other than from a liable relative, is treated as income – as might happen, for example, where the claimant has received a number of gifts over a period of time – it will still be disregarded if it is for an item not covered by supplementary benefit or for a 'leisure or amenity item'; otherwise the excess over £100 will be taken into account and will reduce the supplementary benefit entitlement for one week only.[81]

Capital Resources

Many people still believe that it is necessary to be more or less destitute before one can claim supplementary benefit, and research has shown that the proportion of pensioners entitled to supplementary benefit but not receiving it is particularly high among those who own their homes. It is therefore important to stress that a claimant who owns his or her house and has up to £3,000 in the bank can still qualify for supplementary benefit and that the capital resources will not affect the amount of benefit, except to the extent that they are regarded as available to meet any exceptional needs for which a single payment would otherwise be made.

Valuation

Capital resources must be taken into account at their current market value or surrender value, less any expenses involved in selling them (in the case of land a fixed deduction of 10 per cent is made for selling expenses).[82] The market value is the price a willing buyer would pay to a willing seller.[83]

A special rule applies to National Savings Certificates, which are valued at their purchase price or, if the particular issue had been withdrawn from sale before the preceding 1 July, at the value they would have had if bought on the last day of issue.[84]

The claimant's home

The value of an owner-occupied home is ignored completely,[85] whether it is a house or flat, a caravan or a houseboat. The home, for this purpose, means the accommodation normally occupied by the claimant's household, including a garage, garden and outbuildings, and also any premises which could not reasonably be sold separately from the home.[86] A large family may occupy two adjacent properties as their home, but a home cannot comprise two or more properties in different locations.[87]

If the home has just been acquired and the claimant has not yet moved in, its value will be disregarded if he or she intends to do so within six months of the date of acquisition or such longer period as is reasonable.[88] Similarly, the value of any premises – usually but not necessarily the claimant's former home – which are up for sale is ignored, if it is reasonable to do so, for the time that the adjudication officer estimates it will take to complete the sale.[89]

If a claimant sells his home in order to raise money to live on, he will normally lose his entitlement to supplementary benefit, since his available capital will then be over £3,000. But the proceeds of the sale, together with any interest on the money, will be ignored entirely if the money is to be used to buy another home within six months of the sale or such longer period as is reasonable.[90] If only part of the money will be needed to buy a new home, the remainder will be taken into account as capital.

Savings and other capital

If the capital resources of the claimant and the claimant's wife or husband, excluding the value of their home and any of the other 'disregards' listed below, are worth more than £3,000, there can be no entitlement to supplementary benefit,[91] except perhaps on grounds of urgent need if none of the capital is readily available (see pages 192–3). If the capital resources are worth between £500 and £3,000, the excess over £500 will affect entitlement to single payments for exceptional needs,[92] though the weekly benefit payments will not be affected. The adjudication officer will therefore need full details of any capital resources, even if their value is less than £3,000.

The resources taken into account for this purpose may include cash, bank and building society accounts, stocks and shares, national savings certificates, premium bonds, insurance policies (subject to (e) below), land and house property other than the claimant's home, and investments of all kinds (jewellery, antiques, works of art, etc.). As explained on page 114, resources deliberately disposed of can be treated as if the claimant still possessed them. The only items that are disregarded, apart from the home (or money set aside from the proceeds of the sale of one home for the purchase of another), are:

(a) Personal possessions, including the contents of the home, clothes, books, etc. – but not investments, items which have been acquired in order to get more benefit by taking advantage of this rule, or other items which it would be unreasonable to disregard (see page 116).[93]

(b) Money saved out of income for reasonable living expenses which have to be met periodically, including in particular rent, rates, fuel and telephone bills – to be disregarded to the extent that the adjudication officer considers reasonable, taking into account the expected amount payable and when payment will be due.[94]

(c) Arrears of supplementary benefit, housing benefit, attendance allowance or mobility allowance received in the last twelve months, and any money saved out of a mobility allowance for use in connection with mobility (e.g. to buy a car).[95]

(d) Money paid (e.g. by an insurance company) for loss of or damage to the home or personal possessions and which is to be used for repair or replacement – to be disregarded, normally for up to six months from the date of receipt, if the adjudication officer considers it reasonable; and, similarly, money received as a loan or gift to pay for essential repairs or improvements to the home.[96]

(e) The first £1,500 of the surrender value of any life assurance policies.[97]

(f) Compensation for a personal or criminal injury (including vaccine damage payments) held on trust for a member of the assessment unit – to be disregarded completely if for a child of the claimant, and for a reasonable period (normally not more than two years) if for the claimant or the claimant's wife or husband.[98]

(g) Business assets – to be disregarded for as long as the adjudication officer considers reasonable[99] (but any income from the business will be taken into account, subject to the normal earnings disregard – see pages 120–22). If the business is a limited company the assets belong to the company, not to the claimant, and the claimant's shareholding in the company is taken into account at its market value.

(h) Assets in which the claimant has a 'reversionary' interest[100] – i.e. which will not be available to him or her until some future event occurs, usually the death of a relative.

(i) A deposit paid to a housing association as a condition of occupying the claimant's home[101] (interest on the deposit is taken into account as income – see Table 3, item 15).

(j) Premises that are up for sale (see page 130) or occupied wholly or in part by an aged or incapacitated relative.[102]

If the claimant has debts which are secured on any of his or her assets, the debts are deducted in arriving at the value of the assets.[103] But no deduction is allowed for unsecured debts.[104] This can be very unfair where supplementary benefit is refused because the claimant's gross capital resources are over £3,000 although his net assets, after deducting the money he owes, are less than £3,000. In some cases the problem can be solved by paying off the debts, but this may not be practicable and, even if it is, it may not be in the claimant's interests.

Money owed *to* the claimant, on the other hand, is a capital resource, to be taken into account like any other asset at its 'market value'.[105] This will normally be less than its face value – in fact, an unsecured debt from one individual to another may have little or no market value. The value will depend on the rate of interest, if any, the credit-worthiness of the debtor, and the date when repayment is due or can be demanded.

Resources held on trust, where the trustees have power to make payments to or for the benefit of the claimant or the claimant's wife or children, are treated as belonging to them, wholly or in part, depending on the number of beneficiaries under the trust and the terms of the trust. The special treatment of trust funds resulting from personal or criminal injury is mentioned in item (f) above. In other cases, the resources can be ignored for up to three months if the trustees need time to arrange payments.[106]

Children's Resources

The resources of a child living with the claimant (including a child over 16 who is still treated as a dependant) are normally aggregated with those of the claimant (see pages 51–2). But there are some exceptions, designed to prevent the claimant from losing entitlement to benefit solely by reason of the child's resources.

If the child has capital which, added to that of the parent or parents, would raise their total capital resources above the £3,000 limit and make them ineligible for supplementary benefit, the child's capital is not aggregated with the parents' but is treated as producing an income equal to the child's requirements. The child, in effect, is left out of the benefit calculation – though any payment by a liable relative to or for the child will still be taken into account as part of the claimant's resources. Once the claimant's capital, including that of the child, has been reduced to £3,000 or less, the benefit should be recalculated in the normal way.

If there is more than one child with capital resources, it may not be necessary to exclude them all in order to keep the total within the £3,000 limit. The case is dealt with in whatever way is most favourable to the claimant, excluding one or more children as may be necessary to produce the maximum benefit entitlement.[107]

If the child has an *income* in excess of his or her weekly requirements (the scale rate plus any 'additional requirements'), the excess income is disregarded and does not result in any reduction in the benefit payable for the needs of the rest of the family.[108] In calculating the child's income for this purpose, the normal disregards are allowed: in particular, the child's earnings (apart from those of a school-leaver – see page 120) are entirely disregarded. But if the income includes any maintenance payments by a liable relative, they are left out of the calculation and automatically added to the claimant's resources (see page 126).

REFERENCES

1. Resources Regs. 4(1).
2. S Manual, paras. 6042–3.
3. S Manual, para. 6049.
4. S Manual, para. 6031.
5. Resources Regs. 6(1)(c).
6. Resources Regs. 4(2).
7. S Manual, paras. 6074–6.
8. Resources Regs. 11(2).
9. Resources Regs. 11(4).
10. Resources Regs. 3(2)(a).
11. Resources Regs. 10(5).
12. Resources Regs. 11(4)(d).
13. Resources Regs. 11(2)(l).
14. Resources Regs. 11(4)(m).

15. Resources Regs. 11(4)(*e*).
16. Resources Regs. 11(4)(*i*).
17. Resources Regs. 11(5).
18. Resources Regs. 9(2)(*a*).
19. Resources Regs. 9(2)(*b*).
20. R (SB) 33/83.
21. Resources Regs. 9(2)(*b*).
22. Resources Regs. 9(2)(*cc*).
23. Resources Regs. 10(5).
24. CSB 350/82.
25. Resources Regs. 10(4)(*c*).
26. Resources Regs. 10(4)(*d*); *S Manual*, para. 6368(5).
27. Resources Regs. 9(1)(*a*).
28. Resources Regs. 10(3)(*a*).
29. Resources Regs. 10(3)(*b*).
30. Resources Regs. 10(1).
31. Resources Regs. 11(2)(*f*).
32. Resources Regs. 4(3).
33. *S Manual*, para. 6083.
34. Resources Regs. 10(2)(*b*) and 10(3)(*e*).
35. Resources Regs. 10(1)(*h*).
36. Resources Regs. 10(2)(*c*).
37. Resources Regs. 10(2)(*d*).
38. Resources Regs. 11(4)(*g*).
39. *S Manual*, para. 6808.
40. Resources Regs. 10(2)(*a*).
41. Resources Regs. 9(2)(*d*).
42. *S Manual*, paras. 6482–6538.
43. CSB 521/83.
44. Resources Regs. 4(9).
45. Resources Regs. 4(10).
46. Resources Regs. 10(3)(*d*).
47. Resources Regs. 3(2)(*g*).
48. Resources Regs. 3(2)(*d*).
49. Resources Regs. 11(5)(*a*).
50. Resources Regs. 3(2)(*e*).
51. Resources Regs. 11(2)(*b*).
52. Resources Regs. 11(2)(*c*).
53. Resources Regs. 11(2)(*a*).
54. Resources Regs. 3(2)(*a*).
55. Resources Regs. 11(4)(*a*) and (*b*).
56. Resources Regs. 11(5)(*b*) and (*e*).
57. Resources Regs. 2(1) and 11(2)(*d*).
58. Resources Regs. 11(2)(*e*).
59. Resources Regs. 11(2)(*i*).

60. Resources Regs. 11(2)(*f*).
61. Resources Regs. 11(2)(*l*).
62. Resources Regs. 4(4).
63. Resources Regs. 2(1) and 11(2)(*l*).
64. Resources Regs. 11(4)(*d*).
65. Resources Regs. 13(1).
66. Resources Regs. 2(1).
67. Resources Regs. 12(1)(*a*).
68. Resources Regs. 4(5)(*a*).
69. Resources Regs. 2(1).
70. Resources Regs. 13(4)(*a*).
71. Resources Regs. 13(3).
72. Resources Regs. 13(4)(*b*).
73. Resources Regs. 13(2).
74. CSB 1326/83.
75. Resources Regs. 2(1).
76. Resources Regs. 4(5)(*a*).
77. Resources Regs. 11(4)(*i*).
78. Resources Regs. 11(4)(*j*).
79. Resources Regs. 11(5)(*e*).
80. *S Manual*, para. 6010.
81. Resources Regs. 11(4)(*i*).
82. Resources Regs. 5(*a*).
83. R(SB) 57/83.
84. Resources Regs. 5(*b*).
85. Resources Regs. 6(1)(*a*)(i).
86. Resources Regs. 2(1).
87. R(SB) 30/83.
88. Resources Regs. 6(1)(*a*)(ii).
89. Resources Regs. 6(1)(*a*)(iii).
90. Resources Regs. 6(1)(*b*).
91. Resources Regs. 7.
92. Single Payments Regs. 5.
93. Resources Regs. 6(1)(*c*).
94. Resources Regs. 6(1)(*i*).
95. Resources Regs. 6(1)(*d*) and (*e*).
96. Resources Regs. 6(1)(*g*).
97. Resources Regs. 6(1)(*j*).
98. Resources Regs. 6(1)(*k*).
99. Resources Regs. 6(1)(*a*)(v).
100. Resources Regs. 6(1)(*a*)(vi).
101. Resources Regs. 6(1)(*f*).
102. Resources Regs. 6(1)(*a*)(iii) and (iv).
103. Resources Regs. 5(*a*)(ii).
104. R(SB) 2/83.

RESOURCES

105. R(SB) 31/83.
106. Resources Regs. 4(6).
107. Resources Regs. 8.
108. Resources Regs. 12.

Chapter 7

Single Payments for 'Exceptional Needs'

Supplementary benefit normally takes the form of a weekly payment, calculated as explained in the preceding chapters. But the Supplementary Benefits Act also provides for the payment of benefit in the form of a single payment to meet an exceptional need,[1] and the circumstances in which single payments are to be made are set out in the Single Payments Regulations.

Most single payments are made to people already on supplementary benefit, but the need for a single payment may arise in the case of a person who is entitled to weekly payments of supplementary benefit but has not claimed them. Single payments can be made in these circumstances,[2] but not to people who would not qualify for weekly payments, either because their income or capital is too high or because they are in full-time work or for some other reason are ineligible. Anyone receiving a housing benefit supplement (see pages 107–9) qualifies for single payments because the supplement, although paid by the local authority, is a form of supplementary benefit.

The purposes for which single payments can be made are set out in the regulations. They cover a wide range of needs, some of which occur frequently while others are more rare and affect only a small number of claimants. Provided that the conditions laid down in the regulations are satisfied, single payments are just as much a legal right as weekly benefit payments. Even where the normal conditions are not satisfied or the regulations do not provide for a particular need, a payment can still be made either on grounds of health or safety if there is no other way of meeting the need (see pages 177–9), or if benefit has been underpaid in the past (see page 143).

In the following pages, the general rules about single payments are first explained. Then the rules for each type of payment are explained, in the same order as in the list below. Finally, the operation of the 'safety-net' provision for payments on grounds of health or safety is described.

Needs for which Single Payments Can be Made

Maternity needs
Funeral expenses
Household goods:
   Essential furniture and household equipment
   Repairs to furniture and household equipment
   Hire purchase of furniture and household equipment
   Bedclothes
Housing:
   Deposits and rent in advance
   Legal and survey fees
   Removal expenses
   Repairs and redecoration
   Draughtproofing
   Gardening
   Unpredictable housing costs
   Discharged prisoner's arrears of housing costs
Clothing and footwear
Fuel:
   High fuel bills
   Prepayment meters
   Reconnection charges
Travelling expenses
Expenses on starting work
Debts accrued while abroad
Voluntary repatriation
Prisoners:
   On leave
   Rent arrears, etc. on discharge.

Needs for which Single Payments Cannot be Made

Strikers and other claimants affected by trade disputes (including a claimant whose wife or husband is affected by a trade dispute) cannot receive single payments,[3] though in limited circumstances they can claim urgent need payments instead (see pages 239–40). People in residential accommodation provided or financed by a local authority can claim payments under some but not all of the headings listed above[4] (see page 250).

For *all* claimants, despite the safety-net provision under which payments can be made for purposes not specifically provided for in the regulations, there are some needs which cannot be met by a single payment. These are as follows: [5]

Medical needs (including surgical, optical, aural or dental needs)

Educational or training needs

Distinctive school uniform or sports clothes or equipment

Fares to school

School meals, including meals provided during the holidays (term-time meals should be provided free to children whose parents are on supplementary benefit)

Mobility needs (but fares can be paid for particular purposes – see pages 173–6)

Motor-vehicle expenses, including purchase, running costs, garaging and parking (but the cost of petrol can be met in certain cases – see page 174)

Telephone installation, rental and call charges

Television or radio – purchase, rental, licence or aerial

Holidays

Expenses arising from an appearance in court, including legal costs and fines

Removal expenses for which other provision is available (see page 159)

Domestic assistance provided by a local authority (also excluded in calculating additional requirements – see page 74)

Repairs to council and other public sector housing

Needs occurring outside the United Kingdom.

The exclusion of medical needs applies to weekly payments of supplementary benefit,[6] as well as to single payments, but it mainly affects entitlement to single payments on grounds of health or safety (see page 178).

Where needs arise which fall within one of the excluded categories listed above, it may be possible to get help from a voluntary or charitable source, which will be disregarded for supplementary benefit purposes (see page 128).

Basic Conditions

The fact that a particular item is specified in the regulations does not mean that there is an automatic right to a payment. A single payment can be made only where (a) there is an 'exceptional' need for the item in question and (b) if the payment is for the purchase of a particular item, the claimant does not already possess that item or have a suitable alternative available, and has not unreasonably disposed of such an item or failed to avail himself or herself of it.[7]

Is there a need?

Entitlement to a single payment depends on whether there was a need for the item at the date of the claim.[8] It is not necessary that the need should still exist when the adjudication officer makes a decision on the claim. For example, if a claimant needs blankets and is able to obtain them after claiming a single payment but before a decision is made, a payment must be made provided that all the conditions were satisfied at the date of the claim.

Where the regulations state that a single payment shall be made for the purchase of goods such as furniture, bedclothes or clothing, the need for these items ceases to exist when the items are obtained, whether they have been paid for or not. If an item has been borrowed, it is a question of fact whether the borrowed item meets the need. Where the need is only temporary (e.g. for maternity clothes) and the borrowed items can be retained for as long as the need continues, there will be no further need to be met by a single payment. If the items are borrowed only as a short-term emergency measure and there is a continuing need, the borrowed items should not be regarded as meeting the need.

Where the single payment is not for the purchase of goods but for the cost of a service, the need will continue after the service has been rendered, so long as it has not been paid for. For example, single payments can be made for 'the cost of the removal' where a claimant is moving house, for the 'costs of essential repair' to an item of furniture or to the home, or for 'the fuel costs of the assessment unit'. In any of these cases, the fact that the service has been received or the fuel consumed does not remove the need for money to meet the cost. If the bill has been paid before a single payment is claimed, however, the need will no longer exist, even if it has been paid with borrowed money.[9]

There are two exceptions to the rule that the need must exist at the date of claim. The first is that where a need has to be met immediately and it is impracticable to claim a single payment in advance, the claim can be made within five working days (i.e. a week, except where a strike or public holidays intervene) after the date on which the need first arose.[10] The second is that if a need for which a single payment could have been made has been met by using money intended for normal living expenses, there may still be an entitlement to a single payment.[11] This provision is explained more fully on page 143.

Establishing that a need exists often involves a visit to the claimant's home by a social security officer, but a claim can be dealt with by post if sufficient details are given. A letter from a social worker will be accepted as evidence of a need for clothing or bedclothes. It should state that the claimant does not possess the items in question or have suitable alternative items available to him or her.[12] Where the need is for clothing, the circumstances in which it has arisen should be explained, bearing in mind the conditions that must be satisfied before a payment can be made (see pages 162–8).

Is the item already possessed, available or disposed of?

As with the question of need, it is the situation at the date of the claim that matters.[13] Whether a particular item is a suitable alternative to the one for which a claim is made must be decided subjectively, having regard to the individual needs of the claimant.[14] A raincoat, for example, might be considered a suitable alternative to an overcoat for some claimants but not for others. If the assessment unit has 'disposed or failed to avail itself of such an item', it will be disqualified for a single payment only if it did so unreasonably. An example given in the guidance to adjudication officers of unreasonable failure to avail oneself of an item is 'when it is known that on removal the claimant refused suitable furniture offered by parents/friends or by the local authority or a voluntary organization'.[15] Second-hand furniture that an organization or individual is giving away, however, is often not a 'suitable alternative' to items that the claimant could buy in a second-hand shop. Similarly, if it is suggested that the claimant has unreasonably disposed of suitable alternative items, it is important to consider whether the items were really suitable alternatives, whether they were in fact disposed of (a tribunal of Commissioners has held that a claimant's failure to take sufficient care of her possessions while she was away from home could not be regarded as a 'disposal' or failure to avail herself of them)[16] and, if so, whether in the circumstances at the time of the disposal it was unreasonable. A single payment should be refused on these grounds only if the answer to all these questions is 'Yes'.

Double Payments

The regulations do not place any limit on the number or frequency of single payments, but if a single payment has been made for a particular purpose a second payment cannot be made for the same purpose unless the circumstances giving rise to the payment have changed.[17] Thus, if a payment is made and the money is used for some other purpose it will not normally be replaced. But if some time has elapsed since the first payment, it will often be possible to show that there has been a change of circumstances. A second payment can then be made, provided that the need still exists, even if the change of circumstances was brought about by the claimant's own actions.[18]

Amount of Payment

A single payment must normally be of the amount necessary to meet the need in question. Where goods are to be purchased, it must be enough to pay for items of 'reasonable quality'. If the payment is for services, it must cover the actual cost to the extent that it is reasonable. In the case of clothing and bedclothes, however, the regulations include price lists (see Appendix 3 for clothing and Appendix 4 for bedclothes). Single payments for these items are normally based on the price list.[19] The payment can be *more* than the listed price if a more expensive item of clothing or footwear is needed because the person is 'outsize' or disabled.[20] It will be *less* than the listed price if a cheaper item is obtained and the payment is made in the form of a girocheque payable to the supplier (see page 208).[21]

If the claimant has capital (including that of the claimant's husband, wife or children) of more than £500, the excess is taken into account for this purpose, even though capital of up to £3,000 is ignored for other purposes.[22] For example, if furniture costing £100 is needed and there is capital of £600 or more, the claimant is expected to pay for the furniture out of the capital over £500. If the capital is only £550, £50 is assumed to be available towards the cost of the furniture and a single payment is made for the other £50. But there are some exceptions to these general rules for the treatment of capital:

(a) Capital of £500 or less is taken into account in considering the need for a single payment under the safety-net provisions of regulation 30 (see page 178).

(b) A payment for a discharged prisoner's arrears of housing costs, etc. will be made only to the extent that the debt cannot be met out of his capital resources (see pages 253–4).

(c) Capital over £50 is taken into account in calculating the amount of a single payment for repatriation expenses (see pages 261–3).

(d) Single payments for housing costs which arise irregularly (see page 162) are made without regard to the value of the claimant's capital.

Needs Arising from Underpayment or Failure to Claim Benefit

Single payments are not usually made for day-to-day living expenses of a kind which are assumed to be covered either by weekly supplementary benefit payments or, in the case of rent and rates, by housing benefit. A single payment can, however, be made for any of these purposes if *either* supplementary benefit for a past period was underpaid or not paid at all, *or*, through failure to claim a single payment for some item, the claimant has had to pay for that item with money set aside for living expenses. A payment will be made only for expenses which, as a result of the underpayment or failure to claim, the claimant cannot meet and cannot reasonably be expected to meet but which it is essential that he or she should meet.[23]

Examples

1. A deserted wife delays claiming supplementary benefit and, as a result, is unable to put money aside for electricity. On receiving the bill, she claims benefit but does not satisfy the normal conditions for payment of arrears (see pages 168–72). In addition to future weekly benefit payments she is entitled to a single payment of the amount of the electricity bill or – if this is less – the amount of benefit she has lost by not claiming sooner.

2. An unemployed man has got behind with the rent by spending his rent allowance on blankets, for which he could have claimed a single payment. He is entitled to a single payment for the rent arrears – either the full amount or the amount he would have received for the blankets, whichever is less.

In the first of these examples, if arrears of benefit are awarded subsequently, the single payment will be recovered out of the arrears. The second example illustrates an important exception to the rule that a single payment must be claimed before the need (in this case for blankets) is met.

Savings Deductions

Repeated requests for single payments for clothing or other items of 'normal requirements' (see pages 52–3) may result in a decision to make a weekly 'savings deduction' from the claimant's benefit, so that money is set aside in advance against any future needs of this kind. The decision to do this is taken by the adjudication officer and there is a right of appeal against it. Savings deductions can be made only where, in the officer's opinion, the claimant 'has failed to budget for items to which the category of normal requirements relates but for which the need arises at irregular or extended intervals'.[24] This usually means clothing – housing is not a 'normal requirement' and there are separate arrangements for deductions in respect of fuel costs (see Chapter 9). Requests for single payments for clothing are likely to be interpreted as evidence of failure to budget, but should not be so interpreted if there are good reasons why money that might have been spent on clothing has had to be spent on other things, or if the claimant has recently had to spend more than usual on clothing (the meaning of 'failed to budget' is discussed further on pages 200–201).

It is for the adjudication officer to decide, subject to the right of appeal, how much the weekly deduction should be. The money that has been saved in this way must be paid out as and when the claimant needs to pay for clothing or any other item of normal requirements for which the need arises 'at irregular or extended intervals' – for example, fuel, window-cleaning, cooking utensils, or television licence. Once the adjudication officer is satisfied that the need for any such item has arisen, he is obliged to arrange for a payment to be made of the amount he considers appropriate.[25] Any savings that remain in hand when entitlement to benefit ceases must be paid to the claimant as soon as is practicable.[26]

The fact that savings deductions are being made does not affect the claimant's right to a single payment for any purpose for which specific provision is made in the regulations. For example, payments for maternity needs, furniture or bedclothes should be made in the normal way. The deductions can be used only to pay for 'normal requirements' for which single payments would not normally be available. Even where the need is for clothing or fuel, the savings deductions must not be used if the claimant is entitled to a single payment (see pages 162–72) – but payments would not be made under the safety-net provision of regulation 30 (see pages 177–9) if savings deductions were available.

Maternity Needs

Unless there is sufficient available capital over £500 or the maternity grant is sufficient to meet the need, a single payment must be made 'for the purchase of such items as are necessary to meet the immediate needs of the child' if any member of the assessment unit has recently given birth or her 'expected week of confinement' is not more than six weeks off.[27] Normally the mother or expectant mother would be the claimant or the claimant's wife, but she could also be a dependent child of the claimant, still at school but expecting a baby. The regulations allow similar payments for the needs of an adopted baby.

A list of items that may be covered by the payment is given in the regulations:[28]

Clothing sufficient for a newborn baby
A sufficient quantity of napkins
A sufficient quantity of feeding bottles
A cot
A cot mattress
A pram or carry-cot
A sufficient quantity of cot blankets and sheets
A baby bath

But the list is not exclusive: any other items that are 'necessary to meet the immediate needs of the child', other than medical requirements (see page 139), must be included.

Where a cot, pram, carry-cot or baby bath is needed, the amount to be allowed is the cost of a second-hand item, if available. For other things, the cost of new items is to be allowed – in the case of clothing or bedclothes, at the prices shown in Appendix 3 or Appendix 4.[29] The Chief Adjudication Officer's guidance on the quantities of various items to be regarded as 'sufficient' is as follows:

Clothing: 3 sleeping suits, 1 pramsuit, 1 wrap or shawl, 3 plastic pants, 3 vests.
Nappies: 'allow 18 as the norm but more may be needed if washing/drying facilities are inadequate'.
Feeding bottles: 'allow 4 as the norm'.
Cot blankets and sheets: 3 of each.[30]

The use of the word 'norm' indicates that if the circumstances are abnormal larger quantities may be needed; and even if there are no abnormal circumstances it is open to an appeal tribunal to adopt a more generous view of what is 'sufficient'. Moreover, mothers are not obliged to dress their babies in the particular garments listed in Appendix 3, though a payment for the cost of a more expensive item may be refused on the grounds that it is more than the amount 'necessary to purchase an item of reasonable quality'.[31]

All mothers should receive the £25 maternity grant on or before the birth of their baby. In calculating the amount of a single payment to meet maternity needs, the £25 grant will be taken into account unless it has already been spent on items for which a single payment could have been made.[32]

Entitlement to a single payment for maternity needs does not depend on being in receipt of supplementary benefit on the birth of the child. It arises in any case where supplementary benefit is payable, for however short a period, during the six weeks preceding the week in which the baby is expected, provided that there is a need which cannot be met out of the maternity grant. Similarly, if supplementary benefit does not commence until after the baby is born, a single payment must be made, if needed, provided that the birth occurred 'recently'. The regulations do not state how long ago is 'recently', though it has been held by a Commissioner that, as the baby's normal requirements are provided for in the claimant's weekly benefit payments, the 'immediate needs' for which single payments can be made must be limited to 'such equipment and outfitting for the newborn child as is needed for the inaugural phase only' of the child's membership of the assessment unit;[33] and in another case the Commissioner held that the regulation could not apply where the child was eight months old.[34] If a pushchair or high chair is needed for an older child, a payment can be made under the heading 'furniture and household equipment' (see page 149).

A question that could arise in some cases is whether a mother having her second or third baby has unreasonably disposed of some of the equipment she already had, thereby disqualifying herself for a single payment for those items (see page 141). Unless she disposed of them after she knew that she was pregnant, however, the adjudication officer ought to accept that it is normal for mothers to hand on unwanted baby things.

In the past, difficulties were often caused by the unwillingness of the social security office to make a payment for maternity needs before the birth of the baby. Since the regulations now specify that a payment must be made if the expected week of confinement is not more than six weeks ahead, there should be no question of payments being delayed in this way. Provided that the needs are made known to the social security office in good time, payment should always be made in time for the items to be acquired before the baby is due.

A single payment can also be made for the mother's clothing needs arising from pregnancy or the birth of the child (see page 163).

Funeral Expenses

If a claimant or a claimant's wife or husband takes responsibility for the cost of a funeral or cremation, there may be an entitlement to a single payment to cover essential funeral expenses, but only if the money is not obtainable from any of the following sources:

(a) The death grant (normally £30, but only £15 for a man born before 5 July 1893, or a woman born before 5 July 1898);

(b) A lump sum death benefit under an insurance policy, occupational pension scheme or 'analogous arrangement';

(c) The estate of the deceased, excluding (i) the value of the home unless he/she was the sole occupant and (ii) where the person responsible for the funeral expenses is the widow or widower of the deceased, any personal possessions (except those which would normally be taken into account as resources – see page 116);

(d) Any contribution from a charity or relative (other than a relative to whom (e) applies), after deducting the cost of any items that cannot be included in a single payment (see below for the items that *can* be included) and, in the case of a contribution from a relative, the cost of flowers;

(e) If part of the cost still remains to be met after deducting all the above, any close relative of the deceased (widow, widower, parent or step-parent, child or step-child, brother or sister) is expected to contribute a proportionate share of the remaining cost, except that (i) this does not apply if the deceased was the husband, wife or dependent child of the person responsible for the funeral expenses, (ii) no contribution is assumed from a relative who has not been in touch with the deceased in recent years, who is on supplementary benefit or whose financial circumstances are such that he or she cannot reasonably be expected to contribute, and (iii) relatives are not expected to contribute to the cost of flowers from the person responsible for the funeral.[35]

The fact that the deceased person may have been on supplementary benefit does not entitle the relatives to help with the funeral expenses. It is the financial circumstances of the person who takes responsibility for the cost of the funeral (and who may not be the same person as makes the arrangements) that count. He or she must be entitled to supplementary benefit at the date of the claim for a single payment for the funeral costs, whether actually receiving benefit or not. It does not matter if the funeral has already taken place before the date of the claim, since the 'exceptional need' for which a single payment is made is the *cost* of the funeral, not the funeral itself. What matters is that the bills have not been paid.[36]

To qualify for a single payment, the person responsible for the cost of the funeral must have been either (i) a member of the same household as the deceased, (ii) a close relative (defined as in (e) above) or (iii) a more distant relative if the deceased had had no recent contact with a closer relative; and, in any case, there must be no close relative of the deceased who, having regard to how closely they were related and his or her financial situation, could more reasonably be expected to take responsibility.[37] If the person claiming a single payment is the widow or widower of the deceased, and they had been living together, he or she should always be accepted as the person responsible, even if there is another close relative in the household who could afford to pay and even if someone else makes the arrangements on behalf of the widow or widower.[38]

The deceased must have lived in the United Kingdom (including Northern Ireland) and the funeral must take place in the United Kingdom, though death may have occurred during a temporary absence.[39]

The 'essential expenses' that can be covered by a single payment, to the extent that they are not covered by money derived from the other sources listed above, are:

The cost of necessary documentation (death certificates, etc.)

A plain coffin

Transport for the coffin and bearers, and one additional car

Reasonable cost of flowers from the person responsible for the expenses

Undertaker's fees and gratuities, and chaplain's, organist's and cemetery or crematorium fees, for a simple funeral or cremation

Additional expenses up to £75 arising from a requirement of the religious faith of the deceased

Where the person died away from home, the cost of transporting the body home (if death occurred abroad, only the cost of transport within the United Kingdom).[40]

Travelling expenses connected with the funeral can also be claimed (see page 174). If the person arranging the funeral wants to make more elaborate arrangements or to incur expenses that are not included in this list, they are free to do so but will have to find other ways of meeting the cost. Contributions from relatives or charitable sources may, however, be used to pay for items not covered by the list, without entitlement to a single payment for allowable expenses being affected.

Essential Furniture and Household Equipment

Single payments for furniture and household equipment are available only to certain categories of claimants, as explained below (pages 151–5). A wide range of items defined as 'essential', for which payments can be made, is listed in the regulations:[41]

(a) Sufficient beds and mattresses and dining and easy chairs for all the members of the assessment unit, and a dining table (note that this does not include beds and chairs for boarders and children of working age, who are not 'members of the assessment unit').

(b) Sufficient storage units for clothing, food and household goods (e.g. crockery) for the assessment unit.

(c) A cooker.

(d) Heating appliances, other than parts of a central-heating system.

(e) Fire-guards.

(f) A covered hot-water bottle for an elderly or infirm person.

(g) Curtains (or curtain material) and fittings.

(h) PVC or 'equivalent' floor coverings (Commissioners have held that it was not unreasonable to regard cheap carpeting[42] or Marley tiles[43] as 'equivalent' to PVC).

(i) A washing machine – only where the conditions for a weekly laundry addition are satisfied (see page 73) but there is no accessible laundry or launderette or, if there is one, it cannot be used because of illness or disability.

(j) A vacuum cleaner – only where a member of the assessment unit is allergic to house dust.

(k) A refrigerator – only for a special diet needed for medical reasons.

(l) Minor items such as cleaning implements, cooking utensils, crockery and cutlery – only where the claimant has recently become the tenant or owner of an unfurnished or partly furnished home.

(m) A garden fork or spade and shears, where the home has a garden and digging, or cutting of lawns and hedges, is necessary.

(n) An iron.

(o) Light fittings.

(p) Towels.

(q) A push-chair.

(r) A high chair.

(s) A hot-water cylinder jacket.

(t) Safety gates.

A payment cannot normally be made for an item of furniture or equipment that does not appear in this list, but it may be possible to claim a payment for such an item on grounds of health or safety if there is no other way of obtaining it (see pages 177–9).

The basic conditions of entitlement are the same as for other single payments – that there is a need for the item in question, which cannot be met by using the claimant's capital over £500; that the assessment unit does not already possess it or have a suitable alternative available and has not unreasonably disposed of it or failed to avail itself of it; and, unless there has been a change of circumstances, that a payment has not already been made for the same item. The test of need can usually be satisfied by showing that the item falls within the definition of 'essential' – i.e. that it is included in the above list – and that the assessment unit does not possess it.[44] But it may be more difficult to decide what *quantities* of furniture are needed, particularly where there are children. A young child does not need an easy chair but an older child might. Similarly, a teenager will need a separate wardrobe. Differences of opinion may also arise regarding the amount of storage space needed for food and crockery. If agreement cannot be reached with the adjudication officer, it may be worth appealing against his decision.

The rule that the assessment unit must not already possess the item does not apply if the item it possesses is defective or unsafe and would cost more to repair than to replace, or it would be uneconomic to repair it. Another exception to this rule is a second-hand bed or mattress, for which a payment can be made if it has already been acquired, provided that a single payment is claimed before the bed or mattress is paid for.[45]

The amount of a single payment for furniture is normally the cost of a second-hand item of reasonable quality, if available; otherwise the cost of a new item. But special rules apply in the following cases:

Beds and mattresses. Cost of a new item to be allowed unless the claimant has already acquired or negotiated for a second-hand one (for a squatter, only the cost of a second-hand bed or a new sleeping-bag is allowed).

Cookers and electrical or gas appliances. Cost of a reconditioned item, if available (most second-hand appliances are *not* reconditioned); otherwise a new one.

Curtains, floor coverings and other items of household equipment (not furniture). Cost of a new item, except a push-chair or gardening tools, for which the cost of second-hand items is allowed, if available.[46]

Payments are also made for delivery charges for items (a) to (d) and (h) to (k) in the list above, and installation costs for a cooker, heater, floor covering, washing machine or refrigerator.[47]

It is up to the claimant to find suitable items, whether new or second-hand, and the single payment should cover the actual cost unless the adjudication officer considers that it is more than the amount 'necessary to purchase an item of reasonable quality'. For second-hand articles he should be prepared to say what would be regarded as a reasonable price.[48] Payment is usually made by girocheque payable to the supplier. If this would cause embarrassment, the social security office can be asked to pay the money to the claimant instead – but there is no right of appeal against a refusal to do so (see page 208).

If the furniture is needed for a move to a new home, officers are instructed to 'make every effort to ensure that prior to removal, payment is awarded for all items for which the need can be determined before the move'.[49] If this is done, it should be possible for the claimant to obtain at least the basic essentials of furniture before moving, provided that the local social security office is given reasonable notice of the move.

Who is entitled?

Claimants who qualify for payments for furniture and household equipment fall into four broad groups: (i) those who qualify on grounds of age, sickness, disability, pregnancy or a child in the family; (ii) those who are moving or have moved to a new home; (iii) squatters; (iv) others.

(i) Age, sickness, disability, pregnancy or a child in the family

This category includes all claimants, whether moving to a new home or not, where a member of the assessment unit is a dependent child (under 16 or still at school), or an adult who is over pension age (60 for a woman, 65 for a man), chronically sick, mentally or physically disabled, or pregnant.[50] Whether a person is chronically sick or disabled must be decided by the adjudication officer on the available evidence. Anyone on the local-authority register of disabled persons should be accepted as disabled for this purpose; but registration by the local authority is limited to those who are 'substantially and permanently handicapped', and entitlement to payments for furniture and household equipment is not. Anyone registered as disabled for employment purposes or receiving a disablement pension should also normally be accepted as disabled. Many disabled people are not on any register but are still entitled to these payments.

'Chronic' sickness means an illness that is 'long lasting', 'constantly present' or 'permanent' – it is the duration, not the severity, that matters. It does not imply that the person is unable to work or cannot reasonably be expected to move to furnished accommodation.[51] A

Commissioner decided, for example, that a young man, unemployed and registered for employment, who had suffered from asthmatic bronchitis for ten years and was moving from a furnished to an unfurnished flat, was entitled to payments for furniture and equipment.[52]

(ii) Moving or recently moved to a new home

A claimant who (or whose wife or husband) has recently become the tenant or owner of an unfurnished or partly furnished home, whether he or she has already moved in or not, and who does not qualify on grounds of age, sickness, disability, pregnancy or having a child in the family, can be entitled to payments for furniture and household equipment if one of the conditions (a), (b) or (c) below is satisfied.[53] The regulations do not define 'recently', but in the guidance issued to adjudication officers they are told to take it as meaning 'within the previous three months'.[54] The conditions are that

(a) one of the conditions for payment of removal expenses ((a) to (g) on pages 157–8) is satisfied – whether a single payment is actually made for removal expenses or not; *or*

(b) immediately before acquiring the new home, the claimant was a prisoner, or had been in hospital continuously for more than a year, or was living in a resettlement unit (or similar accommodation provided by a voluntary body) or in accommodation where 'special care and attention' was provided (e.g. a hostel or group home for young people, mentally ill, mentally handicapped or physically disabled people, drug addicts, alcoholics, or a Borstal community home or youth treatment centre); *or*

(c) the claimant is considered by the adjudication officer to have no immediate prospect of employment and has either been on supplementary benefit continuously for 6 months or, within the last 6 months, was the partner of a person who had been on benefit for 6 months ('partners' are either a married couple living together or an unmarried couple living as husband and wife).

To qualify for a payment under (b) or (c), however, it must be shown that 'there is no suitable alternative furnished accommodation available in the area'. This additional condition, as interpreted in an important decision by a tribunal of Commissioners, can prove an insuperable obstacle, even in areas where the chances of obtaining furnished accommodation of a decent standard are very slight. It is important, therefore, when furniture is needed for a new home, to consider whether the claimant is entitled to a payment on other grounds, such as chronic sickness, disability or pregnancy, or by satisfying one of the conditions for payment of removal expenses. If so, the question of the availability of furnished accommodation does not arise. For example, a single man in good health, who has been living with relatives and is offered an unfurnished council flat, will not have to show that no suitable alternative furnished accommodation is available if the home from which he is moving is 'unsuitable either in size or structure',[55] whether or not that is the main reason for the move (see (b) on page 157).

In some cases, however, it is impossible to avoid the 'no suitable alternative furnished accommodation' condition by claiming single payments on other grounds than those of (b) and (c) above. Where the condition applies, the Commissioners' decision mentioned in the previous paragraph places firmly on the claimant the onus of proving, on a balance of probability, that such accommodation is not available. The Commissioners made detailed observations on the wording of the condition. They attached great significance to the word 'no': 'The difficulty of getting accommodation does not come into the matter at all and in order to show that there probably is no such accommodation the claimant must make proper efforts to obtain it and cannot simply rely on the likelihood of it being difficult to obtain.' Similarly, while the fact that accommodation was advertised did not mean that it was 'available' to the claimant, it was for him to show that a particular advertised property which appeared to be suitable for his needs was not in fact available to him: 'For this purpose, it is not necessary for him to show that he has visited and been rejected by *every* landlord of suitable property, provided that he can show by his efforts to obtain such accommodation that, in practice, it is not available to him.' 'Suitable' accommodation, the Commissioners stressed, meant suitable to the needs of the claimant and other members of the household: 'The wishes and desires of these persons are immaterial' – though they did concede that 'bed and breakfast' accommodation, where the user must be off the premises from after breakfast until nightfall, would be 'unsuitable for several, if not all, of the categories of claimant' to whom the condition applied, particularly those 'in need of a more settled way of life'. The possible loss of security of tenure resulting from a move to furnished accommodation, on the other hand, was dismissed as 'of no relevance'. Nor did the Commissioners accept that furnished accommodation might be unsuitable because the rent was more than the claimant would be able to afford when he ceased to draw supplementary benefit, though they accepted that it *would* be unsuitable if the local authority would refuse to meet the rent in full under the housing benefit scheme because it was too high or the accommodation was larger than the claimant needed or situated in an unnecessarily expensive location. Finally, since the condition referred to furnished accommodation available 'in the area', the Commissioners considered the meaning of this term. 'The area', they decided, was that in which the claimant had recently become a tenant or owner, rather than the area from which he was moving. They expressed no view as to how wide that area should be considered to be, apart from saying that 'environmental and geographical factors and the availability of transport' were factors which could be taken into account in any particular case.[56]

In the light of this decision, anyone to whom the 'no suitable alternative furnished accommodation' condition is likely to apply would be well advised to obtain evidence that such accommodation is not available locally, preferably by enquiring about accommodation advertised in the local press, before claiming a single payment for furniture. It will probably be found that many landlords are unwilling to let accommodation to a single person living on supplementary benefit or require immediate payment of rent in advance or a deposit. Although single payments can be made for both rent in advance and deposits, it takes time to obtain these and landlords may not be prepared to wait.

(iii) *Squatters*

A squatter who has the landlord's permission to remain temporarily can get a single payment for a second-hand bed, or, if preferred, a new sleeping-bag, but not for any other furniture or equipment.[57]

(iv) *Others*

Any other claimant who has *not* recently become the tenant or owner of an unfurnished or partly furnished home and is *not* entitled to a payment for furniture on grounds of age, sickness, disability or pregnancy or because there is a child in the family, can still qualify for such a payment under condition (c) above – six months on benefit and no immediate prospect of employment – or if the need is for a cooking or heating appliance.[58] The 'no suitable alternative furnished accommodation' condition does not apply in these cases. This means that a person who has recently moved and is refused a payment for furniture on the grounds that there is suitable furnished accommodation in the area can apply again once the move has ceased to be recent – and, as noted above, this is taken to mean three months after becoming the tenant or owner of the home. But the need must still exist at the time of the claim. If furniture has been borrowed meanwhile, there will still be a 'need' provided that the borrowed items have to be returned in the near future.

Repairs to Furniture and Household Equipment

If an item of furniture or household equipment listed on page 149 is in need of repair, a single payment must be made 'to meet the costs of essential repair' provided that, if the claimant did not already possess the item in question, he or she would be entitled to a single payment to purchase it. A single payment for repairs will not be made if it would be cheaper to replace the item or if the cost of repair would be 'un-economic having regard to the future viability of the item'.[59] In that case, a single payment is made for the replacement of the item instead (see page 150).

A payment for repairs must be enough to cover the reasonable cost, to the extent that it cannot be met out of capital over £500. It is advisable to obtain an estimate and get it agreed as reasonable by the social security office before the repair is done. If a claim is made for repair or replacement of a cooker, heating appliance, washing machine, vacuum cleaner or refrigerator, the social security office may ask for an estimate of the cost of repair and a single payment will then be made for any cost incurred in obtaining the estimate.[60]

Hire Purchase of Furniture and Household Equipment

If the claimant or the claimant's wife or husband is buying furniture or household equipment on hire purchase, a single payment can be made to clear the outstanding debt or part of it.[61] It must be hire purchase, not a credit sale agreement. The items for which the payment is made must be things for which a single payment could be made if the claimant did not already possess them (see page 149). And the claimant must, in the adjudication officer's opinion, be likely to remain on supplementary benefit for the whole period covered by the HP agreement. If not, a single payment will not be made but the claimant may be entitled to help with the HP instalments on a weekly basis (see pages 79–80).

If the outstanding debt is not more than would have been allowed as a single payment to purchase the item in question, a payment will be made of the full amount needed to clear the debt, after deducting any capital over £500 that the claimant may have.

If the debt is more than would have been allowed as a single payment to purchase the item, a single payment of up to that amount will be made only if (i) the HP agreement was entered into before the claimant became entitled to claim supplementary benefit, and (ii) the HP instalments will be reduced to an amount that can be met out of disregarded earnings and any other income covered by the £4 disregard (item 40 in Table 3 – see pages 118–19).

Bedclothes

A single payment must be made for any of the items listed in Appendix 4 – sheets, blankets, pillows, pillow-cases and eiderdowns – of which, in the adjudication officer's opinion, the assessment unit's stock is inadequate for its needs, unless the items needed can be bought out of their capital over £500. The payment must be based on the price list in Appendix 4. In assessing the needs, the adjudication officer must take into account any additional need arising, in particular, from the state of health or physical disability of a member of the assessment unit – for example, extra blankets, extra sheets where frequent washing is needed,[62] or extra pillows for a person who has to sleep propped up. For normal cases where there are no special needs, officers are told to regard the stock of bedclothes as inadequate if, for each bed in use, there are less than:

3 blankets (or two and an eiderdown)
3 sheets
1 pillow per person
2 pillow-cases per person.[63]

Even when there are no health problems, this standard should be applied flexibly. The number of blankets needed varies between individuals (elderly people, even in normal health, may need more) and depends on the quality and age of the blankets. The temperature of the bedroom is also relevant: an unheated bedroom in Scotland will need more blankets than a centrally heated or even unheated room in the south of England.

A single payment for bedclothes can cover only the needs of the assessment unit – claimant, wife or husband and dependent children – not those of lodgers and other non-dependent members of the household.

Deposits and Rent in Advance

A claimant who (or whose wife or husband) has to pay a deposit to a landlord to secure the tenancy of a new home is entitled to a single payment of the amount of the deposit, up to a maximum of eight weeks' rent. The deposit must be returnable: a single payment cannot be made for a non-returnable premium or 'key-money', which in any case is usually illegal.[64]

The regulations do not say that, to qualify for a payment for this purpose, the move should be necessary or the new rent reasonable. If the adjudication officer considered the move unnecessary, however, a payment might be refused on the general grounds that there was no 'need' (see page 140).

A payment can also be made for up to four weeks' rent payable in advance, other than to a local authority, but only if there were reasonable grounds for the move.[65] If such a payment is made, the amount will be deducted from the rent allowance paid by the local authority (see page 106).[66] This may mean that the problem of finding a month's rent out of a week's income is merely postponed until the second month of the tenancy. The local authority may, however, be willing to spread the deductions over a longer period if there are good grounds for doing so.

Legal and Survey Fees

A single payment is made for reasonable legal fees (but not stamp duty) in connection with the renewal or extension of the lease of the claimant's home, provided that he or she does not intend to dispose of the lease within twelve months.[67]

If survey fees are incurred in connection with a loan or mortgage for repairs which are necessary to maintain the fabric of the home or keep it in habitable condition, a single payment can be made for the reasonable amount of the fees.[68]

Removal Expenses

A single payment is made for the cost of moving house in *any* of the following circumstances (with the exceptions noted on page 159):

(a) Where the existing home is structurally deficient or insanitary.

(b) Where the existing home is unsuitable in size or structure or because it is too far from close relatives (husband or wife, parents, children, brothers or sisters) – and factors to be taken into account in deciding whether it is unsuitable include the age, state of health or any physical disability of a member of the assessment unit and the number of people living in the home.

(c) Where the move is in consequence of the death of the claimant's husband or wife, divorce, or any other breakdown of the marriage (or of the relationship if the couple are unmarried but were living as husband and wife).

(d) Where the move will significantly improve the employment prospects of the claimant or the claimant's wife or husband or enable him or her to take up an offer of employment.

(e) Where the move will make it possible to take in a close relative (husband, wife, parent, child, brother or sister) of the claimant or of the claimant's wife or husband, who is over pension age, chronically sick or mentally or physically disabled, a hospital patient, a child in the care of a local authority, or a person living in residential accommodation.

(f) Where the claimant's supplementary benefit or housing benefit entitlement is reduced because the housing costs are excessive or the accommodation is too large or in an expensive area or the rent too high (see pages 93–4 and 104–5).

(g) Where the claimant's benefit includes (or recently included) an additional requirement for furniture storage (see page 80).[69]

This list covers most circumstances in which a claimant is likely to move. The existing home may, for example, be unsuitable in size because it is either too large or too small. It may be unsuitable in structure because of stairs that an elderly claimant cannot manage or because it lacks basic amenities such as an indoor lavatory. 'Structure' also includes the location of the home within the building: e.g., a twenty-fourth floor flat was held to be 'unsuitable in structure' for a single mother with a two-year-old child.[70] If a move to unfurnished accommodation follows the breakdown of a marriage or relationship, it can be 'in consequence of' the breakdown even if it occurs several months later and the claimant has meanwhile lived in furnished accommodation at one or more addresses.[71] If the move results from a fire, flood or other disaster, and the removal expenses cannot be paid on any of the grounds listed above, emergency relief may be payable (see page 191).

A single payment for removal expenses cannot be made in any of the following cases:

(a) Where the claimant is permanently rehoused because of a compulsory purchase, redevelopment or closing order (a payment can be made by the local authority under the Land Compensation Act 1973, which is intended to cover the cost of the move).

(b) On a compulsory exchange of local authority tenancies (the authority has power to assist with removal costs).

(c) Where the removal costs are met by the Manpower Services Commission under the employment transfer scheme.[72]

(d) Where the local authority has power to help under the Housing (Homeless Persons) Act 1977 – even though local authorities may refuse to use this power.

(e) Where supplementary benefit will be restricted because the housing costs for the *new* home are excessive, unless there are disregarded earnings or other disregarded income of at least the amount by which benefit is restricted.[73] The fact that *housing* benefit may be restricted because the new home is 'unsuitable' (see page 104) does not affect entitlement to a single payment for the removal.

(f) Where the move is to or from somewhere outside the United Kingdom.[74]

It is advisable to make a claim for a single payment before the removal, since a Commissioner has held that the words 'is moving to a new home' in the regulation mean that a claim by a person who has already moved cannot succeed.[75] In any case, the claimant is required to produce two competitive estimates of the cost of removal, unless the social security office agrees on grounds of urgency or of the claimant's age or state of health that only one estimate need be produced.[76] The estimates should normally be obtained before the move but can be submitted to the social security office after the move if necessary. If no written estimate was obtained, the social security office can accept a receipted account as the estimate.[77]

The single payment will be for the amount of the estimate or, where two estimates are required, the lower of the two, after deducting any capital over £500 and a proportionate share of the cost attributable to any non-dependent members of the household, unless they are also on supplementary benefit or, having regard to their financial circumstances, cannot be expected to contribute.[78] A non-dependant's share is calculated on the basis of the number of people in the household, counting a child as half.[79] A non-dependant who is staying, or moving separately, should not be expected to contribute.

A claimant who qualifies for a single payment for removal expenses is also entitled to payments for travelling expenses to the new home (see page 174), for the reasonable cost, if any, of re-installing a cooker, heating appliances, floor coverings (including carpets), a washing machine and a refrigerator, and for the purchase of any additional furniture and household equipment that are needed (see page 152).

Repairs and Redecoration

Claimants who own their homes or are responsible for all structural repairs are entitled to a weekly 'maintenance and insurance' allowance of £1.80 in the calculation of their supplementary benefit (see page 91). If this is not enough to meet the actual cost, a single payment may be obtainable for this purpose.

If a bill for essential routine minor maintenance is more than the amount unspent out of the weekly allowance, a single payment is made for the balance. The amount unspent is calculated by taking the total weekly maintenance and insurance allowance for the past 52 weeks, or since benefit commenced if that is more recent, and deducting the amount spent during that period on these items, including the weekly cost of house insurance if the claimant is responsible for it. If the claimant has any capital it is ignored completely for this purpose.[80]

The regulations do not define 'essential routine minor repairs or maintenance' but, if the repair is not regarded as being of this kind, more stringent rules apply. A single payment can be made for the reasonable cost of repairs and any resulting redecoration, if the repairs are 'essential to preserve the home in a habitable condition', do not cost more than £325 (including redecoration), and the claimant cannot reasonably be expected to meet the cost out of the weekly maintenance and insurance allowance and is 'unable to finance the repairs in any other way'.[81] 'Any other way' includes capital over £500, but not the first £500 of capital.[82] It might also include a grant or loan from the council, a mortgage, and possibly even help from relatives. If the cost of a repair is more than £325, a single payment cannot be made for part of the cost – it is all or nothing. But if several repairs are needed, totalling more than £325, a payment should be made for each separate repair costing £325 or less, provided that it is essential to keep the house in a habitable condition.[83] If money has to be borrowed for a larger repair bill, the claimant may be entitled to a weekly addition to cover the loan interest (see page pages 89–91).

Where redecoration is needed, unconnected with any major repair, renovation or alteration of the property, a single payment is made for the cost of materials (but not labour) if the claimant has lived there for at least a year and is responsible for internal redecoration, either as the owner or leaseholder or under the terms of the tenancy. The payment will not cover external redecoration. Non-dependent members of the household are expected to contribute their share of the cost if they can afford to, and the payment will be reduced by their assumed contribution.[84] To qualify for a payment, the redecoration must be 'essential', but this does not mean that it must be necessary in order to prevent insanitary conditions or structural deterioration,[85] but only that there should be 'substantial need, judged by the modest standard of living to the provision of which the award of supplementary benefit is directed' (these words were used by a Commissioner in the case of an elderly widow with restricted mobility, living alone, who was awarded a payment for the redecoration of her kitchen which had not been decorated for five years).[86] Redecoration may also be regarded as 'essential' in the case of a council tenant who needs to move but will not be offered a new tenancy until the present home is redecorated.[87]

Draughtproofing

Where the home is draughty and the draughts would be reduced by simple measures, a single payment is made for the cost of the materials. 'Simple measures' include the usual forms of draught excluder, but not double glazing.[88] A payment can be made for fitting plastic sheeting over windows, if this is done as a draughtproofing measure and not simply to improve insulation.[89]

Gardening

Payments can be made for basic garden tools under the heading of 'household equipment' (see page 149). If nobody in the household is able to look after the garden and, as a result, it is in such a state that a summons from the local authority or a notice to quit has been received, a single payment can be made for the costs incurred by a voluntary organization in doing the necessary work.[90] Payments cannot be made for the cost of regular maintenance of the garden, only for the immediate need arising from the summons or notice to quit.

Unpredictable Housing Costs

Certain expenses connected with housing, for which it is not practicable to make a fixed weekly allowance because their amount is not known in advance, are met as they arise by means of single payments. These include, in particular, charges for emptying a cess-pit or septic tank. The claimant's capital, including any capital over £500, is ignored for this purpose.[91]

Discharged Prisoner's Arrears of Housing Costs

The rules regarding payments for arrears of housing costs or storage charges to a prisoner discharged after less than a year are explained in Chapter 14 (pages 253–4).

Clothing and Footwear

Because clothing and footwear are regarded as 'normal requirements', the cost of which is allowed for in the scale rates (see page 52), single payments are made for them only in abnormal circumstances or if there has been a previous underpayment of benefit.

The most straightforward case is where the need arises on admission to hospital or 'a similar institution'. A payment should be made for any item of clothing included in the clothing price list in Appendix 3 that is needed for the stay in hospital and which the patient does not already possess.[92] The adjudication officer should take a reasonable view of the need to replace worn-out items which might be usable at home but which the patient would be ashamed to wear in hospital.

A similar provision applies to a person whose need arises on admission to a re-establishment centre, whether residential or not (see pages 231–2).

In other cases, a single payment is made where there is a need for clothing listed in Appendix 3 which has not arisen either 'by normal wear and tear' or 'in the normal course of events (for example where an item of clothing or footwear is outgrown)'. The regulation gives four examples of cases where the need is regarded as arising 'otherwise than by normal wear and tear' (though a payment may still be refused if the need arose 'in the normal course of events'). Note that these are only examples, and there may be other circumstances in which it can be argued that the need has not resulted from normal wear and tear. The four examples are:

Where the need has arisen because of

(a) Pregnancy, the birth of a child, or rapid weight loss or gain;

(b) Heavy wear and tear on clothing or footwear resulting from any mental or physical illness, handicap or disability (except where an additional requirement is applicable (see page 78));

(c) The accidental loss of, damage to or destruction of an essential item of clothing or footwear;

(d) Physical or mental illness or disability which necessitates the purchase of a particular or additional item of clothing or footwear.[93]

Adjudication officers are given detailed guidance on the meaning of these examples, on which there have also been some Commissioners' decisions. The officers are told to regard as *rapid weight loss or gain* 'a weight loss resulting from, e.g., a serious operation or illness so that items of clothing no longer fit and must be replaced, or a gain due to, e.g., a glandular condition or period of drug treatment' – but not 'normal growth including "growth spurts" by children or adolescents'.[94] This should not be taken to mean that children's growth can never give rise to a need for which a single payment can be made. Although payments cannot be made 'where the need has arisen in the normal course of events (for example where an item of clothing or footwear is outgrown)', a Commissioner has expressed the view that 'this is a reference to the items being outgrown in the normal course of events and not to an item being outgrown because of some abnormal or exceptional circumstances such as very rapid growth such that a child requires replacement of clothing very much more quickly than is normal'. In another case, the same Commissioner said that a 'rapid increase in size, e.g. of feet, or in height' could qualify for a payment, just as a rapid increase in weight can, provided that it was 'such as to take it out of the category of need arising in the normal course of events'.[95]

On *example (b)*, wear and tear resulting from an illness, handicap or disability, officers are told that this would include a case where a leg iron causes heavy wear on trousers or shoes, or where incontinence causes heavy wear on underclothing from repeated laundering.[96] The illness or handicap can be either physical or mental. The test is not the severity of the illness or handicap but its effect on wear and tear of clothing or footwear. The words in brackets in example (b) refer only to additional requirements for abnormal wear and tear (see page 78).[97] If the extra cost is already being met in this way, by an addition to the weekly benefit payments, single payments are not made for clothing needs arising from the same cause. But if the weekly benefit is not actually increased, because of the £1 offset in long-term cases (see page 67), officers are told that they can make single payments.[98] A Commissioner has said that a single payment can be made for needs of this kind which exist at the time of an initial claim for supplementary benefit, even if the future cost of heavy wear and tear is to be met by a weekly addition.[99]

Officers are given very little guidance as to the meaning of 'accidental loss, damage or destruction' in *example (c)*; in fact most of the guidance issued by the Chief Supplementary Benefit Officer (now the Chief Adjudication Officer) when the regulations were introduced in 1980 has now been withdrawn. For example, officers were told that 'the clothing needs of children such as shoes kicked out playing football in the playground or trousers torn climbing trees should not be accepted as damage or destruction within the meaning of this regulation; such circumstances should be regarded as normal wear and tear'.[100] This was clearly wrong. It is a matter of judgement at what point the rough treatment of children's shoes ceases to be normal wear and tear, but the tearing of clothes while climbing trees is certainly 'accidental damage' and, especially if the clothes are fairly new, can hardly be regarded as 'normal wear and tear'. Losses arising from theft, though not mentioned in the guidance to officers, should also be accepted as 'accidental' from the claimant's point of view. Claims for single payments resulting from loss or destruction of clothing are likely to be treated with some suspicion. Any supporting evidence, such as a letter from a witness of the events leading to the loss, will therefore be helpful.

Example (c) specifies that the accidental loss, damage or destruction must be of an *essential* item of clothing or footwear. This presumably means more than the normal test of 'need' which applies to all single payments (see page 140), and suggests that a payment will not necessarily be made for an item that is lost, damaged or destroyed merely because it appears in the price list in Appendix 3. Whether it is essential depends on the needs of the person concerned and whether he or she possesses other items of a similar kind. Officers are given the list on page 165 as a guide to the levels below which the claimant's stock of particular items is to be regarded as inadequate and therefore justifying a single payment for some or all of the items lost, damaged or destroyed.

For example, if a claimant has lost two pairs of shoes but still has a third pair, a single payment will be made for only one pair, bringing his stock of shoes up to two pairs – the quantity shown in the list.[101] Some items of clothing listed in Appendix 3 are not included in this list but may still be essential – e.g. a dressing-gown and slippers for a housebound person. The list is only a guide to officers and is in

Men/boys		*Women/girls*	
Item	Quantity	Item	Quantity
Overcoat or raincoat	1	Overcoat or raincoat	1
Jacket or anorak	1	Jacket or anorak	1
Cardigan, pullover or sweater	1	Cardigan, pullover or sweater	1
Trousers or jeans	2 pairs	Dresses	2
Socks·	3 pairs	Stockings/tights or (for girls) socks	3 pairs
Shoes	2 pairs	Shoes	2 pairs
Shirts	2	Slips	2
Vests	2	Vests	2
Underpants	3	Knickers/briefs	3
Pyjamas	2 pairs	Pyjamas/nightdress	2
		Corset/pantie girdle	1
		Brassière	2

no way binding on an appeal tribunal. A Commissioner has held that a payment can be made for only one of each item of clothing, since that is sufficient to satisfy the immediate need;[102] but this seems an unduly restrictive interpretation and is unlikely to be applied in cases where it can reasonably be argued that more than one of a particular item is needed.

If the loss, damage or destruction results from a 'disaster' of any kind and a single payment is not otherwise available, it can be made by way of emergency relief under the Urgent Cases Regulations (see page 189).

On *example* (*d*) on page 163 – particular or additional items needed because of physical or mental illness or disability – the guidance to officers includes the following:

A *particular* item could be a dressing-gown for an elderly, bedridden person, or a raincoat for a bronchitic whose existing topcoat does not keep him dry; an *additional* item could be an extra pullover for a person with tuberculosis.[103]

The item must be one of those listed in Appendix 3, though it may be of a more expensive kind than would normally be needed, in which case the payment may be more than the amount shown in Appendix 3 (see page 167).

A person's size does not count as a physical disability, except possibly if it is due to illness.[104] If a person needs clothing of a non-standard size or fitting, however, an additional requirement can be allowed to meet the extra cost on a weekly basis (see pages 78–9).

Clothing needed on grounds of health or safety

Payments for clothing and footwear can also be made under regulation 30 of the Single Payments Regulations if the case does not fit into the conditions described above – for example, where the need arises from normal wear and tear or normal growth – and there is no other way of preventing serious damage or serious risk to the health or safety of a member of the assessment unit. The restrictions on the use of regulation 30 are explained more fully below (pages 177–9). The guidance to officers stresses that the damage or risk to be prevented must be *serious* and that, for example, the fact that a child has to stay away from school for lack of clothing is not, in itself, a serious risk to health, and even shoes that let in water are not necessarily a serious risk (a statement which, regrettably, has the support of a Commissioner's decision).[105] Examples of conditions which, officers are told, could give rise to serious damage or risk to health are:

(a) Frail elderly people (70 or over) suffering from a physical or mental disability or illness (e.g. chronic bronchitis or rheumatism) or getting over an operation.

(b) Adults suffering from a serious disability, e.g. multiple sclerosis, or recovering from a severe operation.

(c) Children suffering from a chest condition such as bronchitis, asthma or tuberculosis, a heart condition, or mentally retarded.

Where any of these conditions would be aggravated by the lack of an item of clothing, officers are told to accept that there is serious risk to health. They are also told that very exceptionally, in a family with 'multiple problems', a single payment may be the only way of preventing a deterioration which would result in serious damage or risk to health, 'e.g. further neglect of children, self-neglect by the claimant, even the risk of suicide'.[106]

The rule that a payment under regulation 30 must be the *only* means of preventing serious damage or serious risk to health or safety is interpreted with some flexibility. Officers are told not to regard the following as other means of meeting the need:

(a) Jumble sales;

(b) Help from the local authority social services department under the Children and Young Persons Act (or, in Scotland, from the social work department under the Social Work (Scotland) Act);

(c) Charities and voluntary bodies unless it is known that they can help with the particular item;

(d) The WRVS, which has stores of mostly second-hand clothing.

Thus, if a payment can be made under regulation 30, the claimant should not normally be expected to seek help from charitable sources or from the social services department. Other means of meeting the need which, officers are told, *may* be available include clothing clubs, provident cheques, mail order catalogues and other credit facilities; but a Commissioner has held that compelling evidence of the availability of credit facilities to a supplementary benefit claimant would be needed.[107]

Amount of payment

If a single payment is made for an item of clothing or footwear which appears in the list in Appendix 3, the amount paid must be the price shown in Appendix 3, unless a higher price has to be paid because the person is 'outsize' or disabled. The lists of boys' and girls' clothing in parts IV and V of Appendix 3 apply to children under 14 and the adult lists in parts I and II to those aged 14 and over; but if a child under 14 is large for his or her age, the adult price list must be used. The boys' and girls' clothing lists give prices for small and large sizes, leaving it to the adjudication officer to decide on a figure within these limits according to the child's size. Payments can be made under regulation 30 for items of clothing not included in the price lists, in which case the normal rule applies – that the payment must be sufficient to purchase an item of reasonable quality.[108]

Work or school clothing

Single payments can also be made for working clothes and footwear to enable a person to start a job (see page 176). A single payment cannot be made, even under regulation 30, for a distinctive school uniform or sports clothes.[109] The reason for this is that the local education authority has powers to help with the cost of schoolchildren's clothing. Most education authorities have a school-uniform grant scheme, under which parents whose incomes are below a certain level can claim a grant of a fixed amount, with smaller grants for those with slightly higher incomes. The details, including the size of the grants and the qualifying levels of income, are left to each local authority to decide. There are wide variations between one area and another and a few authorities do not give school-uniform grants at all. Where schemes exist, they are usually confined to secondary-school children, though some primary schools require uniforms; and most authorities insist on an interval of two years between grants for the same child, while some refuse to give a grant during the child's last year at school.

Local education authorities also have a more general power to provide clothing (sometimes referred to as 'necessitous clothing') for a schoolchild of any age who appears 'unable by reason of the inadequacy or unsuitability of his clothing to take full advantage of the education provided at the school'. Again, there are wide variations between different authorities in the way in which this power is used, some having fixed limits as for school-uniform grants while others consider each case 'on its merits'. Where there is an entitlement to a single payment for clothing under the normal rules, an application to the education authority for 'necessitous clothing' will not be necessary. In considering whether a payment should be made for reasons of health or safety under regulation 30, however, the adjudication officer will take into account any help that is available from the education office.

High Fuel Bills

Fuel, like clothing, is a 'normal requirement' covered by the scale rates. If a claimant is likely to have large fuel bills because he or she is elderly or there is a young child in the family, or because of ill health or the high cost of heating the accommodation, a weekly 'additional requirement' is allowed (see pages 68–72). For claimants who get in difficulties with their fuel bills, there are arrangements for payment of part of their benefit directly to the fuel board to ensure that the supply is not disconnected (see pages 202–5).

In certain cases a single payment can be made to enable a claimant to meet the whole or part of a fuel bill. The right to a single payment can arise from the fact that benefit was underpaid for an earlier period or a single payment was not claimed on a previous occasion (see example 1 on page 143). The safety-net provision of regulation 30 can also be used to pay for fuel where there is no other way of preventing serious damage or risk to the health or safety of the claimant or the claimant's wife, husband or child (see pages 171–2). If fuel consumption has been unexpectedly heavy, however, entitlement to a single payment under the provisions explained below should be considered, before turning to regulation 30.

Unexpectedly high fuel consumption

Single payments are made for fuel costs which are more than the amount of money the claimant has put aside to pay for fuel, either because *exceptionally severe weather* has resulted in higher than normal fuel consumption (see below) or because the claimant has recently moved or acquired a new heating system and is *unfamiliar with the cost* of running it (see page 170).[110] Payments can be made for any kind of fuel, or for more than one kind. Money saved with the intention of using it for fuel bills is regarded as 'put aside' for this purpose, whether it is kept physically separate from any other savings or not. The mere fact that the claimant has enough money to meet the bills, however, does not mean that it has been 'put aside' for fuel costs; nor does it mean that a single payment can be refused on the grounds that there is no 'need'.[111]

Exceptionally severe weather

The regulation provides for a single payment to be made where the fuel costs are more than the amount put aside for them because 'a period of exceptionally severe weather has resulted in consumption greater than normal, having regard to any available information on previous levels of consumption'. The single payment must be of the amount needed to pay for the excess over normal consumption.[112] The responsibility for deciding whether the weather has been 'exceptionally severe' and, if so, how much above the normal level the claimant's fuel consumption has been, rests on the adjudication officer dealing with the individual claim. In practice, however, adjudication officers are guided by information from the Meteorological Office, based on the temperatures recorded at one of seventeen weather stations in different parts of the country. If the temperatures during a given week are low enough, it is automatically regarded as a week of exceptionally severe weather in the area covered by the weather station. The Met Office figures are also used to calculate what proportion of the fuel consumed in that week can be regarded as excess consumption and, similarly, what proportion of the fuel consumed in the period covered by a gas or electricity bill (normally eight or thirteen weeks) is excess consumption for weeks of exceptionally severe weather during that period. A single payment is made for the full cost of that excess consumption, excluding any standing charge.[113]

The standard applied in deciding whether the weather has been

169

exceptionally severe is so low that in most parts of the country it has been reached in only three or four weeks in the last twenty years. But this standard is not binding on appeal tribunals, which are free to take a more reasonable view. If an adjudication officer's decision that the weather has not been exceptionally severe seems unreasonable, therefore, the claimant should appeal against the refusal of a single payment.

Although the regulation requires the adjudication officer to have regard to available information on previous levels of consumption, the single payment is normally calculated by the formula described above, without taking into account the extent to which the fuel consumption of the individual claimant is above that of previous years. If evidence can be produced showing that the single payment does not cover the full increase (bearing in mind that only an increase in consumption, not an increase in price, counts for this purpose), the adjudication officer should be prepared to recalculate the payment accordingly.

Unfamiliar heating system

To qualify for a single payment under this heading, the claimant and any other members of the assessment unit must be 'unfamiliar with the cost of running the heating system', either because they recently moved or because the system was recently installed, and the fuel bills must, as a result, be more than the amount they have put aside for them. The amount of the single payment is half the fuel costs for any period during the first six months' use of the heating system.[114] It is not necessary to wait until the end of the six months before a payment can be made; each quarterly bill can be dealt with as it arrives. The single payment is not limited to the amount by which the bills exceed the amount set aside for them.[115]

There is some doubt as to what 'fuel costs' include. The guidance to officers says that standing charges are to be excluded,[116] but this seems wrong, since the standing charge is clearly part of the cost of fuel. In some cases an adjustment is made for the estimated amount of fuel used for purposes other than heating, and this practice has been endorsed by a tribunal of Commissioners;[117] but the regulation states that the single payment is to be half the fuel cost, not half the heating cost. Claimants should, therefore, ask for a payment of half the total fuel bill, including the standing charge; and where more than one fuel is used, claims should be made for each of them.

It is often difficult to calculate the amount of fuel consumed during the first six months' use of the heating system. Consumption may have been estimated by the gas or electricity board because the meter could not be read and a subsequent meter reading may suggest that the estimate was wide of the mark. There may be some doubt as to when the heating system was first used (if the same system provides both hot water and space heating, it is the date when the space heating was switched on that counts). And, even if a precise date is known, it is unlikely that the meters will have been read both at the beginning and at the end of the six-month period, and it will therefore be necessary to apportion the quarterly bills, bearing in mind that consumption may be either higher or lower in the first half of the quarter than in the second, depending on the time of year, the weather and other factors.

For all these reasons, where a single payment is made, details of the calculation should be requested and carefully checked. If the payment seems too low, the claimant should write to the social security office asking for it to be recalculated and, if this is refused, should consider appealing against the refusal.

Health or safety risk

If a payment cannot be made under the provisions explained above and there is no other way of preventing serious damage or serious risk to the health or safety of any member of the assessment unit (claimant, wife or husband, or a dependent child), a single payment must be made under regulation 30 (see pages 177–9). This regulation can be used to meet current fuel needs – for example where the family relies on solid fuel for heating. But it is more likely to be used to pay a fuel debt or provide an alternative to the normal fuel supply which has been or is about to be cut off. Whether having a fuel supply cut off is likely to cause serious damage or serious risk to health or safety depends on the circumstances, including the age and state of health of members of the family, the time of year, the purposes for which the fuel is used, and whether any other fuel is available. The guidance issued to officers gives the following examples of situations in which it can be assumed that serious damage or serious risk will follow if the fuel supply is cut off:

(1) Disconnection will deprive the claimant of *lighting* during the period October–April and there are in the assessment unit:

  (a) children under 11;
  (b) elderly people over 70; *or*
  (c) disabled people,
who will be at risk of injury through fire (if candles are used) or through falling downstairs; *or*
(2) disconnection will deprive the claimant of *heating* during the period October–April and there are in the assessment unit:
  (a) children under 5; *or*
  (b) anybody who is disabled or in poor health (e.g. suffering from chronic bronchitis), whose condition could be seriously aggravated by loss of heat ... *or*
(3) disconnection will deprive the claimant of *cooking* facilities and:
  (a) there are children under 2 in the assessment unit; *or*
  (b) hot meals are medically essential to any member of the assessment unit.[118]

But these are only examples and clearly do not cover all the circumstances in which there may be a serious health or safety risk. For example, living in an unheated home in a cold winter would pose a serious health risk to an able-bodied adult, not just to children under five and people in poor health. Similarly the suggestion that only children under two are at risk from lack of cooked meals is highly questionable.

A single payment cannot be made under regulation 30 unless it is the *only* means of preventing serious damage or serious risk to health or safety. Adjudicating officers therefore have to consider whether any other means are available. As with payments for clothing, they are told not to refer the claimant to the local authority social services or (in Scotland) social work department. Other means which may be available include installation of a prepayment meter, direct payment of part of the weekly benefit to the fuel board (see pages 202–5) or other arrangements for paying off the debt over a period.[119]

Although there is a right to a single payment if it is the only means of preventing serious damage or serious risk to health or safety, the payment will not necessarily be of the amount needed to get the fuel supply reconnected or to avoid disconnection. Officers are told, where this is practicable, to make a payment for an alternative means of lighting, heating or cooking, as the case may be.[120] If the suggested alternative does not seem a reasonable way of meeting the need, however, and especially if it would itself involve a safety risk, the officer should be asked to make a payment which will enable the normal fuel supply to be maintained.

Prepayment Meters

Where a prepayment meter is necessary to help the claimant to budget for the cost of gas or electricity, a single payment is made for the installation charge. Whether a meter is necessary is a matter of judgment, but if the claimant has got seriously behind with quarterly payments this should normally be accepted as sufficient evidence of the need. If the claimant already has a prepayment meter but, because of chronic sickness or disability, has difficulty in reaching it, a single payment is made for the cost of having it moved.[121]

Fuel Reconnection Charges

A single payment is made for the reconnection charge where gas or electricity has been cut off for non-payment of a debt and arrangements are made for paying the debt either by a single payment (see pages 168–72) or by paying part of the weekly benefit to the gas or electricity board (see pages 202–5) – but not if the debt is paid in any other way.[122]

Travelling Expenses

Single payments are made for travelling expenses within the United Kingdom in a variety of circumstances, set out in regulation 22 of the Single Payments Regulations:

Visits to people in hospital and residential accommodation. Visiting someone in hospital, a nursing home or residential accommodation (e.g. a home for elderly or disabled people), provided that the person being visited was previously a member of the same household or is a close relative (husband, wife, parent or step-parent, child or step-child, brother or sister) or is a more distant relative whom no other relative has visited recently or intends to continue visiting; but a payment will not be made if the claimant is entitled to a weekly addition to pay for regular visits (see pages 80–82). If the visitor cannot travel alone, travelling expenses for an escort are also allowed.[123] Urgent need payments can be made for visits to a person who is critically ill but not in accommodation of the kinds mentioned above, or where the visitor is not entitled to supplementary benefit, e.g. because he or she is in full-time work or a student (see page 196).

Domestic crises. (a) A journey by a child (with an escort if necessary) going to stay with relatives because of a domestic crisis, or returning home; or a visit to the child by one or both of the parents.[124]

173

(b) A journey to look after a relative's child, whose parents cannot do so because of a domestic crisis.[125]

Visiting a child pending a decision on custody. A visit by a parent to a child who is with the other parent pending a court decision on custody.[126]

Funerals. A journey connected with the arrangement of a funeral or attendance at the funeral, by a close relative of the deceased or a person who qualifies for a single payment for funeral expenses (see pages 147–8).[127]

Employment. (a) A journey to seek employment in another area, which would mean moving to that area, provided the adjudication officer considers that the claimant has reasonable prospects of finding a job there. A payment will not be made if travelling expenses can be claimed from the Manpower Services Commission (the jobcentre will advise on this).[128]

(b) Going for a job interview more than ten miles from home, where travelling expenses are not payable in advance by the prospective employer or the Manpower Services Commission.[129]

(c) Seeking a job within ten miles of home at the instigation of an unemployment review officer (see page 228).[130]

(d) Travelling to work at the start of a new job or on returning to work (see page 176).[131]

Single homeless persons. A journey to take up suitable accommodation which has been offered within reasonable travelling distance (the regulation does not define a reasonable distance).[132]

Moving to a new home. The journey to a new home, provided that the move qualifies for a single payment for removal expenses (see pages 157–9).[133]

The amount payable for travelling expenses is normally the cost of second-class public transport by whatever method is used, other than air travel. Where private transport is used, a payment is made for the cost of petrol, but not exceeding the cost of public transport where available. Taxi fares will be paid if public transport is not available or for a physically disabled person who cannot use other transport. If it is impracticable to make the return journey in one day, the cost of a night's lodging (or bed and breakfast where an inclusive charge is made) will be added. If it is reasonable to stay more than one night, for example when visiting a child in hospital or searching for a job, the cost of lodging or bed and breakfast will be met for whatever period is reasonable.[134]

Help with travelling expenses can be obtained from a number of sources in addition to the supplementary benefit scheme. Some of these are as follows:

Fares to the social security office. If a claimant or somebody acting for a claimant visits an office of the Department of Health and Social Security in connection with a supplementary benefit claim, and the matter could not have been dealt with satisfactorily and more cheaply by writing, telephoning or in some other way, he or she may be able to claim travelling expenses for the journey. Payments for this purpose do not count as supplementary benefit and there is no right of appeal against a refusal. Travelling expenses are paid only for visits made 'for good reason' – for example, if the claimant has been asked to attend at the office, or calls to inquire about a possible error in the benefit calculation or to report a change of circumstances – or if the claimant is entitled to emergency relief or other urgent need payments. The claimant, unless getting urgent need payments at the reduced rate (see pages 185–6), is expected to meet the first 80p of the cost of the first or only visit to the office in any week. A payment is made for the remainder of the cost and for the whole cost of any subsequent visits in the same week. If the claimant has to be accompanied by his or her wife, husband or children, or by an escort or interpreter, their fares are paid in full. Payments are based on the cost of the cheapest form of public transport or, if none is available or the person is too disabled to use it, the cost of petrol or the taxi fare.[135]

Hospital treatment. Hospital patients receiving supplementary benefit or family income supplement can have their fares to and from the hospital paid by applying at the hospital and producing their order-book. Fares should be claimed at the time of the visit, but can be claimed later if necessary. Payment is normally made by the hospital. Patients not receiving supplementary benefit or family income supplement may also be entitled to help with fares if, by supplementary benefit standards, they cannot afford to meet the cost themselves. They should obtain a form from the hospital giving dates of the visit or visits and take or send it to the social security office. These arrangements apply to both in-patients and out-patients. If the patient cannot travel alone, the travelling expenses of an escort will also be paid. There are special arrangements for war disablement pensioners undergoing hospital treatment for their war disablement, whose expenses are paid by the Department of Health and Social Security without any inquiry into their financial situation. The fares of patients attending a venereal disease clinic can also be paid without a means test where the journey to the clinic is fifteen miles or more for a single visit, or five miles or more for regular visits at weekly or shorter intervals.

Visits to relatives in prison. Help with the cost of visits by the wife or other close relative of a person serving a prison sentence of more than three months is provided by the Home Office. If the relative is entitled to or in receipt of supplementary benefit, the social security office will deal with the question of fares and the claim should be made there. Those not entitled to supplementary benefit because they are in full-time work, but with incomes around or below supplementary benefit level, should apply to a probation officer. Visits are normally allowed every four weeks but extra visits may be paid for on the recommendation of the prison governor if, for instance, the prisoner is seriously ill or it is necessary to discuss urgent domestic matters, or if the prisoner's solicitor confirms that a visit is necessary for the purpose of discussing arrangements for an appeal. In addition to the fares, the cost of overnight accommodation is paid if this is necessary. The travelling expenses of children named on the visiting order are also paid.

Visits to children in the care of a local authority. The social services department (social work department in Scotland) of the local authority can, where necessary, assist parents with the cost of visiting children in care.

Expenses on Starting Work

If a member of the assessment unit has to incur expenses which are not reimbursed by the employer in order to take up a job that has been offered (including a part-time job if it is for at least fifteen hours a week on average), or to continue in a job that commenced within the last two weeks, a single payment is made for these expenses. The payment can cover the cost of basic tools, any of the working clothes listed in part III of Appendix 3, a driving licence (but not driving lessons), fees for a medical examination, and up to £35 for any other items. The actual costs are allowed (subject to the normal deduction for any capital over £500), except in the case of working clothes, for which the price list in Appendix 3 is used unless they are supplied more cheaply by the employer.[136]

A single payment can be claimed for travel and removal expenses where a change of home is necessary, unless the expenses are being paid by the Manpower Services Commission under the employment transfer scheme.[137] Whether a change of home is involved or not, a claimant starting or restarting work is entitled to a single payment for travelling expenses between home and work while still in receipt of supplementary benefit – normally for up to fifteen days after starting work (see page 267).[138]

Debts Accrued while Abroad

As explained on page 259, supplementary benefit is sometimes payable while the claimant is out of Great Britain, but only for up to four weeks. If, on returning to Great Britain after an absence of less than twenty-six weeks, the claimant is again entitled to supplementary benefit, a single payment is made for a debt that has built up during the period of absence. But the debt must be for a 'continuing commitment' for which provision would have been made in calculating supplementary benefit entitlement – e.g. mortgage interest, HP instalments or gas and electricity standing charges. The single payment cannot be more than the amount of supplementary benefit that was not paid because of the absence. Subject to that limit, it must cover the full amount of the debt that has accrued during the period of absence less any capital over £500.[139] (Adjudication officers are told to exclude debts accrued during the first four weeks' absence,[140] but this seems incorrect.)

A claimant who is not entitled to benefit for at least part of the first four weeks of absence cannot claim a single payment for a debt that has accrued during the absence.

Voluntary Repatriation

The circumstances in which single payments are made for this purpose are explained on pages 261–3.

Prisoners on Leave and Discharged Prisoners

The rules regarding single payments to meet the needs of a prisoner on pre-release leave and for arrears of rent or other housing costs of a prisoner discharged after less than a year are explained in Chapter 14 (pages 253–4).

The Safety Net

Before 1980, a single payment of supplementary benefit could be made for any exceptional need. Since 1980, such payments have normally been available only in the particular circumstances set out in the regulations and explained in the preceding sections of this chapter. When the regulations were drawn up, however, it was recognized that there were bound to be cases of real need which were not covered by the rules. Regulation 30 of the Single Payments Regulations, referred to above in connection with payments for clothing (pages 166–7) and fuel (pages 171–2), was intended to fill these gaps. It applies only to people already on supplementary benefit – not to a person who would be entitled to benefit but has not claimed it, though he or she might qualify for an urgent need payment instead (see page 184). If the conditions for a payment under regulation 30 are satisfied, however, there is a legal entitlement to it, just as much as to a payment under any other regulation.

Regulation 30 can be used to make a payment *either* for an exceptional need provided for in the regulations (e.g. clothing) but for which the claimant does not satisfy the normal conditions, *or* for an exceptional need which is not otherwise provided for – but it cannot be used to make a payment for any of the items listed on page 139, for which single payments are never available.

The most important condition that must be satisfied before a payment can be made under regulation 30 is that, in the opinion of the adjudication officer, 'such a payment is the only means by which serious damage or serious risk to the health or safety of any member of the assessment unit may be prevented'. A health risk can be either physical or mental; for example, in the case of a young man suffering from depression because he lacked the tools needed for a new job, a Commissioner held that it was open to an appeal tribunal to conclude that there was a serious risk to his health.[141] But it is not enough to show that there is a risk to health or safety: it must be a *serious* risk.

Similarly, it is not enough to show that a single payment will prevent the damage or risk: it must be the *only* means of preventing it. As noted above in connection with payments for clothing and fuel, this requirement is not interpreted literally, since officers are told to ignore certain sources from which, in some cases, the need could be met – in particular, claimants are not expected to apply to charities (unless there is definite reason to think a particular charity will be able to meet the need in question) or social services departments, presumably because the Department of Health and Social Security does not want to be accused of evading its responsibilities at the expense of these bodies. Borrowing or buying on credit, on the other hand, is regarded as a possible alternative means of meeting the need, though 'compelling evidence' of the availability of credit facilities is required (see page 167).

As with other single payments, the need for the item in question must exist at the date of the claim. It is also at that date that a single payment must be the only means of preventing the damage or risk to health or safety. This condition can be satisfied even if, by the time a decision is made on the claim, some other way of meeting the need has been found, provided that it was not available at the time of the claim. As a Commissioner put it, 'the greater a claimant's need the likelier it may be that some external agency may step in if there is delay and provide some means of ending a crisis or averting some serious hazard. It would be quite wrong if this were then taken to show that a single payment was not the "only means" for the purpose of the regulation.'[142]

REFERENCES

1. SB Act, sec. 3(1).
2. Single Payments Regs. 4(b).
3. Single Payments Regs. 6(1)(b).
4. Single Payments Regs. 6(3).
5. Single Payments Regs. 6(1)(d) and 6(2).
6. SB Act, sec. 1(3).
7. Single Payments Regs. 3(2); R(SB) 21/84.
8. R(SB) 26/83.
9. R(SB) 47/83.
10. Claims and Payments Regs. 5B.
11. Single Payments Regs. 28(1)(b).
12. S Manual, para. 7012.
13. R(SB) 26/83.
14. R(SB) 1/84.
15. S Manual, para. 7079.
16. R(SB) 26/83.
17. Single Payments Regs. 6(1)(a).
18. R(SB) 15/81.
19. Single Payments Regs. 3(3) and (4).
20. Single Payments Regs. 27(2).
21. Single Payments Regs. 3(5).
22. Single Payments Regs. 5.
23. Single Payments Regs. 28.
24. Claims and Payments Regs. 15(1).
25. Claims and Payments Regs. 15(2).
26. Claims and Payments Regs. 24(a).
27. Single Payments Regs. 7(1).
28. Single Payments Regs. 7(2).
29. Single Payments Regs. 7(3).
30. S Manual, para. 7103.

31. Single Payments Regs. 3(3)(*b*)(i).
32. Single Payments Regs. 7(4).
33. R(SB) 7/82.
34. CSB 1101/83.
35. Single Payments Regs. 8(3).
36. R(SB) 47/83.
37. Single Payments Regs. 8(1)(*a*) and (*b*).
38. *S Manual*, para. 7122.
39. Single Payments Regs. 8(1)(*c*).
40. Single Payments Regs. 8(2).
41. Single Payments Regs. 9.
42. R(SB) 19/82.
43. CSB 641/83.
44. CSB 1068/82 and CSSB 6/83.
45. Single Payments Regs. 10(2)(*b*).
46. Single Payments Regs. 10(3).
47. Single Payments Regs. 10(5).
48. *S Manual*, para. 7214.
49. *S Manual*, para. 7218.
50. Single Payments Regs. 10(1)(*a*)(ii) and 10(1)(*b*)(i).
51. CSB 139/83 and R(SB) 41/84.
52. CSB 598/83.
53. Single Payments Regs. 10(1)(*a*).
54. *S Manual*, para. 7175(1).
55. Single Payments Regs. 13(1)(*b*).
56. R(SB) 8/84.
57. Single Payments Regs. 10(1)(*b*)(iv).
58. Single Payments Regs. 10(1)(*b*)(ii) and (iii)
59. Single Payments Regs. 10(4).
60. Single Payments Regs. 10(2A).
61. Single Payments Regs. 11.
62. Single Payments Regs. 12.
63. *S Manual*, para. 7237.
64. Single Payments Regs. 14.
65. Single Payments Regs. 21A.
66. Housing Benefits Regs. 1982, 16(4A).
67. Single Payments Regs. 15.
68. Single Payments Regs. 17(4).
69. Single Payments Regs. 13(1).
70. CSB 642/82.
71. CSB 78/83.
72. Single Payments Regs. 6(2)(*k*).
73. Single Payments Regs. 13(2).
74. Single Payments Regs. 13(1).
75. R(SB) 39/84.

76. Single Payments Regs. 13(3).
77. CSB 1140/82.
78. Single Payments Regs. 13(4) and (5).
79. *S Manual*, para. 7261.
80. Single Payments Regs. 21.
81. Single Payments Regs. 17(1).
82. R(SB) 35/84.
83. CSB 191/83.
84. Single Payments Regs. 19.
85. CSB 1107/83.
86. R(SB) 10/81.
87. CSB 143/81.
88. Single Payments Regs. 18.
89. CSB 109/82.
90. Single Payments Regs. 17(5).
91. Single Payments Regs. 21.
92. Single Payments Regs. 27(1)(*b*).
93. Single Payments Regs. 27(1)(*a*).
94. *S Manual*, para. 7463(2).
95. CSB 48/83; CSB 866/83.
96. *S Manual*, para. 7463(3).
97. CSB 485/82.
98. *S Manual*, para. 7463(3).
99. CSB 945/82.
100. Chief Supplementary Benefit Officer, *Guidance to Supplementary Benefit Officers: Claims for single payments*, 1980, para. 39(2).
101. *S. Manual*, para. 7472.
102. CSB 822/82.
103. *S Manual*, para. 7463(4).
104. R(SB) 3/83.
105. *S Manual*, para. 7546; R(SB) 8/82.
106. *S Manual*, paras. 7547–51.
107. *S Manual*, paras 7567–9; R(SB) 9/82.
108. Single Payments Regs. 27(2) and (3) and 30(3)(*a*)(i) and (ii).
109. Single Payments Regs. 6(2)(*b*).
110. Single Payments Regs. 26.
111. R(SB) 22/84.
112. Single Payments Regs. 26(1)(*a*) and (2)(*a*).
113. *S Manual*, paras. 7427–35.
114. Single Payments Regs. 26(1)(*b*) and (2)(*b*).
115. R(SB) 22/84.
116. *S Manual*, para. 7454.
117. R(SB) 22/84.
118. *S Manual*, para. 7557.
119. *S Manual*, paras. 7567–9.

120. *S Manual*, para. 7558.
121. Single Payments Regs. 20(*a*) and (*b*).
122. Single Payments Regs. 20(*c*).
123. Single Payments Regs. 22(1)(*a*), (*d*) and (*l*).
124. Single Payments Regs. 22(1)(*b*)(i) and (ii) and 22(1)(*d*).
125. Single Payments Regs. 22(1)(*b*)(iii).
126. Single Payments Regs. 22(1)(*c*).
127. Single Payments Regs. 22(1)(*i*).
128. Single Payments Regs. 22(1)(*e*).
129. Single Payments Regs. 22(1)(*f*).
130. Single Payments Regs. 22(1)(*g*).
131. Single Payments Regs. 22(1)(*h*).
132. Single Payments Regs. 22(1)(*k*).
133. Single Payments Regs. 22(1)(*j*).
134. Single Payments Regs. 22(2) and (3).
135. Claims and Payments Regs. 29.
136. Single Payments Regs. 23.
137. Single Payments Regs. 22(1)(*j*).
138. Single Payments Regs. 22(1)(*h*).
139. Single Payments Regs. 24.
140. *S. Manual*, para. 7387.
141. CSB 1141/82.
142. CSSB 76/82.

Chapter 8

Urgent Needs

This chapter deals with a variety of circumstances in which supplementary benefit would not normally be available but can be paid under the special rules laid down in the Urgent Cases Regulations. Many of these are also referred to in other chapters. The information is brought together here because of the special conditions to which urgent need payments are subject – in particular, the fact that they are only available as a last resort or in an emergency and in some cases they may have to be repaid later. Because of these special conditions, benefit should be paid wherever possible under the normal rules of the scheme rather than in the form of urgent need payments.

Who Can Get Urgent Need Payments?

Urgent need payments can be made to people who are entitled to supplementary benefit under the normal rules (with the exceptions noted below), whether they are actually receiving it or not. In addition, urgent need payments can be made to people who would not otherwise be entitled to benefit because they are in one of the following situations:

(a) In full-time employment.

(b) Not complying with the requirement to be available for work (see page 34).

(c) Not complying with a direction to attend a re-establishment course (see pages 231–2).

People who *cannot* receive payments under the Urgent Cases Regulations are:

(a) Strikers (including a claimant whose husband or wife is on strike), except for emergency relief after a disaster[1] – but in some circumstances they can get other urgent need payments under the Trade Disputes Regulations (see page 239).

(b) People in 'residential accommodation' – except that they *can* get travelling expenses for visiting a critically ill relative (see page 250).[2]

(c) NHS hospital patients.[3]

(d) Full-time students, except emergency relief or during vacations.[4]

(e) Members of religious orders.[5]

(f) Prisoners.[6]

(g) Visitors from abroad, other than from EEC countries and other countries covered by the European Social Assistance Convention – but they *can* get emergency relief after a disaster, or temporary help and travelling expenses in the circumstances explained on pages 195–6 and 197.[7]

Urgent need payments can be made for normal living expenses or as single payments for particular needs; but a single payment cannot be made, even on grounds of urgent need, for any of the items listed on page 139 (needs that cannot be met by a single payment)[8] or for needs arising outside Great Britain other than travelling expenses within the United Kingdom.[9]

Two urgent need payments cannot be made for the same need where the circumstances are unchanged.[10] There is also a curious provision in the regulations to the effect that, apart from emergencies and payments under the 'safety net' regulation (see below), if the claimant has had a similar need in similar circumstances in the past, no payment is to be made 'unless it is reasonable for that need to be met'.[11] This was presumably intended to discourage repeated claims for needs which could have been avoided, but there can be few cases in which payments are refused on these grounds.

The Safety Net

The Urgent Cases Regulations include a provision, almost identical to the 'safety net' provision of the Single Payments Regulations (see pages 177–9), under which urgent need payments can be made to people who either do not otherwise satisfy the conditions for a payment or have urgent needs for which the regulations do not specifically provide. Such payments are to be made if, and only if, in the opinion of the adjudication officer, it is the only way of preventing serious damage or serious risk to the health or safety of any member of the assessment unit.[12]

Other Resources

The normal rules allowing the claimant's capital resources to be disregarded up to a limit of £3,000 for purposes of entitlement to weekly benefit payments and £500 for single payments do not apply to urgent need payments. Nor do the rules regarding income disregards.

An urgent need payment can be made only where 'the item in question, or funds for that item or funds to meet the expenses in question are not readily available to the assessment unit from its own resources or from any other source' – including, for example, friends, relatives, credit facilities, a voluntary organization or, in the case of emergency relief, a local authority or relief fund.[13]

In calculating the claimant's resources for this purpose, all available income is taken into account but certain types of capital are disregarded. These are items (a) to (j) listed on pages 131–2, other than item (d) – i.e. money received as compensation for loss or damage to the claimant's home or possessions or to pay for repairs or improvements to the home *is* treated as available to meet an urgent need. Money held from the sale of a home and intended for the purchase of a new home is, similarly, regarded as available for this purpose, though it would be disregarded under the normal rules.[14] But if either capital or income, whether derived from these or other sources, is not in fact readily available, it should not be taken into account. In deciding whether a payment should be made by way of 'emergency relief' or under the 'safety net' regulation, the adjudication officer has a discretionary power to disregard any resource if it would be reasonable to do so,[15] but he is unlikely to do so if the resource is in fact available.

Amount of Payment

The rules for calculating the amount of a *single payment* for an urgent need are similar to the rules relating to other single payments (see Chapter 7). In particular, the Urgent Cases Regulations provide that a payment for the purchase of any item must be enough to pay for an item of reasonable quality, and a payment for services must cover the costs of the services to the extent that they are reasonable.[16] More detailed rules regarding particular items are set out in schedules 1 and 2 to the regulations and are explained in the following sections of this chapter.

Where urgent need payments are made in the form of a *supplementary pension or allowance*, special rules apply for the purpose of calculating the claimant's requirements for the first fourteen days and any further days before the start of the next 'benefit week':

(a) The scale rates for 'normal requirements' of married couples, single householders, and non-householders are the 'ordinary' (short-term) scale rates reduced by 25 per cent (the long-term scale rates are not used, even if the claimant is over pension age).

(b) The requirements of children of all ages (including those over 16 still at school) are assessed at the full rate for a child under 11.

(c) Nothing is allowed for additional or housing requirements ('standard' housing benefit is payable for this period but not housing benefit supplement – see Chapter 5).

(d) For a boarder, the 'ordinary' (short-term) personal expenses allowance (see page 60) is reduced by 25 per cent and the usual allowance for any meals not included in the board and lodging charge is added; but the board and lodging charge itself is met (subject to the normal limits) only if it falls due in the period covered by the payment.[17]

The reduced rates applicable for the first two weeks, based on November 1984 benefit rates, are as follows:

Married couple	£34.20
Single householder	21.05
Non-householder:	
18 or over, or under 18 with a child	16.85
Under 18 without a child	13.00
Dependent child (any age)	9.60
Boarder – personal expenses allowance	6.95

If urgent need payments are made for a longer period, requirements are assessed in the normal way from the third week and 'certificated' housing benefit is payable. Even if benefit is refused for the first two weeks on the grounds that the claimant's resources are above the reduced rates, it can still become payable under the normal rules from the third week.[18] If this were not the case, a person who failed to qualify for benefit for the first two weeks would never become entitled, however long the need continued.

Recovery of Urgent Need Payments

Section 4(2) of the Supplementary Benefits Act provides that urgent need payments are to be recoverable from the claimant, except to the extent that regulations provide otherwise. Generally speaking, urgent need payments are recoverable unless they are very small or the claimant is not in a position to repay them because his or her resources are at or below supplementary benefit level, but there are some other exceptions. Regulation 25 of the Urgent Cases Regulations sets out the precise circumstances in which the payments are *not* recoverable. If the case is not covered by regulation 25, the social security office will normally proceed to recover the money. They may, however, decide that it would be wrong or impracticable to do so – for example, where the claimant's financial position unexpectedly worsens. There is a right of appeal against the adjudication officer's decision that the payments are recoverable; but the decision as to whether, if they *are* recoverable, the power to recover them should be enforced is not subject to a right of appeal.

Some types of urgent need payment are automatically exempt from recovery. Others may or may not be recoverable, depending on the claimant's financial position. The exempt categories are as follows:

(a) Payments for the period preceding the first normal benefit pay day.

(b) Payments to a person failing to comply with the requirement to be available for work or to attend a re-establishment course.

(c) 'Hardship' payments to a person (usually a woman) living as a member of an 'unmarried couple' (see page 222).

(d) Payments made because one member of a married or unmarried couple is not being maintained by the other, if it is subsequently found that the other member would have been entitled to supplementary benefit for the same period (see pages 194–5).

(e) Interim payments made where the appropriate deduction for income from subletting cannot be ascertained immediately (see page 92).

(f) Payments of the following kinds, if it is subsequently found that the claimant is entitled to the money under the normal rules:

  (i) Interim payments where entitlement to benefit has not been established or the claimant's requirements or resources are not immediately ascertainable, or benefit has been suspended because of a doubt as to entitlement.

  (ii) A payment to a claimant with no fixed address for a deposit for accommodation.

(g) Any payment or series of payments totalling £10 or less.

Urgent need payments which do not fall into any of these categories are recoverable, but not from a person whose resources are, and are expected to remain for more than six months from the date of the urgent need payment, at or below supplementary benefit level. The way in which this is defined depends on whether the person is still in receipt of supplementary benefit. If so, urgent need payments will not be recovered if he or she has no earnings, no other income qualifying for the £4 disregard (item 40 in the table on pages 118–19), and no capital resources other than his or her home or other items which are disregarded under the normal supplementary benefit rules (see pages 130–32). If the person is no longer on supplementary benefit, the same capital rule applies but the total income, without any disregards, must be below supplementary benefit level.[19]

Urgent need payments can be recovered either by making deductions from subsequent benefit payments or 'in any other manner'.[20] The benefits from which deductions can be made include supplementary benefit, FIS, and most other social security benefits – but not child benefit or maternity or death grant.[21] Where deductions are made from supplementary benefit payments for this purpose, the maximum deduction is:

(a) If the claimant has savings or other capital resources, £10 a week.

(b) If there are no capital resources, half the total of any disregarded earnings and other income that qualifies for the £4 disregard – but no deduction of 50p a week or less is to be made, and if the disregarded income is also the subject of deductions for recovery of overpayments or for direct payment of fuel costs, those deductions take precedence over the recovery of urgent need payments.

Whether the deduction is in respect of capital or disregarded income, the claimant must be left with supplementary benefit of at least 10p per week (or 5p if paid with another benefit, e.g. retirement pension).[22]

Emergency Relief

Emergency relief under regulation 8 of the Urgent Cases Regulations is available where a person 'is affected by a disaster', as a result of which he or she is in need of money for living expenses or for clothing, repair or replacement of furniture or household equipment, house repairs, fuel, or travelling and removal expenses. It can take the form of a supplementary pension or allowance to cover living expenses for a period after the disaster or single payments for particular items, or both. The regulation does not define a disaster but gives as examples 'a fire or a flood'. The provisions of regulation 8 normally apply for fourteen days after the disaster, but the period can be extended by direction of the Secretary of State.[23]

Emergency relief is available both to people in full-time work[24] and to people who would normally be in work but, in the period after the disaster, are neither going to work nor available for employment (the requirement to be available does not apply in this situation).[25] Strikers, too, can get emergency relief in the same way as other claimants.[26] So can visitors from abroad. And full-time students can receive emergency relief, though they are not entitled to other urgent need payments except during vacations.[27]

The amounts payable by way of emergency relief are calculated in accordance with the rules that apply to all urgent need payments (see pages 185–6). The detailed rules regarding single payments are as follows:

Clothing and footwear. Emergency relief payments can be made for any of the items of clothing or footwear listed in Appendix 3 that are needed as a result of the disaster (if the claimant is already getting supplementary benefit, the payments can be made under the normal rules – see pages 162–8). The boys' and girls' clothing lists in parts IV and V of Appendix 3 are to be used for children under 14 unless they are large for their age, in which case the adult lists in parts I and II are to be used. The amount payable is the full cost of buying the clothes, provided that it is not more than the amounts shown in the appendix – but a higher amount can be allowed if the person is outsize or disabled.[28]

Furniture and household equipment. Payments can be made for any of the following items lost, damaged or otherwise needed as a result of the disaster:

(a) Beds and mattresses, sufficient for all members of the assessment unit (the payment must cover the cost of new items).

(b) Bedclothes, the need for which is to be judged on the same basis as where a single payment is made for bedclothes in other circumstances (see page 156), except that in addition to the factors normally taken into account the adjudication officer must have regard to the circumstances of the disaster (for example, extra blankets may be needed because power supplies have broken down). Payments are based on the price list in Appendix 4.

(c) A cooker and heating appliances (reconditioned, if available; otherwise new).

(d) A table and enough chairs for all members of the assessment unit (second-hand if available; otherwise new).

(e) Essential cleaning materials, cooking utensils, crockery and cutlery.

(f) A fireguard.

Delivery and installation costs are also met for items under (a), (c) and (d).[29]

If the items in question can be repaired, however, the cost of essential repairs (including removal and re-installation where appropriate) will be met instead, unless it would be cheaper to replace them or the repair would be 'uneconomic having regard to the future viability of the item'.[30]

A claimant who is already on supplementary benefit may be entitled to payments for these items under the normal rules (see pages 151–5), but emergency relief payments can also be made to claimants who would not otherwise be entitled.

House repairs. Payments can be made for the reasonable costs of 'emergency minor repairs to the home . . . in respect of damage caused by the disaster (for example, so as to secure the building temporarily such as by boarding up windows and patching the roof)'.[31] A claimant already on supplementary benefit may be entitled under the normal rules (see page 160).

Fuel. Payments can be made for the cost of essential fuel for cooking, heating, hot water, lighting and, after a flood, drying out the home and personal possessions.[32]

Travelling expenses. Payments can be made for travelling expenses to enable people to leave the place where the disaster occurred and stay with relatives or friends until their home is habitable; or, in the case of a visitor, to return home (a visitor from abroad can have the fare paid to the point of departure from the United Kingdom or, if without means of completing the journey home, to the nearest representative of his or her country in the UK). Payments can also be made to enable either a resident or a visitor to get to his or her workplace. Second-class fares by public transport are paid, or the cost of petrol or taxi fares where public transport is not available. Taxi fares are paid for a physically disabled person who cannot use other transport.[33]

Removal expenses. Where removal is necessary as a result of the disaster and the local authority has no power to assist under the Housing (Homeless Persons) Act 1977, the cost can be met, based on the lower of two estimates, unless the social security office decides that, in view of the urgency, only one estimate need be obtained.[34]

Other Urgent Need Payments for Living Expenses

Apart from emergency relief after a disaster, urgent need payments to meet daily living expenses can be made in the circumstances mentioned below, but only to the extent needed to meet the claimant's require- ments, initially at the reduced level explained on page 186. Unless otherwise stated, the payments may be recoverable. The rules regard- ing recovery are explained on pages 186–8. Details of the items for which single payments can be made on grounds of urgent need, other than by way of emergency relief, are given on pages 196–8.

Period before normal payments start or while they are suspended. If the claimant has no resources to tide him or her over to the first day on which supplementary benefit is payable, an urgent need payment can be made for the intervening days, starting from the day on which the claim was decided. In the case of a boarder, a payment can be made for the board and lodging charge if it falls due at any time between the date of the claim and the first normal benefit pay day.[35] These payments are not recoverable.[36]

Similarly, where there is a delay in establishing entitlement to benefit after a claim is made, or payment of benefit has been suspended tempor- arily while a doubt about entitlement is cleared up, urgent need pay- ments can be made if in the opinion of the adjudication officer it is 'appropriate and reasonable' to do so.[37] If the payments are needed because entitlement to benefit has not been established, they are limited to three working days (e.g. if the claim is made on a Friday, an urgent need payment can be made for the period from Friday to Tuesday).[38] In a case where the claimant's entitlement is not in doubt but the precise amount of requirements or resources cannot immediately be ascertained, urgent need payments can be made instead of the normal benefit payments, on the basis of estimated figures, while the necessary information is obtained, if the adjudication officer considers it 'ap- propriate and reasonable'. If the uncertainty is about income from subletting, a fixed amount is assumed for each sub-tenant but, apart from that, the special rules for calculating urgent need payments do not apply. In all these cases, if it is eventually decided that at least the amount paid on grounds of urgent need was due under the normal rules, the urgent need payments are treated as payments on account and are not recoverable.[39]

Loss of money. If a benefit girocheque is lost or stolen, it can be replaced at once provided that the loss is accepted as genuine; but the decision on whether to replace it is not made under the supplementary benefit regulations and there is no right of appeal against a refusal. Urgent need payments can be made to replace any other money, including cheques and postal orders, that has been lost, stolen or destroyed. The payments are limited to the amount needed to meet living expenses until other resources become available.[40]

Income adequate for living expenses but spent on other needs. A person whose resources are too high to qualify for supplementary benefit in the normal way, but who would otherwise be entitled, and who has used current income to pay for an item for which, if he or she had been on supplementary benefit, a single payment would have been made (for details of such items, see Chapter 7), can get an urgent need payment for living expenses, up to the amount of the single payment.[41] The most common situation in which this might occur is where a person whose income is just above supplementary benefit level has had to meet a large bill. It could also be a person with capital above the £3,000 limit, none of which is 'readily realizable'; but this situation is covered by the more general provision explained below (see '*Unrealizable capital over £3,000*').

Income due but not received. Where a payment to which the claimant is entitled is not received but has been taken into account as a 'notional' resource (see page 116) for a particular week, an urgent need payment can be made, of not more than the amount of the missing payment. This provision can be used, for example, where a private pension or other income is held up by a postal strike. But it does not apply where the missing payment consists of earnings or a student's grant or parental contribution.[42] Nor does it apply to social security benefits paid late, which cannot be treated as notional resources but should simply be ignored until they are paid.

Unrealizable capital over £3,000. A claimant who has capital resources (excluding those of dependent children) over £3,000, and is therefore not entitled to benefit under the normal rules, can claim urgent need payments if none of the capital is readily realizable. The adjudication officer decides what is a reasonable time within which the capital should be realized (i.e. turned into cash). Urgent need payments continue beyond that period only if the claimant is taking reasonable steps to realize the capital.[43]

Assumed income not available. Where supplementary benefit entitlement is either reduced or extinguished by notional resources which the claimant does not actually possess, urgent need payments can be made for current living expenses. The notional resources are ignored for this purpose. The types of case to which this provision applies are:

(a) Where a person is assumed to have access to money held on a discretionary trust (see page 132).

(b) Where part of a claimant's seasonal or intermittent earnings for a past period are treated as current earnings (see pages 122–3).[44]

Starting work. A claimant who has just started or restarted full-time work is entitled to benefit under the normal rules for the first fifteen days (see page 267). Urgent need payments can be made:

(a) for a further period of up to sixteen days where the claimant is still in need, e.g. because the earnings are paid monthly; *or*

(b) for up to a month if the claimant is not entitled under the normal rules for the first fifteen days because the present job started soon after the end of the previous one.

But payments are not made in either of these cases if the employer is prepared to meet the need by an advance of earnings (a 'sub').[45]

A claimant who qualifies for an allowance for living expenses in these circumstances can also claim single payments for fares to work (see page 197).

Unpaid or part-paid holidays, etc. If a claimant has to take time off work without pay or on reduced earnings but is not entitled to benefit under the normal rules because still regarded as 'engaged in remunerative full-time work', urgent need payments can be made for up to a month from the beginning of the period of unpaid or part-paid absence.[46] This enables payments to be made during compulsory unpaid holidays and in other circumstances where an employee has to take time off for reasons beyond his or her control.

Failure to be available for work. Urgent need payments can be made to an unemployed claimant not otherwise entitled because not available for work (or not registering for work if under 18); but only if, in the adjudication officer's opinion, there is no other way of preventing serious damage or serious risk to the health or safety of the claimant or any member of the assessment unit. The payments must not be more than would be payable under the normal rules if a deduction were made for 'voluntary unemployment' (see page 228).[47] They are not recoverable.[48]

Failure to attend a re-establishment course. A claimant who is directed to attend a re-establishment course and fails to do so, or drops out after starting it, loses entitlement to benefit but can receive urgent need payments if it is the only means of preventing serious damage or risk to the health or safety of the claimant or a member of the assessment unit. The payments are limited for the first six weeks to the amount payable under the normal rules where a 'voluntary unemployment' deduction applies (see page 228).[49] They are not recoverable.[50]

Husband's (or wife's) failure to maintain. The provisions explained below can apply where a couple are living together, whether married or as an 'unmarried couple' (see page 218), and the partner who would be the claimant under the normal rules is not maintaining the other partner. The following paragraphs refer to the situation where the husband would normally be the claimant and fails to maintain his wife; but the rules are the same where the couple are not married or where it is the woman who is failing to maintain the man.

Urgent need payments are not the only way of dealing with such situations. It may be possible to 'switch' claimants if the wife is eligible to claim in place of the husband (see page 39). If there has been no previous claim by the husband, there will be no need to 'switch': the wife can simply make the initial claim, if she is eligible. But this may not solve the problem, because the husband's resources will be taken into account in assessing her benefit entitlement, if any. Another possible solution, if the husband is already receiving supplementary benefit, is to arrange for his benefit to be paid to the wife as a 'third party' (see pages 207–8).

If none of these solutions is available or seems appropriate, the wife can claim urgent need payments for her own needs and those of any dependent children.[51] The adjudication officer will need to be satisfied that the couple are members of the same household (if they are not, the wife should be able to claim under the normal rules, rather than for urgent need payments) and that he is failing to maintain her. The husband's resources are ignored, but any payments the wife receives from him, in cash or in kind, are taken into account. The urgent need payments are recoverable from the wife, and action can be taken against the husband for failing to maintain her (see Chapter 10).

Probably the most common situation in which this provision applies is where the husband is temporarily absent and, for whatever reason, the wife has not received money from him to maintain herself and the children, if any. But it can also apply where the husband is present but not maintaining her.

Finally, it is important to note that the provision applies equally to unmarried couples living together as husband and wife. If the man refuses to maintain the woman and she has no other means of support, she can claim urgent need payments for as long as the situation continues. The payments are recoverable from her if she is later in a position to repay them, but there is no question of action being taken to recover the money from the man, since he is not a 'liable relative', unless there are children in the family of whom he is the father.

Unmarried couple. The circumstances in which non-recoverable urgent need payments can be made to a member of an unmarried couple (usually the woman) who would not otherwise be entitled to benefit are explained on page 222. Since the couple's combined resources are taken into account, the payments are likely to be much smaller than those made on grounds of 'failure to maintain', which are based on the requirements of the woman (or man) and children only (see above).

People from abroad. A visitor from abroad who would not normally be allowed to receive supplementary benefit (see page 261) can get urgent need payments in two types of situation. The first is where a person who has leave to remain in the United Kingdom for a limited period has supported himself or herself through an earlier period without help from public funds (apart from any payments under this provision), is temporarily without money, for example because payments from abroad have been disrupted, but there is a reasonable expectation that the supply of funds will be resumed. Urgent need payments can be made for up to forty-two days in any one period in the UK.

The second type of situation is where a person has applied for extension or renewal of leave to remain in the UK; is awaiting the results of an immigration appeal or of representations to the Home Secretary; has entered the UK illegally but been allowed to stay; or is awaiting removal under a deportation order. Urgent need payments can be made pending a favourable decision or the person's departure from the country, as the case may be.[52]

Single Payments for Urgent Needs

The Urgent Cases Regulations provide for single payments, other than by way of emergency relief, in a number of situations where a payment could not be made under the normal rules explained in Chapter 7 and the claimant has no other means of meeting the expense.[53] Details are given in the following paragraphs. Apart from deposits for accommodation and payments of £10 or less, the payments may be recoverable (see pages 186–8).

Travelling expenses. Urgent need payments for travelling expenses can be made for the following purposes:

Visiting sick relatives. Visiting someone who is critically ill and is a close relative (parent or step-parent, child or step-child, brother or sister), a more distant relative who has not been visited recently by any closer relative who intends to continue visiting, or someone who, before the illness, was a member of the household (including the claimant's husband or wife). The expenses of an escort can be met if the person cannot travel alone, and accommodation for one or more nights and one main meal a day will be paid for if the return journey cannot be completed in a day or a longer stay is reasonable (e.g. for a parent visiting a child in hospital). These payments, unlike those made under the Single Payments Regulations (see page 173), are not limited to cases where the sick person is in a hospital or home. Strikers can get similar payments under the Trade Disputes Regulations (see pages 238–9).

Stranded away from home. A person who is stranded without means of travel can be paid the fare home (or, if the home is in an EEC country or certain other European countries, to the port of departure from the United Kingdom), or to his or her destination if that would be cheaper. The cost of overnight accommodation and one main meal a day will be paid if necessary. Payments will not be made for an unaccompanied child under 16 – the police or social services department should be informed.

Fares to work. Fares can be paid during the first month after starting or resuming work, pending receipt of wages, in a case where urgent need payments are made for living expenses during that period (see page 193).

Arriving in the United Kingdom. A person with a right of residence in the UK who arrives penniless can have the fares paid to his or her destination, plus the cost of one main meal a day (but not overnight accommodation).

Leaving the United Kingdom. Visitors from abroad who satisfy the conditions for urgent need payments (see pages 195–6) can have their fares and those of their family paid to the port of departure from the UK or, if they have no means of completing the journey, to their country's nearest representative in the UK (see also *'Stranded away from home'* above).

The normal rules regarding payment of travelling expenses apply: the cost of second-class public transport is paid, or the cost of petrol or a taxi where public transport is not available, and taxi fares are paid for a physically disabled person who cannot use other transport.[54]

Leaving a resettlement unit. A person moving into unfurnished or partly furnished accommodation on leaving a DHSS resettlement unit, who would not be entitled to single payments for furniture, household equipment and bedclothes under the normal rules because he is in full-time work, can claim urgent need payments instead, for the items listed on pages 149 and 156. If he already possesses items of furniture or equipment which are in need of repair and it would be cheaper to repair than to replace them, a payment will be made for the repair.[55] The normal rule that a person moving from a resettlement unit is entitled to single payments for furniture only if there is no suitable alternative furnished accommodation available in the area (see page 152) does not apply to a person in full-time work claiming payments under this provision.

Deposit for accommodation. A single payment can be made under the normal rules for a deposit to the landlord where the claimant has already found accommodation and has to pay the deposit as a condition of the tenancy (see page 157). Under the Urgent Cases Regulations, a person with no fixed address can receive a single payment on account to put him or her in a position to put down a deposit on finding accommodation, or for accommodation already found if a payment cannot be made under the normal rules. Such payments are made only if it is 'reasonable' to do so, and officers are told to make them only if (a) it is known that suitable accommodation is available in the area, (b) it is considered likely that the payment will be used for its intended purpose, and (c) the proposed accommodation is suited to the claimant's needs which, in the case of a single, unemployed person who is known to 'sleep rough', will usually mean a lodging-house or hostel.[56]

Discharged prisoners. A discharged prisoner who cannot get a single payment for expenses on starting work, under the normal rules (see page 176), because he or she has received a discharge grant, can claim an urgent need payment for the same items.[57]

REFERENCES

1. Social Security (No.2) Act, 1980, s. 6(1)(c); Urgent Cases Regs. 6(1)(b); Trade Disputes Regs. 4(1).
2. Urgent Cases Regs. 6(1)(c).
3. Urgent Cases Regs. 6(1)(i).
4. Urgent Cases Regs. 6(1)(e).
5. Urgent Cases Regs. 6(1)(h).
6. Urgent Cases Regs. 6(1)(d).
7. Urgent Cases Regs. 6(1)(g).
8. Urgent Cases Regs. 6(2).
9. Urgent Cases Regs. 6(1)(f).
10. Urgent Cases Regs. 6(1)(a).
11. Urgent Cases Regs. 6(3).
12. Urgent Cases Regs. 24.
13. Urgent Cases Regs. 3(1).
14. Urgent Cases Regs. 2(1) (definition of 'capital otherwise disregarded').
15. Urgent Cases Regs. 5(4)(b)(ii).
16. Urgent Cases Regs. 4(1)(b).
17. Urgent Cases Regs. 5(3).
18. CSB 894/82.
19. Urgent Cases Regs. 25(2)–(6).
20. SB Act, s. 4(2).
21. Urgent Cases Regs. 26(1).
22. Urgent Cases Regs. 26(2).
23. Urgent Cases Regs. 8.
24. Urgent Cases Regs. 3(2)(c).
25. Urgent Cases Regs. 3(2)(b).
26. Trade Disputes Regs. 4.

27. Urgent Cases Regs. 6(1)(e).
28. Urgent Cases Regs., schedule 1, para. 1.
29. Urgent Cases Regs., schedule 1, para. 3.
30. Urgent Cases Regs., schedule 1, para. 4.
31. Urgent Cases Regs., schedule 1, para. 5.
32. Urgent Cases Regs., schedule 1, para. 7.
33. Urgent Cases Regs., schedule 1, para. 2.
34. Urgent Cases Regs., schedule 1, para. 6.
35. Urgent Cases Regs. 12.
36. Urgent Cases Regs. 25(2).
37. Urgent Cases Regs. 17, 19 and 20.
38. Urgent Cases Regs. 17.
39. Urgent Cases Regs. 25(3).
40. Urgent Cases Regs. 10.
41. Urgent Cases Regs. 13.
42. Urgent Cases Regs. 11.
43. Urgent Cases Regs. 18.
44. Urgent Cases Regs. 18.
45. Urgent Cases Regs. 14.
46. Urgent Cases Regs. 15.
47. Urgent Cases Regs. 16.
48. Urgent Cases Regs. 25(2).
49. Urgent Cases Regs. 16.
50. Urgent Cases Regs. 25(2).
51. Urgent Cases Regs. 22.
52. Urgent Cases Regs. 21.
53. Urgent Cases Regs. 9(a).
54. Urgent Cases Regs., schedule 2, para. 1.
55. Urgent Cases Regs., schedule 2, paras. 2, 2A and 3.
56. Urgent Cases Regs., schedule 2, para. 5; *S Manual*, para. 8281.
57. Urgent Cases Regs., schedule 2, para. 4.

Chapter 9

Payments to Third Parties

In some cases, supplementary benefit may be paid wholly or partly to somebody other than the claimant. If the claimant is incapable of handling his or her own affairs, for example because of mental illness or handicap, somebody else can be appointed by the Secretary of State to deal with the claim and receive benefit payments. This arrangement is explained at the end of the chapter, on pages 208–9. The remainder of the chapter is concerned with less extreme cases where there are grounds for making payments to a third party, usually for particular items of expenditure.

Apart from single payments and urgent need payments, nearly all decisions to pay benefit to a third party must be made by an adjudication officer and are therefore subject to a right of appeal to the local tribunal. If the adjudication officer refuses to make such a decision, for instance in a case where the claimant has asked for fuel payments to be made direct to the electricity or gas board, it seems that there may be no right of appeal against the refusal, since an appeal must be against a determination of an adjudication officer and not against a refusal to make a determination. In the case of a single payment or an urgent need payment, the decision to pay the money direct to the supplier (see page 208) is made on behalf of the Secretary of State; [1] it is entirely discretionary and there is no right of appeal.

The circumstances in which an adjudication officer can decide that benefit, other than a single or urgent need payment, is to be paid to a third party are explained below, but in most cases one of the conditions is that the claimant, in the opinion of the officer, 'has failed to budget', 'is incapable of budgeting' or 'wilfully refuses to budget' for certain expenses. The precise meaning of these terms will probably be decided in due course by the Social Security Commissioners. For the present, officers must apply their common sense in interpreting them. Clearly the fact that a claimant has difficulty in meeting a particular expense is not necessarily due to failure to budget for it. It may be due to failure to budget for some other expense of a more pressing nature, or to unpredictable events which have unbalanced the household's finances. At the very least, failure to budget must imply that, in allocating his weekly income, the claimant has not taken into account the need to set aside a reasonable amount towards the expense in question. If he *has* taken it into account but has still not succeeded in making sufficient provision for the expense, it is doubtful whether he can be said to have failed to budget for it. The definition of a 'person who is incapable of budgeting' offered by the weekly paper *Community Care* – 'any claimant who cannot choose between eating properly, wearing decent clothes, or being warm and therefore attempts to do two or more of them at once' – has at least a grain of truth in it.

Payment in Kind

In certain circumstances, goods or services of equivalent value may be supplied in place of cash payments of supplementary benefit. But there is no question of goods being bought by the social security office and handed over to the claimant. Payment 'in kind' must take the form of either a voucher to be presented to the supplier of particular goods or services or a travel warrant. In effect, therefore, it is simply another way of making payments to a third party.

Any urgent need payment (see Chapter 8) can be made in the form of a voucher, and any single payment for travelling expenses (see pages 173–4) can take the form of a travel warrant. A voucher for board and lodging can be issued where it is 'necessary to secure residential accommodation' (some hostels and lodging-houses for single people insist on payment by voucher rather than cash). Finally, vouchers can be issued where, in the officer's opinion, the claimant is 'incapable of managing' a cash payment.[2]

Multiple Deductions

As explained below, where deductions are made from the weekly benefit to pay off a debt for gas, electricity, rent or other housing expenses, the amount deducted is normally £2.85 or £1.45 per week, plus the amount currently needed to meet the expense in question (other than rent, for which separate provision is made – see Chapter 5). If deductions are made for two or more debts, the most that will be deducted for the debts is £4.35 (excluding any additional amount that may be deducted where the claimant has disregarded income – see page 204).[3] If deductions are being made to recover an overpayment of benefit, as well as to pay off a fuel or housing debt, the combined amount deducted for these purposes must not exceed £5.95 (see page 48). Where deductions cannot be made for all the outstanding debts, the following order of priority must be observed:

(a) Rent or mortgage payments.

(b) Fuel debts (priority between gas and electricity debts is to be decided by the adjudication officer, having regard to the circumstances and any request by the claimant).

(c) Other debts for housing expenses.

All of these have priority over deductions to recover an overpayment of benefit,[4] except that any additional amount deducted out of disregarded income must be used first to clear an overpayment[5] and the additional £1.60 that can be deducted where there has been an overpayment can only be used for recovery of the overpayment.

Direct Payment of Fuel Costs

A claimant who has difficulty in paying his fuel bills may, in certain limited circumstances, be entitled to a single payment towards the debt (see pages 168–72). In most cases, however, the only direct help with fuel debts provided by the supplementary benefit scheme consists of the power to make deductions from the weekly benefit and pay the money direct to the gas or electricity board. This does not increase the claimant's total resources in any way, but it may prevent disconnection of the fuel supply.

The gas and electricity industries operate a 'code of practice' regarding disconnections, the main features of which are:

(a) If the bread-winner is on supplementary benefit or unemployment benefit or all the people in the house are pensioners, the fuel board and the local social security office should be informed. The supply will then not be cut off for fourteen days or possibly longer if the social security office is still looking into the case.

(b) A similar arrangement applies if there are children under 11 or the family is on FIS (see page 270); but in these cases the local council's social services department (social work department in Scotland) should be informed instead of the social security office.

(c) If the customer is blind, severely sick or disabled, the fuel board should be informed so that an acceptable method of payment can be agreed and disconnection avoided.

(d) If payments for gas or electricity are made to the landlord and the debt is in his name, the fuel board and (in England or Wales) the local council should be told and the supply will not be cut off for fourteen days.

(e) The supply will not be cut off at all if the customer agrees (and keeps to the agreement) to make regular payments in future and to pay off the debt by instalments in a reasonable period.

(f) The supply will not be cut off: (i) for a hire purchase debt; (ii) if a slot meter is installed and set to recover the debt in a reasonable period; (iii) between 1 October and 31 March if all the people in the house who have an income are pensioners, unless it is clear that they can pay the bill; (iv) if the debt is in the name of a past customer and the supply has been properly transferred; (v) if there is no adult in the house, unless prior warning has been given and, if it is necessary to enter the home, the board has obtained an entry warrant.

Direct payment of benefit to the fuel board is a way of ensuring that an agreement under (e) to make regular payments and to pay off the debt by instalments will be complied with and will therefore be acceptable to the fuel board. It is for the adjudication officer to decide that direct payment should be arranged. He is never obliged to make such a decision and he can do so only if *all* the following conditions are satisfied:

(a) The claimant (or the claimant's wife or husband) has failed to budget for the fuel – gas or electricity – and there is still a need for the supply of that fuel.

(b) Direct payment, in the adjudication officer's opinion, would be in the interests of the claimant or of the family. Officers have been told by the Chief Adjudication Officer that this will normally be the case if the claimant has been advised that the fuel supply will be cut off (or it has already been cut off) and no other fuel is available for the same purpose; and that in these circumstances they should *always* accept that direct payment is in the interests of the persons concerned if there is a risk to health or safety, e.g. because there are children under five in the family or the claimant or the claimant's wife or husband is over seventy, disabled or long-term sick. But they are instructed not to agree to direct payment if the fuel board is willing to instal a prepayment meter and set it to collect part of the debt.[6]

(c) The debt must be at least £29.

(d) It is more than the claimant (or the couple) can pay out of their savings, and there is no other member of the household who can reasonably be expected to pay it or at least to reduce it below £29.

(e) The amount of supplementary benefit payable after deducting the amount to be paid direct to the fuel board will be at least 10p a week (or at least 5p if paid with another benefit, e.g. a retirement pension or attendance allowance).[7]

The amount to be deducted weekly and paid direct to the fuel board is £2.85 towards the outstanding debt (or, if there are debts for both gas and electricity, £1.45 for each), plus the estimated average weekly cost of the fuel in question unless this is being paid for by some other means such as a prepayment meter. But the weekly deductions can be increased by up to one half of the disregarded earnings of the claimant or the couple and half of any income disregarded under the £4 'other income' disregard (item 40 in Table 3 on pages 118–19). The total weekly deduction for the debts (i.e. excluding the amounts added for the weekly cost of fuel), however, must not exceed the limit of £4.35; and if the total deduction (including the weekly fuel cost but excluding the amount added for disregarded income) amounts to 25 per cent or more of the sum allowed for 'normal requirements' (see Appendix 2), the deduction must not be made without the claimant's consent. If the full deduction cannot be made because the claimant would no longer receive benefit payments of at least 10p or 5p a week (see (e) above), the amount deducted towards the debt can be reduced from £2.85 to £1.45.[8]

The adjudication officer has to rely on the fuel board to estimate the amount to be deducted for the average weekly cost of the fuel. The formula normally used for this purpose has been agreed between the gas and electricity industries and the Department of Health and Social Security. The cost at current prices of the claimant's actual consumption over the past twelve months is calculated, and an adjustment is made for any expected price increase. The calculation is normally revised at six-monthly intervals and, if the actual fuel consumption has been more or less than the estimate, an adjustment is made in the deductions for the following period. The formula may have to be modified, for example where fuel consumption figures are not available for the full twelve months.[9]

The fuel board does not normally supply details of its calculation of average weekly consumption but should be asked to do so if the resulting deduction seems unduly high. The claimant has a right of appeal against the amount of the deduction. Provided that the formula has been correctly applied, however, an appeal is unlikely to succeed – and if it did, the result might be a refusal by the fuel board to accept a lower figure and a renewed threat of disconnection. If there is any difficulty in obtaining details of the calculation it may be worth appealing, since the social security office should then ask the fuel board for full details and include them in the documents sent to the claimant before the appeal hearing.[10] If the calculation seems correct, the appeal can be withdrawn at that stage.

Direct payment will normally continue only until the debt has been cleared, but it can be extended if the adjudication officer still considers that it is in the claimant's interests. In that case, the deductions will be reduced to the amount estimated to be needed to pay for current consumption.[11]

Direct Payment of Rent

If the claimant is a householder, all or most of the rent will normally be covered by housing benefit (see Chapter 5). In the case of a council tenant, the housing benefit includes a rent rebate which is automatically set off against the rent payable. Private or housing association tenants get a rent allowance which is normally paid to them monthly or weekly but can be paid direct to the landlord in some circumstances.

If there are rent arrears of at least four times the *full* weekly rent, part of the supplementary benefit can be paid to the landlord provided that either:

(a) there are at least thirteen weeks' rent arrears and the landlord has asked the social security office to do this; *or*

(b) in the adjudication officer's opinion it would be in the 'overriding' interests of the assessment unit (claimant, wife or husband, and children if any).

In calculating the number of weeks' rent arrears, any part of the rent which is treated for housing benefit purposes as the share of a non-dependent member of the household (see page 105) is ignored.

The amount of benefit that can be deducted weekly and paid to the landlord includes:

(a) any charge included in the rent for amenities (heating, hot water, lighting and cooking) and deducted in the housing benefit calculation (see page 101); and

(b) £1.45 per week towards the rent arrears.

Deductions will not be made unless the claimant will be left with supplementary benefit of at least 10p a week (5p if paid with another benefit). If the weekly benefit is enough to cover the amenity charge but not the additional £1.45, a deduction can be made for the amenity charge alone. The deduction for rent arrears will cease as soon as the arrears (other than a non-dependant's share) are cleared. Deductions for both arrears and amenity charges will cease if the claimant moves and no longer has the same landlord.[12]

Direct Payment of Mortgage Interest and Other Housing Requirements

It is possible, though less usual, for a similar arrangement to be made for payment of arrears of mortgage interest direct to the building society or other lender. Before this can be done, the following conditions must be satisfied:

(a) The mortgage interest payable by the claimant (or the claimant's wife or husband) is in arrears and they have failed to budget for it.

(b) The adjudication officer considers that direct payment would be in their interests.

(c) Either they have not made, in total, at least two mortgage payments in the past twelve weeks or, in the adjudication officer's opinion, direct payment is in the 'overriding' interests of the assessment unit.

The amount of the weekly deduction for this purpose is £1.45 plus the amount needed to meet the current interest payments, and deductions for the current interest payments can continue after the arrears have been cleared. The claimant must, however, be left with benefit payments of at least 10p a week (5p if paid with another benefit), and if necessary the deductions must be reduced accordingly.

Only the interest on the mortgage can be paid direct in this way. Supplementary benefit does not provide for mortgage capital repayments (see page 86).

Similar arrangements can be made for direct payment of other 'housing requirements' (see pages 84–5), such as water charges, provided that the debt is at least half the annual charge for the item in question (this condition replaces (c) above).[13]

Other Accommodation Charges

A similar power to pay the board and lodging charge direct to the landlord applies where the claimant is a boarder, subject to the same conditions – that, in the opinion of the adjudication officer, the claimant has failed to budget for the board and lodging charge and that direct payment would be in his or her interests.[14] In the case of a resident in 'residential accommodation' (see pages 249–52), these conditions do not apply and the charge for the accommodation can be paid direct to the local authority in any case where the resident fails to pay it – the regulations do not specify any period over which the failure to pay must have continued.[15] For certain special types of accommodation, the adjudication officer can decide that the charge should be paid direct without showing that there has been any failure to budget or to pay similar charges in the past. These are residential re-establishment centres, resettlement units and the DHSS home for Poles. And, finally, where a claimant is staying in accommodation provided by a voluntary body for purposes similar to those of resettlement units (see page 253) or in a centre for alcoholics or drug addicts, the board and lodging element in the benefit payment can be paid direct with the agreement of the voluntary body or centre.[16]

In addition to these powers of direct payment, board and lodging charges can be paid 'in kind', by means of vouchers, where this is necessary to secure the accommodation or the adjudication officer considers the claimant incapable of managing cash payments (see page 201).

General Power to Pay Benefit to a Third Party

In any case where, in the opinion of the adjudication officer, the claimant is either incapable of budgeting for any item covered by the supplementary benefit assessment (other than items covered by the arrangements for direct payment for fuel and housing needs, described above) or 'wilfully refuses' to do so, the adjudication officer can decide that all or part of the benefit should be paid to another person in the interests of the assessment unit.[17] This would normally be done only where, in the words of the *Supplementary Benefits Handbook*, 'a claimant because of improvidence or eccentricity neglects his responsibilities to support his partner or dependent children'.[18] The payments can be made to the claimant's wife or some other responsible person. The possibility of making arrangements of this kind is an important protection for wives who cannot themselves claim supplementary benefit (see pages 36–40) and whose husbands fail to provide for the needs of the family. Adjudication officers, however, will be reluctant to use this power unless they are convinced that it is absolutely necessary, since it constitutes a major interference in the family's affairs. It can anyway only be used where supplementary benefit is already payable. In other cases where a husband fails to maintain his wife and children while they are living as one household, if the wife cannot satisfy the normal conditions for claiming benefit, she may be able to claim urgent need payments (see pages 194–5).

Benefit can also be paid to another member of the household where the claimant is for some reason temporarily away from home.[19]

Single Payments and Urgent Need Payments

Where a single payment or urgent need payment is made for a specific item or items, rather than for general living expenses, it can be paid to the supplier instead of to the claimant, normally by sending the claimant a girocheque payable to the supplier;[20] and, as noted on page 201, any urgent need payment can be made by voucher in favour of a supplier. Single payments for large items such as furniture, removals or funeral expenses are likely to be made by girocheque payable to the supplier, although social security officials are told to consider using this method only where 'there is good reason to believe that payment to the claimant may be misused'.[21] The responsibility for the decision is that of the Secretary of State, not the adjudication officer. In other words, it is regarded as an administrative decision, against which there is no right of appeal. If it will cause embarrassment, however, the social security office should be prepared to pay the money to the claimant instead, unless there are good reasons for not doing so in the particular case.

Appointees

If a person is or becomes incapable of dealing with his or her own claim for supplementary benefit, special arrangements can be made for somebody else to act on the claimant's behalf and receive the benefit payments. If the person's affairs are already being looked after by a receiver appointed by the Court of Protection (or, in Scotland, by a curator, factor or other legal guardian), that person will act for him or her in relation to the supplementary benefit claim. If not, some other responsible person can be appointed by the Secretary of State for Social Services for this purpose.[22] It is generally best for the appointee to be either a close relative or somebody who has no financial interest in the claimant's affairs. The appointment of the proprietor of a private old people's home, for example, is in principle undesirable, though in practice it is not unusual.

Anybody wishing to act as an appointee for a particular claimant should apply in writing to the social security office. If appointed, he can resign at any time after giving a month's notice in writing, and the Secretary of State can revoke the appointment at any time without notice.[23] Anybody who suspects that an appointee may be abusing his position should not hesitate to convey his suspicions to the local social security office.

It may happen that a claim for supplementary benefit is made, or has been made in the past, on behalf of a person who is unable to act, for example because of mental handicap, by someone who at the time of the claim has not been formally appointed by the Secretary of State. The Social Security Commissioners have held that, while an adjudication officer has a duty to decide such a claim, it does not follow that the decision must be given an effect that is prejudicial to the person on whose behalf it is made. In particular, it should not prevent a subsequent claim by that person or by an appointee from being backdated on the grounds that there was 'good cause' (e.g. mental handicap) for the delay in claiming (see pages 42–4, 'Late claims').[24]

REFERENCES

1. Claims and Payments Regs. 25.
2. Claims and Payments Regs. 12.
3. Claims and Payments Regs. 18(1)(a).
4. Claims and Payments Regs. 18(3).
5. Duplication and Overpayment Regs. 7(3).
6. S Manual, paras. 9212–13.
7. Claims and Payments Regs. 17.
8. Claims and Payments Regs. 17(2) and (4).
9. Supplementary Benefits Handbook, 1984 edition, Appendix 2; Claims and Payments Regs. 17(2B)(a).
10. S Manual, para. 9228.
11. Claims and Payments Regs. 17(2B)(b).
12. Claims and Payments Regs. 15B.
13. Claims and Payments Regs. 16.
14. Claims and Payments Regs. 19.
15. Claims and Payments Regs. 20.
16. Claims and Payments Regs. 21.
17. Claims and Payments Regs. 23(b).

18. *Supplementary Benefits Handbook*, 1984 edition, p. 81.
19. Claims and Payments Regs. 23(*a*).
20. Claims and Payments Regs. 25.
21. *S Manual*, para. 9511.
22. Claims and Payments Regs. 26(1).
23. Claims and Payments Regs. 26(2).
24. R(SB) 9/84.

Chapter 10

Family Responsibility

Entitlement to supplementary benefit is based on the needs of the basic family unit of husband, wife and dependent children, as long as they are living in the same household. If a husband and wife separate, they become two separate units for supplementary benefit purposes and each of them can claim benefit for himself or herself and for the needs of any dependent children living with him or her. Similarly, an unmarried person bringing up a child single-handed can claim benefit for his or her needs and those of the child. In both cases, the benefit will be calculated without taking any account of the resources of the absent husband, wife or parent, except to the extent that he or she actually contributes to the household income. Under the Supplementary Benefits Act, however, a man is legally liable to maintain his wife and children, including illegitimate children of whom he has been adjudged the father (in Scotland he becomes liable for an illegitimate child if he admits paternity or it is otherwise legally established); and a woman is similarly liable to maintain her husband and her children, including illegitimate children.[1] If they fail to do so, supplementary benefit may be available to fill the gap. Before awarding benefit in this situation, however, the adjudication officer must satisfy himself that the failure is genuine; and if it is, the Department of Health and Social Security will want to recover as much as possible of the money it is paying out from the 'liable relative' and to ensure that he (or she) does not default in future.

Liability to maintain, for the purposes of the Act, does not normally extend beyond the responsibility of husbands and wives for each other and that of parents for their dependent children. Whether grown-up children support their elderly parents, and whether parents support their children once they are over 16, is a matter for their consciences, not for the law (even though the Act treats a child in full-time education as 'dependent' up to the age of 19).[2] But in two respects, the Act goes further. One is of only minor importance – the legal liability for somebody who has sponsored an immigrant to fulfil the undertaking he has given (see page 127). The other, far more important, is what was formerly known as the 'cohabitation rule'. The effect of this rule, explained more fully in Chapter 11, is that a man and woman who are living together as husband and wife, though not under any legal obligation to maintain each other, are treated for supplementary benefit purposes in the same way as a married couple.

Separated Wives

If a woman claims supplementary benefit as a result of separation from her husband (whether he has left her or she him), her requirements and those of her children who are living with her are assessed in the normal way. In calculating the resources to be set against the family's requirements to arrive at the amount of benefit payable, the husband's resources are ignored, only the amount he is actually paying to or for the wife and children being taken into account (for the treatment of maintenance payments, see pages 126–7). At the beginning of a separation, benefit may have to be reassessed from week to week until the situation has become stable.

A separated wife applying for benefit for the first time may be questioned in some detail about the circumstances of her separation. Such inquiries may be necessary to enable the Department of Health and Social Security to decide what action, if any, should be taken to induce the husband to fulfil his obligations. Moreover, cases of 'collusive desertion' have been known to occur, in which the wife denies knowledge of her husband's whereabouts although he is in fact living with her or his temporary absence has been arranged to enable her to claim benefit. The adjudication officer will therefore need to be satisfied that the husband is not, in fact, still a member of the household.

If the husband's whereabouts can be established and he is not already making regular maintenance payments under a court order, he is contacted by a specially trained officer of the Department of Health and Social Security known as a 'liable relative officer' (LRO). The husband is asked to fulfil his obligation to maintain his wife and children, at least to the extent necessary to remove the need to pay her supplementary benefit. If it is not reasonable to expect him to do so, for example because his income is low or he has other commitments (he may be living with another woman and supporting her children), the DHSS may agree to his making smaller payments or even none at all. If he is himself drawing supplementary benefit, he will probably be unable to pay anything to his wife, since his benefit will cover only his own needs and those of his new family, if any. But in any case he will not be expected to reduce his standard of living below supplementary benefit level (based on the 'ordinary' scale rates – see Appendix 2), and he will be allowed to retain a quarter of his net earnings in addition.[3]

If the husband refuses or fails to make reasonable provision when able to do so, several courses of action are open to the DHSS:

(a) The wife's right to apply to the court for a maintenance order is explained to her. But it is not the Department's policy to put any pressure on her to take her husband to court, and her entitlement to supplementary benefit is not affected if she decides not to.

(b) If the wife does not apply for a maintenance order, the DHSS may do so.[4]

(c) As a last resort, the DHSS can take criminal proceedings against a person who persistently refuses or neglects to maintain another person whom he or she is liable to maintain and whose needs, as a result, have to be met by supplementary benefit. For this purpose, the DHSS can apply for an arrest warrant. On conviction the offender is liable to up to three months' imprisonment and/or a fine of up to £500.[5]

Provided that whatever payments the husband has undertaken or been ordered to make are made regularly, the wife should receive supplementary benefit to meet the balance of her weekly requirements and those of the children living with her, subject to the normal conditions (e.g. if she has no children under 16 she will normally have to be available for employment). If the maintenance payments are not made regularly, however, the amount of benefit she is entitled to may vary from week to week, causing a good deal of anxiety and inconvenience. To prevent this, the husband is usually asked to make his payments to the DHSS instead of to his wife; or, if payments are made under a court order, she can authorize the magistrates' clerk to pay any money received from her husband to the DHSS instead of to her. A supplementary benefit order book can then be issued for the full amount she would be entitled to if the husband made no payments, giving her an assured weekly income whether the maintenance payments are made regularly or not. She is free to cancel this arrangement at any time and revert to receiving the money direct from the clerk's office. In Scotland, maintenance payments are not made through the court, but it may still be possible to arrange for the DHSS to receive them either direct from the husband or via the wife's solicitor.

This method of relieving a separated wife of the uncertainty of maintenance payments generally works well, but it can only be used with the agreement of the social security office. If the wife's income, including the full maintenance payments, is below supplementary benefit level, she will normally be asked to arrange for the payments to be made to the D H S S. If the maintenance payments would normally be enough to remove the need for supplementary benefit, however, the Department will want to be sure that they are unlikely to be made regularly before agreeing to such an arrangement. From the woman's point of view, there is no point in transferring the payments to the Department if she is likely to need supplementary benefit only occasionally when the maintenance payments are not made on time.

A husband who is thinking of returning to his wife may be worried about the possibility of being asked to repay the supplementary benefit she has received in his absence. The official *Handbook*, in fact, warns that this will happen if the D H S S could not contact him while he was away, provided that his financial circumstances allow him to repay the money.[6] He cannot, however, be compelled to do so unless the Department obtains a court order under section 18 of the Act; and in making an order the magistrates must have regard to his financial situation at the time when his wife was receiving benefit, ignoring any improvement that may have taken place since then.[7] In practice, the Department would be unlikely to take a man to court in these circumstances unless his current resources were well above the family's requirements by supplementary benefit standards.

Divorced Women

Once a couple are divorced, their liability to maintain each other under section 17 of the Supplementary Benefits Act ceases, though there may be a court order or voluntary maintenance agreement. Each of them remains liable under section 17 for the support of the children but, again, the division of responsibility between them will usually be the subject of a court order or agreement. The question of 'collusive desertion' will not arise, so the woman should have no difficulty in obtaining supplementary benefit if she is eligible for it, once the legal position has been made clear.

A court order in favour of a divorced woman or her children can be 'signed over' to the D H S S in the same way as that of a separated wife. First, however, an application must be made to have the divorce court order registered in the magistrates' court – a simple procedure on which the magistrates' clerk will advise. As with separated wives, different arrangements have to be made in Scotland.

Unmarried Mothers

As in the case of a separated wife, an unmarried mother who is eligible to claim supplementary benefit (i.e. is over 16, not in full-time work, etc.) is entitled to an income sufficient to meet her requirements and those of her child or children, whether the father is maintaining them or not; and the DHSS has a duty to take all reasonable steps to ensure that the father of an illegitimate child supports the child financially, if he is in a position to do so, at least to the extent necessary to avoid the need for payment of supplementary benefit to meet the child's needs. He is not legally liable for the maintenance of the mother but, if his maintenance payments, whether voluntary or under a court order, exceed the supplementary benefit 'requirements' of the child, the balance will serve to reduce the benefit payable for the mother's requirements. Where the question of paternity has not been decided by the court, a man may be treated as the father even though he denies it and, as explained on page 126, payments he is making for the child's support may be treated as evidence of paternity for supplementary benefit purposes. This has direct consequences for the mother, since payments by a liable relative, whether to her or to the child, are taken into account in full in assessing her entitlement to supplementary benefit.

The methods of persuading the father to meet his responsibilities are much the same as in the case of an absent husband. The mother can apply for an affiliation order, normally within three years of the birth of the child in England or Wales. If she is unwilling the application can be made by the Secretary of State under section 19 of the Supplementary Benefits Act. Once the court has made an order, if the father still fails to pay, he can be prosecuted under section 25 of the Act. The Department's policy regarding applications to the court is the same as in the case of a separated wife: the mother is advised about making her own application but should not be persuaded to do so. Once an order has been made, she is normally allowed to sign over the payments to the DHSS in the same way as a separated wife.

Unless maintenance payments are already being made or the mother is taking legal action, the DHSS will want to contact the alleged father and get his agreement to voluntary payments or, if necessary, take court proceedings against him. But the mother does not have to reveal the father's identity and should never be persuaded to do so against her will. As the official *Handbook* explains: 'It is made quite clear to her at the outset that she does not have to give this information and that she will continue to receive her full supplementary benefit entitlement whatever she decides.' Similarly, she is not obliged to assist in any proceedings taken against the alleged father by the DHSS.[8]

Mothers Under 16

There are no exceptions to the rule that a person under 16 cannot claim supplementary benefit. A girl under 16 who has a baby is therefore not eligible for benefit in her own right, though she can claim free milk and vitamins on grounds of low income (leaflet MVII, from any post-office or social security office, gives details and a claim form) and child benefit – including the £4.25 'one parent benefit' (see page 22). If she is living with either or both of her parents who are themselves receiving or claiming supplementary benefit or a family income supplement, both the girl and her baby can be counted as their dependants in assessing their entitlement to either of these benefits.[9]

Separated Husbands and Fathers

The rules regarding the supplementary benefit entitlement of a man who is separated from his wife or the mother of his child are the same as for a woman in a similar situation. His benefit payments will not cover her needs or those of any children not living with him, even though he may have a legal liability to maintain them. If he can no longer afford to comply with a court order for maintenance, he should apply to the court to vary the order. If he is left to look after the children and has to give up work for this purpose, the question of the mother's liability to maintain the children (and the father if they are married) may arise and will be dealt with in the same way as in the case of a separated wife or mother, except that there will normally be no difficulty in establishing the mother's identity.

REFERENCES

1. SB Act, s. 17.
2. SB Act, schedule 1, para. 3(2).
3. *Supplementary Benefits Handbook*, 1984 edition, p. 115.
4. SB Act, s. 18.

5. SB Act, s. 25.
6. *Supplementary Benefits Handbook*, p. 115.
7. SB Act, s. 18(4).
8. *Supplementary Benefits Handbook*, pp. 116–17.
9. Aggregation Regs. 3(2); and Family Income Supplements Act 1970, s. 1(1)(c).

Chapter 11

Unmarried Couples

For the purpose of entitlement to supplementary benefit, a married couple are treated as a single unit. Either the husband or the wife, but not both, may be entitled to claim and receive benefit – the rules for deciding which of them should claim are explained on pages 36–40. The effect of these rules may be that a man or woman (more commonly a woman) who would be entitled to claim benefit as a single person is prevented from claiming because only the other partner would satisfy the conditions; and if that partner is also unable to claim because he or she is in full-time work, the benefit entitlement is lost altogether.

The same rules apply to an 'unmarried couple', defined in the Supplementary Benefits Act as 'a man and a woman who are not married to each other but are living together as husband and wife otherwise than in prescribed circumstances'.[1] The 'prescribed circumstances' in which, for a short time, they are not treated as an unmarried couple are explained on pages 221–2 – in particular, that one of them (usually the woman) has a child of whom the other is not a parent. There are also provisions in the Urgent Cases Regulations which can help to prevent hardship resulting from a man and woman being treated as an unmarried couple (see page 222). The basic principle, however, is that two people who are living together as if they were married should be treated no differently from a couple who have gone through a marriage ceremony. Thus, for example, if a woman who has been receiving supplementary benefit for herself and her children starts living with a man who has a full-time job, and an adjudication officer decides that they are 'living together as husband and wife', she can lose the whole of her benefit entitlement from one day to the next.

Meaning of 'Living Together as Husband and Wife'

The question whether a couple are living together as husband and wife can only be decided by looking at their relationship and living arrangements as a whole and asking whether they can reasonably be said to be those of a married couple. The official *Supplementary Benefits Handbook* sets out 'the main criteria which are taken into account':

1. *Members of the same household.* The couple must be living in the same household and neither partner will usually have any other home where they normally live. This implies that the couple live together, apart from absences necessary for employment, visits to relatives, etc.

2. *Stability.* Living together as husband and wife clearly implies more than an occasional or very brief association. When a couple first live together, it may be clear from the start that the relationship is similar to that of husband and wife (for example, if the woman has taken the man's name and has borne his child), but in cases where at the outset the nature of the relationship is less clear it may be right not to regard the couple as living together as husband and wife until it is apparent that a stable relationship has been formed.

3. *Financial support.* In most husband and wife relationships one would expect to find financial support of one party by the other, or sharing of household expenses, but the absence of any such arrangement does not of itself prove that a couple are not living together.

4. *Sexual relationship.* Similarly, a sexual relationship is a normal part of a marriage and therefore of living together as husband and wife. But its absence at any particular time does not necessarily prove that a couple are not living as husband and wife, nor does its presence prove that they are.

5. *Children.* When a couple are caring for a child or children of their union, there is a strong presumption that they are living as husband and wife.

6. *Public acknowledgement.* Whether the couple have represented themselves to other people as husband and wife is relevant. However, many couples living together do not wish to pretend that they are actually married. The fact that they retain their identity publicly as unmarried people does not mean that they cannot be regarded as living together as husband and wife.[2]

An earlier version of these criteria was described by Mr Justice Woolf, in a High Court judgement on a 'living together' case, as 'an admirable signpost'. The judge added that 'the approach indicated in that handbook cannot be faulted'.[3] More recently, the criteria were endorsed by a Social Security Commissioner.[4] In most respects, the current version of the criteria, quoted above, is identical to the one referred to in these judgements, and can therefore be regarded as having the force of law. But there have been some changes, notably in the fourth criterion, the first sentence of which previously read as follows:

A sexual relationship is a normal and important part of a marriage and therefore of living together as husband and wife.[5]

The omission of the words 'and important' suggests that the existence or otherwise of a sexual relationship is not a particularly important consideration. This is plainly wrong. The absence of a sexual relationship may not be conclusive evidence but it would usually be a strong indication that the couple were not living as husband and wife.

The guidance issued to officers suggests some other points that should be taken into account:

(a) How the couple got to know each other, why they decided to live in the same household and, if one of them is said to be there temporarily, what has been done to find permanent lodgings.

(b) If one of them is said to be a boarder, whether he or she is paying more or less than the commercial rate for board and lodging.

(c) Whether they visit friends and relations, go to social events and other places, or go on holiday together.

(d) Whether they wish to marry (whether or not they are free to do so).

(e) Whether either of them, in claiming other benefits, has put the other down as a 'dependant'.

(f) Whether they appear under the same name on the electoral register.[6]

In cases where a doubt arises as to whether a claimant is living with another person as husband and wife, he or (more usually) she is visited by a specially trained officer who, after explaining the 'living together' rule, asks a number of questions designed to throw light on the nature of the relationship. The officer is forbidden to ask any questions about a sexual relationship or sleeping arrangements, or to inspect bedrooms unless invited.[7] If the couple sleep separately or do not have a sexual relationship, therefore, the claimant should say so; otherwise the opposite may be assumed.

On the basis of the information given during this interview and any other evidence, the adjudication officer then decides whether, on a balance of probabilities, the couple are living together as husband and wife. The guidance issued to officers indicates that, in a case where in other respects the couple seem to be living as husband and wife, it may be appropriate to treat them temporarily as not living as husband and wife if one of them shows signs of reluctance to accept financial responsibility for the other's support and that of any children. In other words, *if there is a risk that the withdrawal of benefit will break up the relationship, it can be continued for a time.* This is not done if the couple have been living together for four months or more or the woman has taken the man's name or had children by him. Where it is done, the claimant is warned that, if the situation continues for a few months, this may be taken to mean that there is a 'husband and wife' relationship. They are visited again between four and six months after the first interview and, if there has been no change in the situation, a decision that they are living as husband and wife is then issued.[8]

Prevention of Hardship

Short-term

A decision that a couple are living together as husband and wife takes effect immediately. The claimant has a right of appeal but it usually takes a month or more for the appeal to be heard. Meanwhile, the social security office will proceed on the assumption that the decision was correct, unless the adjudication officer decides to review it on the grounds that it was based on a mistake of either fact or law or that new facts have come to light (see pages 274–5).

It does not necessarily follow from a 'living together' decision that no benefit is payable. Since the couple will now be treated as a single unit, either of them may be entitled to claim benefit for their combined needs, provided that he or she satisfies the conditions set out on pages 37–8. If neither of them satisfies these conditions, however, the effect on their financial situation, if the benefit that one of them was receiving is suddenly withdrawn, can be catastrophic. In certain cases, therefore, where the claimant has at least one dependent child, the regulations allow benefit to continue, temporarily at least, but generally at a much reduced rate.

Payment of benefit in respect of the children's requirements only can continue, normally for four weeks (known as the 'period of adjustment'), if all the following conditions are satisfied:

(a) At least one of the children is not a child of the other member of the couple.

(b) Neither the man nor the woman would be entitled to benefit if they claimed as a couple.

(c) Complete withdrawal of benefit would cause a 'disproportionate' drop in their combined income.

The temporary allowance is calculated by taking the scale rates for the children who are eligible (excluding any child of whom the couple are the father and mother) and deducting any child benefit, FIS or maintenance payments in respect of those children, and any other income of the children except earnings. The four weeks adjustment period for which the allowance is payable may be extended for up to another six weeks if the couple's combined income is expected to increase soon – for instance, if they are claiming FIS.[9]

Long-term

To qualify for an allowance for the children's needs during the 'adjustment period', it is not necessary to show that withdrawal of benefit will cause hardship, but only that the fall in income would be 'disproportionate'. But if the fall in income, in a case where conditions (a) and (b) above are satisfied, would be so severe that the couple's net income, after deducting any maintenance payments the other member of the couple is making and any hire purchase payments of a kind for which single payments can be made (see pages 155–6), would be below the level of their requirements, and they have no readily available capital, benefit payments to the claimant can be continued indefinitely under the Urgent Cases Regulations. These payments are at the lower of the following rates:

(a) the amount that would be payable to the claimant if the couple were not living as husband and wife; *or*

(b) the amount needed to raise the couple's total income (including any income that would normally be disregarded), less maintenance and hire purchase payments, to the level of their requirements.[10]

In calculating the amount payable under (a), the claimant must be treated as still being a single parent; thus, half of any earnings between £4 and £20 is disregarded in addition to the normal £4 earnings disregard. In practice, however, the amount payable under (b) will usually be less.

The payments, although made under the Urgent Cases Regulations, are not recoverable.[11]

Failure to Maintain

If, despite the decision that the couple are living as husband and wife, the man refuses to maintain the woman and her children – or, if he was the claimant, the woman refuses to maintain him and his children – the partner who is left without support can claim urgent need payments for as long as is necessary (see pages 194–5). The non-claimant partner should make it clear, as soon as the question of withdrawal of benefit arises, that he or she is not prepared to accept this responsibility, and a claim for urgent need payments should be made as soon as possible after receiving the 'living together' decision. The claimant may have to repay the money later if her or his circumstances improve.

Administration of the 'Living Together' Rule

In view of the difficulties inherent in the administration of the 'living together' rule, it is not surprising that the DHSS sometimes resorts to some unsavoury methods of obtaining evidence, particularly in cases where the claimant is suspected of concealing the facts. A report by the Supplementary Benefits Commission on the administration of the 'cohabitation' rule (as it was then called), published in 1971, admitted that inquiries might be set off by 'an anonymous letter which may be spiteful and unfounded' and that 'special investigators' (officers trained to deal with cases of suspected fraud) might 'have to make local enquiries without the knowledge of the claimant or to watch a house to see who lives there'. This, the Commission wrote, 'is distasteful work, to the investigator as well as to the claimant and others concerned. But it is the price that has to be paid for administering the cohabitation rule.' The report said nothing about the damage such investigations might do to the reputation of the victims of 'spiteful and unfounded' allegations. It admitted, however, that the evidence on the basis of which a woman could lose her sole source of income might be far from conclusive, since the decision to withdraw benefit had to be taken 'on the balance of probabilities'.

Subsequently, the Fisher Committee on abuse of social security benefits, in its report published in 1973, expressed its distaste for the practice of obtaining evidence of 'cohabitation' from 'persons who are in a position to have knowledge of those persons who live in the accommodation, e.g. other residents, landlords, etc.' (the words were quoted from the instructions issued to special investigators). The committee recommended that 'such techniques should be used only as a last resort, when other methods have either been tried and failed, or are for some reason impossible, but none the less serious grounds for suspicion remain'. On the practice of spying on persons suspected of cohabiting, the committee wrote: '. . . it should take place, so far as is practicable, in such a way that the fact that observation is taking place should not become apparent to the neighbours. If the circumstances are such that this is clearly impossible, then it should not take place at all.' Both these recommendations, however, were rejected by the government.

The questioning of neighbours and open spying activities are therefore still permitted.

Since innocence is not an automatic protection from these methods of investigation, there is no way of guaranteeing that a single woman receiving supplementary benefit will not be subjected to them. It must, however, be stressed that visits from a male friend, whether he stays the night or not, and however much disapproval they may arouse among the neighbours, cannot justify the withdrawal of benefit. For the question of a 'husband and wife' relationship to arise, the couple must be living in the same household. The presence of a non-dependent member of the household will affect the *amount* of supplementary benefit or housing benefit payable, whatever the relationship between the claimant and the non-dependant may be (see pages 92–3 and 105–6), and is therefore a relevant fact which the claimant is under a duty to report to the social security office. Provided that she does so, she should be spared the attentions of special investigators, though if the non-dependant is a man and not a close relative she must expect to be interviewed and subjected to questioning on the lines explained above.

REFERENCES

1. SB Act, s. 34(1).
2. *Supplementary Benefits Handbook*, 1984 edition, p. 33.
3. *Crake* v. *S.B.C.* [1980].
4. R(SB) 17/81.
5. *Supplementary Benefits Handbook*, 1979 edition, p. 25.
6. S Manual, paras. 2546, 2556–8.
7. S Manual, paras. 2554(4), 2559.
8. S Manual, paras. 2583–90.
9. Aggregation Regs. 7; Requirements Regs. 10(1) and schedule 3, para. 11.
10. Urgent Cases Regs. 23.
11. Urgent Cases Regs. 25(2).

Chapter 12

Unemployment

Availability for Work

Anyone under sixty claiming supplementary benefit because they are unemployed will normally have to be 'available for employment'[1] and attend as required – usually once a fortnight – at the unemployment benefit office to sign a statement that they are unemployed and available for employment.[2] This procedure is the same as for unemployment benefit: there is no need to sign twice where both benefits are payable. A claimant aged under 18 must, in addition, register at a careers office or jobcentre.[3] Older claimants can register at the jobcentre if they wish but they are not obliged to.

Availability is normally defined in the same way for supplementary benefit purposes as for unemployment benefit[4] and has been the subject of numerous Commissioners' decisions. The claimant must be able and willing to accept any suitable offer of employment and, with some exceptions, must not restrict the kinds of job he or she is prepared to take in such a way as to remove any reasonable prospect of finding employment. The exceptions – where, in spite of imposing such restrictions, the claimant is still regarded as available for employment – are:

(a) if the lack of job prospects is due to temporarily bad industrial conditions;

(b) if the restrictions are reasonable in view of the claimant's physical condition; *or*

(c) if the restrictions are reasonable in view of the claimant's usual occupation and length of unemployment (i.e. the claimant can refuse, for a reasonable time, to consider employment in an unfamiliar occupation).[5]

The claim form which has to be completed on first applying for benefit at the unemployment benefit office asks, 'Would you take any full-time job which you can do?' A claimant who answers 'No' is asked to complete another form, giving detailed information about the kind of job he or she is willing to take, where, for what hours if not full-time, for what wage, and whether he or she has transport and, if necessary, can arrange for children to be looked after during working hours. If the adjudication officer does not consider the answers satisfactory, or the claimant fails to complete the form,[6] benefit may be refused on grounds of non-availability.

People Who Cannot be Treated as 'Available for Employment'

Certain categories of people cannot be treated as available for employment, even if they are in fact willing to take any job that is offered. This means that they are not entitled to supplementary benefit (except urgent need payments) unless they fall within one of the categories listed on pages 34–6, who are not required to be available for employment. The list of people who are not to be treated as available, other than those already mentioned, is as follows:

(a) Students (see pages 255–6).

(b) Share fishermen who do not satisfy the conditions imposed on them for unemployment benefit.

(c) A person who, without good cause, has refused or failed to apply for a suitable job properly notified to him or her, or refused such a job when it was offered – but the non-availability decision can only remain in force while the job remains vacant, and anyway not for more than six weeks (within these limits it is for the adjudication officer to decide for how long the decision should run, subject to the normal right of appeal if the claimant feels that the penalty is excessive).

(d) A person who, having failed without good cause to attend at the social security office or jobcentre for an interview with an 'unemployment review officer' (see page 228) about job prospects, is notified of a second appointment within fourteen days and again fails without good cause to attend for interview. The non-availability decision runs from the date of the second appointment until such time as the claimant attends for an interview. In the case of a claimant whose benefit entitlement, at the time when the first appointment is given, is reduced on grounds of 'voluntary unemployment' (see page 228), the non-availability decision runs from the failure to keep that appointment.

(e) A person who, in the circumstances explained below, 'has failed to avail himself of a reasonable opportunity of short-term work which is available in the area in which he lives'.[7]

Short-term Work

Category (e) above could include claimants in any part of the country where short-term jobs are available, but in practice it operates only in areas where the Manpower Services Commission reports that short-term work is readily available – mainly seaside resorts and agricultural areas. It applies only to claimants aged 18 or over but under 45 and having no dependent children. In the case of a married (or unmarried) couple, both must also be under 45 and the wife not pregnant. The adjudication officer must be satisfied that withdrawal of benefit on the grounds of availability of short-term work 'would not be inappropriate' in the circumstances of the case, including the state of health of the claimant and his or her partner.[8] It is not necessary that a particular job should have been offered and refused – only that short-term work is available in the area and that the claimant has had a reasonable opportunity of obtaining it and has failed to do so. The maximum period for which benefit can be withdrawn is six weeks.[9]

Before operating this procedure, officers are instructed to warn claimants that, if they have not found work within a certain time, they will be interviewed by an unemployment review officer and their benefit may be cut off. The time allowed for the claimant to find a job is at least two weeks if he or she has just arrived in the area and up to six weeks otherwise.[10] After the interview, if the adjudication officer decides that benefit should be withdrawn, another two weeks' written notice must be given before this is done.[11] At that stage the claimant can appeal against the decision, though the appeal is very unlikely to be heard until after the two weeks have expired and benefit has been cut off.

Part-time Study

There are special provisions to allow a claimant to undertake a part-time course of study during a period of unemployment without losing entitlement to supplementary benefit. See pages 258–9.

Voluntary Unemployment

A number of provisions of the Act and regulations are intended to discourage or prevent people who are fit for work from deliberately or unnecessarily becoming or remaining idle at the taxpayers' expense. These measures are described in the following paragraphs. An important part in their enforcement is played by specially trained 'unemployment review officers' (UROs). The UROs' task is both to help and encourage people who have difficulty in finding suitable work or problems which prevent them from holding down a job, and at the same time to exert pressure on claimants who are suspected of being workshy or of making too little effort to find work. Their normal method of work is to ask the claimant to come to the social security office for an interview, during which the efforts he or she has made to find a job and the reasons for failing to do so are discussed. Failure to attend for an interview may result in withdrawal of benefit on the grounds that the claimant is not available for employment (see page 226). During the interview, it is important to avoid saying anything which might throw doubt on the claimant's availability or willingness to work.

Reduction of Benefit

A claimant who is regarded as being responsible for his or her own unemployment can be disqualified for unemployment benefit for up to six weeks. Governments have always taken the view that supplementary benefit should not be paid at the normal rate in this situation, since in many cases it would give the claimant exactly the same weekly income as if unemployment benefit had been payable. The claimant's 'normal requirements' are therefore reduced by 40 per cent of the scale rate for a single person, or by 20 per cent if a member of the assessment unit is pregnant or seriously ill and the claimant does not have capital of more than £100. The amounts to be deducted, based on the scale rates which came into force in November 1984, are:

	40 per cent	20 per cent
Single householder or married	£11.20	£5.60
Single non-householder:		
Aged 18 or over	9.00	4.50
Under 18	6.90	3.45
Boarder (single or married)	3.70	1.85

The deductions for boarders are 40 or 20 per cent of the allowance for personal expenses (see page 60). No deduction is made if the claimant is in 'residential accommodation' (see pages 251–2).[12]

The circumstances in which these deductions are to be made are that the claimant is required to be available for employment as a condition of receiving benefit (i.e. is classified as unemployed) but is disqualified for unemployment benefit for one of the reasons set out in section 20(1) of the Social Security Act 1975 (see below). The deduction must also be made if the claimant would be disqualified but for the fact that he or she has not claimed unemployment benefit or the claim has been disallowed on other grounds; or if the unemployment benefit claim has not yet been decided but, in the adjudication officer's opinion, 'a question as to disqualification arises'.[13] The officer may decide that 'a question as to disqualification arises' if the unemployment benefit office has suspended payment of unemployment benefit pending a final decision – for example where the last employer has reported that the claimant left voluntarily without a good reason. But the adjudication officer may also decide, without any prompting from the unemployment benefit office, that 'a question as to disqualification arises', on the basis of the statements made by the claimant on the supplementary benefit claim form or in the course of an interview at the social security office.

The grounds for disqualification are summarized well in the DHSS leaflet on unemployment benefit (NI 12, February 1984 edition):

If you left your job voluntarily
You will not get unemployment benefit for a period of up to six weeks if you left your job voluntarily without a good reason.
Your former employer will be asked to say why you left.
If it is found that you left voluntarily, it will be for you to show that you had a good reason for leaving.

If you were dismissed for misconduct
You will not get unemployment benefit for a period of up to six weeks if you lose your job through your misconduct.
'Misconduct' can mean simply that you have done something, or failed to do something, which would make a reasonable employer consider you no longer fit to hold your job. For example, it could mean refusing to carry out a reasonable instruction from your employer, or repeatedly staying away from work without explanation or permission.
Misconduct must be proved, so both your former employer and you will be asked to say why your employment ended.

If you refuse to take a job
You will not get unemployment benefit for a period of up to six weeks if, without good reason, you:
refuse or fail to apply for, or refuse to accept, a suitable job notified to you by an officer of the Manpower Services Commission, or of some other recognized

agency, or by a local education authority careers officer, an employer or someone on behalf of an employer

or

fail to take some other reasonable chance of a job

or

refuse, or fail, to carry out reasonable recommendations (given to you in writing by an officer of the Department of Employment, Manpower Services Commission, or local education authority) to help you to find a suitable job

or

refuse, or fail, to accept a reasonable opportunity of receiving approved training to help you to get regular work.

Range of jobs

You would normally be expected to be willing to do a job in your usual occupation; and after a reasonable time other work will be regarded as suitable also. You will not lose your benefit for refusing to take a job if:

the wages and conditions were not as good as those generally paid by agreement between associations of employers and employees, or if there were no such agreement, those generally paid by good employers

or

the job had become vacant because of a stoppage of work due to a trade dispute.

Once it has been decided that the claimant is disqualified for unemployment benefit on one of the grounds mentioned above, the adjudication officer *must* make the appropriate deduction from the supplementary benefit entitlement. If the claimant appeals against disqualification and wins the appeal, the deduction will be cancelled and arrears paid accordingly. Similarly, where the deduction is made without a formal decision that the claimant is disqualified for unemployment benefit, if it is subsequently decided that unemployment benefit is payable, any money already deducted will be repaid.

The deduction, at whichever rate (40 or 20 per cent) is appropriate, continues for the same period as the unemployment benefit disqualification (usually six weeks, but sometimes less if there are extenuating circumstances). Where there is no disqualification because unemployment benefit has not been claimed or is disallowed for other reasons, the deduction is made for what would have been the period of disqualification. If the deduction is made in anticipation of the unemployment benefit decision, it will normally commence with the first payment of supplementary benefit and continue for up to six weeks; but when the decision is known, the supplementary benefit already paid must, if necessary, be adjusted to bring the deduction period in line with the unemployment benefit disqualification period (or to cancel the deductions if there is no disqualification). The disqualification period may start before supplementary benefit is payable, in which case the 40 or 20 per cent deduction can be made only for the remainder of the period, not for the full six weeks.[14]

For these arrangements to work efficiently, it is essential that, in any case where a deduction is imposed before the unemployment benefit decision is known, the social security office should be informed of that decision by the unemployment benefit office, so that arrears can be paid if there is no disqualification or if the period for which deductions were made does not coincide with the disqualification period. In the past it frequently happened that the social security office was not informed of the decision or failed to make the repayment that was due. If a claimant suspects that benefit may have been wrongfully withheld in this way, the social security office should be asked to confirm that the weeks in which deductions were made were in fact weeks of disqualification for unemployment benefit.

Re-establishment Courses

The DHSS runs courses at centres located in various parts of the country, at which 'persons who are in need of re-establishment through lack of regular occupation or lack of instruction or training may be afforded the occupation, instruction or training required to fit them for entry into, or return to, regular employment'.[15] A man (there are no centres for women) who has been unemployed for a long time and shows no signs of finding work may be asked by an unemployment review officer whether he would be prepared to attend a re-establishment course. If he is not prepared to go voluntarily, he may in certain circumstances, explained below, be ordered to go under the threat of withdrawal of supplementary benefit if he refuses.[16]

Re-establishment centres do not provide training in particular skills. Their object is to help long-unemployed men to reacquire the habit of regular work. The work done at the centres is mainly simple woodwork or metalwork, or gardening, kitchen and other domestic work around the centre. The centres vary in quality but the best of them achieve a fair degree of success in terms of the proportion of men who find work on leaving them. Of the nineteen centres, one has residential facilities.

The DHSS regards it as highly desirable that those attending should do so voluntarily. In theory most do, but in many cases their decision is probably influenced by the knowledge that the adjudication officer has the power to issue a direction requiring them to attend. A direction can be issued only where all the following conditions are satisfied:

(a) The claimant is required to be available for employment as a condition of receiving supplementary benefit.

(b) He is not receiving unemployment benefit.

(c) He appears to be refusing or neglecting to maintain himself or his wife or children.

The direction must be given in writing in the form set out in the regulations.[17] It does not come into force at once. The claimant has 28 days in which to appeal against it and, if he does so, further time is allowed for the tribunal to hear the appeal and make a decision. By lodging an appeal towards the end of the 28 days, therefore, a claimant can obtain well over a month's delay – possibly two or three months – before having to attend a re-establishment centre. Even without an appeal, the direction cannot be enforced until the end of the 28 days.[18]

Once the direction is in force, supplementary benefit is not normally payable for any period during which the claimant does not comply with it.[19] Urgent need payments can, however, be made if the health or safety of the claimant or his family is seriously threatened (see page 194). In practice, odd days of absence are likely to be overlooked.

The requirements of a person attending a non-residential course are assessed in the normal way. For a period at a residential centre, if the claimant is married, normal benefit payments continue during his absence from home, increased by the charge made for board and lodging at the centre. A single claimant staying in a residential centre gets the board and lodging charge, a personal expenses allowance of £9.35 a week and, if necessary, a discretionary payment to cover a retaining fee for lodgings.[20]

Prosecution

Section 25 of the Supplementary Benefits Act provides that if a man persistently refuses or neglects to maintain himself or his wife and children under 16, or a woman persistently refuses or neglects to maintain herself or her husband and children under 16, and as a result supplementary benefit has to be paid in respect of any of them, he or she is guilty of an offence, punishable by up to three months' imprisonment, a fine of up to £500, or both. Anybody faced with a prosecution or the threat of prosecution under this section should obtain legal advice at once. Prosecution, however, is used only as a last resort when other methods of persuasion have failed. It is always preceded by an interview during which the claimant is warned of the possible consequences of his or her behaviour.

The power to prosecute for failure to maintain cannot be used where the failure is due entirely to the consequences of a strike.[21]

REFERENCES

1. SB Act, s. 5.
2. Claims and Payments Regs. 4.
3. Conditions of Entitlement Regs. 5.
4. Conditions of Entitlement Regs. 7(1).
5. Conditions of Entitlement Regs. 8(1)(*f*).
6. Conditions of Entitlement Regs. 8(1)(*g*).
7. Conditions of Entitlement Regs. 8(1) and (2).
8. Conditions of Entitlement Regs. 8(1)(*e*).
9. Conditions of Entitlement Regs. 8(2)(*c*)(ii).
10. *S Manual*, para. 1468.
11. Conditions of Entitlement Regs. 8(2)(*c*)(i).
12. Requirements Regs. 8(2) and (3).
13. Requirements Regs. 8(1).
14. Requirements Regs. 8(4).
15. SB Act, schedule 5, para. 1(1).
16. SB Act, s. 10(4).
17. SB Act, s. 10(1); Conditions of Entitlement Regs. 12(2) and schedule 1.
18. Conditions of Entitlement Regs. 12(2A).
19. SB Act, s. 10(4).
20. Requirements Regs., schedule 3, para. 6.
21. SB Act, s. 25(2).

Chapter 13

Strikes and Other Trade Disputes

There are special rules regarding the entitlement to supplementary benefit of persons who are on strike or who are without employment because of a 'stoppage of work due to a trade dispute' – a term which covers both strikes and lock-outs. The broad effects of these rules are that benefit is not payable in respect of the person involved in the dispute but only for his/her wife/husband and children; that strike pay of £16 a week is taken into account whether actually paid or not; that income from some other sources is treated less generously; and that the provisions relating to additional requirements, single payments and urgent need payments are more restrictive than for other claimants. There are also special arrangements for recovering any benefit paid in the fifteen days after return to work. All these provisions are explained more fully in the following paragraphs.

Exclusion of 'Persons Affected by Trade Disputes'

Under section 8 of the Supplementary Benefits Act, if a person is without employment as a result of 'a stoppage of work which is due to a trade dispute at his place of employment' and has not taken another job during the stoppage, his or her requirements are to be disregarded for supplementary benefit purposes. This applies only to the person affected by the dispute. Thus a striker can claim benefit to meet the needs of other members of the assessment unit; and similarly, if a claimant's wife or husband is on strike, only the striker's requirements are excluded by section 8.

Section 8 does not apply if the person can prove that he or she 'is not participating in or directly interested in the trade dispute which caused the stoppage of work'.[1] The section follows closely the provisions of section 19 of the Social Security Act 1975, under which a person who has lost employment as a result of a trade dispute is disqualified from receiving unemployment benefit. Because of the similarity of these provisions, the adjudication officer dealing with a supplementary benefit claim relies on the decision made for unemployment benefit purposes as to whether the trade dispute disqualification applies. Until that decision is made, if the adjudication officer does not feel able to decide the matter himself, he must assume, once the question has arisen, that it will be decided against the claimant;[2] but arrears of benefit are paid if it is subsequently decided in the claimant's favour.

There is a considerable body of national insurance case-law on the meaning of 'participating in' and 'directly interested in' a trade dispute. Strikers should be able to get advice on legal questions of this kind through their trade union. Generally speaking, however, it can be assumed that anybody employed at the same workplace whose pay or conditions of employment are likely to be affected by the outcome of the dispute will not be entitled to supplementary benefit to meet his or her own needs while out of work as a result of the dispute. The fact that a particular worker may be opposed to the strike and may have tried to prevent it is no protection. Moreover, section 8 places on the individual concerned the onus of proving that he or she is not participating or directly interested in the dispute.

Single Strikers

Once it is established that the case is one to which section 8 applies, if the claimant is a single person with no dependent children, the effect of disregarding his or her requirements is that no supplementary benefit is payable, except in the very limited circumstances where urgent need is recognized (emergency relief after a disaster, an allowance for a very expensive diet, repair or replacement of a cooker or heater, or travelling expenses to visit a sick relative – see pages 238–40). Until 1980, a single striker with no means of support could get urgent need payments for normal living expenses. However 'undeserving', a striker was not allowed to starve. This protection no longer exists. A single striker can, however, claim 'standard' housing benefit (but not housing benefit supplement) from the local authority (see Chapter 5). The amount of housing benefit payable depends on how the local authority assesses the striker's income. They may agree to award, or re-assess, housing benefit for a short period on the basis of the claimant's income while on strike, thus giving the maximum benefit during that period; or they may take the loss of earnings into account in estimating the average income on which the claimant's housing benefit is based over a longer period.[3]

Strikers' Families

Only the requirements of the striker are excluded by section 8. Benefit can still be paid to meet the needs of the striker's wife or husband and their children, if any – or, if the striker is a single parent, for the children's needs. The payments are, however, reduced by £16 a week[4] – the amount that the trade union concerned is expected to contribute by way of strike pay. The reduction is made whether strike pay is actually available or not, and whether the strike is official or unofficial.

In the case of a married couple (or an unmarried couple living as husband and wife), where either the husband or the wife is on strike, the other partner's requirements are assessed by taking the 'ordinary' scale rate for a 'non-householder'[5] (£22.45 a week) and adding any housing requirements (e.g. mortgage interest) and the normal scale rates for any children. In the case of a single parent, or a couple who are both off work because of a trade dispute, only the requirements of the children and any housing requirements are taken into account; and if there are no children, the couple are in the same position as two single strikers – apart from the limited 'urgent need' exceptions, they have no entitlement to supplementary benefit.

The effect of these rules in the case of a married couple, one of whom is on strike, is to reduce the normal supplementary benefit entitlement by £39.10 a week, up to £16 of which can be made good by strike pay where available (see below). For a single parent who is a householder, the reduction is £44.05 a week, less up to £16 strike pay. Further reductions may result from the treatment of strikers' resources, explained below.

If, in spite of these reductions, some supplementary benefit is still payable, the claimant will qualify for 'certificated' housing benefit. If not, it is always possible to claim 'standard' housing benefit (but not housing benefit supplement). As with single strikers, the amount of housing benefit payable will depend on whether the local authority bases it on the actual income during the period of the strike or on an estimated average income over a longer period.

The Treatment of Resources

One of the main differences between the treatment of resources of strikers and other claimants is mentioned above: the striker is assumed to have strike pay of £16 a week, which is deducted from the benefit payable for the family's needs whether it is actually paid or not. The way this rule works is:

(a) £16 is deducted from the weekly benefit, whether it is the claimant or the claimant's wife or husband who is on strike (if both are on strike, only one deduction is made).[6]

(b) If strike pay from a trade union (but not from any other source) is received or available, the first £16 a week of it is ignored.[7]

Thus, if the strike is official and the union can afford to finance it, the £16 deduction can be made good by strike pay; but if there is no strike pay or it is less than £16 a week, the family's income is reduced below the needs of the striker's family (his or her own needs having already been excluded). The deduction increases annually, roughly in line with the rate of inflation.[8]

If a striker receives any other income 'by reason of being without employment', for example from a hardship fund, it is taken into account in full[9] – unlike similar payments to a person who is laid off but not participating or directly interested in the dispute, which qualify for the £4 disregard.

There are special rules for the treatment of earnings received before or during the strike. The striker is treated as if in full-time work and therefore not entitled to benefit for the period covered by the earnings, in the same way as a person whose job has come to an end.[10] In addition, however, if the last week's earnings are more than two and a half times the scale rates for the assessment unit as a whole (including the striker), the excess is carried forward as income for the following week.[11]

Certain types of earnings are taken into account (subject to the normal disregard of £4 a week – see page 120) if received by a striker, though in other cases they would be disregarded: the first £10 of a Christmas bonus from an employer (see page 121) and the part-time earnings of lifeboat men, auxiliary coastguards, firemen and members of the territorial or reserve forces (see page 123).[12]

Additional Requirements

Since the striker's own requirements are excluded in calculating the benefit payable for the family's needs, it follows that no allowance is normally made for any additional requirements the striker may have for heating or other needs mentioned in Chapter 3. The Requirements Regulations do allow certain additional requirements of members of the assessment unit other than the striker; and in other cases, payments can be made on grounds of 'urgent need' under the Trade Disputes Regulations for extra needs, including those of the striker. Urgent need payments, however, are made only if the need in question cannot be met out of savings, disregarded income (including the first £16 a week of strike pay), or by any other means, including help from any source to which the assessment unit can reasonably be expected to look – working members of the household, other individuals, the local authority, trade union or emergency relief fund, etc. – or credit facilities.[13]

The relevant provisions are explained below, distinguishing between needs that can be met under the Requirements Regulations and those to which the more stringent conditions of the Trade Disputes Regulations apply.

Heating. An addition of £5.20 is allowed under the Requirements Regulations if the person in need of extra heating is not the striker and the need arises under heading (f) or (g) on page 69.[14]

Blindness. The addition of £1.25 a week, or payment of the full householder rate in place of the non-householder rate, is allowed under the Requirements Regulations if the blind person is not the striker[15] (see page 67).

Diet. An addition for diet is allowed under the Requirements Regulations if the person requiring the diet is not the striker and the diet is not one to which the lower rate of addition (£1.55) would apply[16] (see pages 72–3). If the striker needs a special diet, an addition of £10.35 a week is allowed as an urgent need payment under the Trade Disputes Regulations if he or she is undergoing renal dialysis. In other cases the extra weekly cost of a striker's special diet is allowed, also as an urgent need payment, only if it is £10.35 a week or more.[17]

Visits to people in hospital and residential accommodation or critically ill. Additions are allowed for the cost of the journey under the normal rules (see pages 80–82) provided that the person making the visits is not the striker. The visits must be regular.[18] In addition, urgent need payments can be made for:

(a) Visits by the striker to his wife (or, if a woman, her husband) in hospital.

(b) Visits by a striker who is a single parent to a child in hospital.

(c) Visits by another member of the assessment unit to a hospital patient who is a close relative of the visitor (parent or step-parent, child or step-child, brother or sister) or who before going into hospital was a member of the same household, if an addition is not allowed under the normal rules because, for example, the visits are not regular.

(d) Visits by any member of the assessment unit, including the striker, to a critically ill person who is either a close relative or was, until the illness, a member of the household.

The urgent need payments can include the cost of an overnight or longer stay where necessary, and the expenses of an escort if the visitor is not the striker and cannot manage the journey alone. Although these payments are described in the regulations as being for 'additional requirements', they are made as required to meet the actual cost of visits rather than as a regular addition to the weekly benefit payments. The amount payable is calculated in the same way as under the Requirements Regulations, with similar deductions where the patient is a member of the assessment unit (see page 81); but only journeys within Great Britain, not to Northern Ireland, can be paid for.[19]

School transport costs for a handicapped child. Urgent need payments are made under the Trade Disputes Regulations for the cost of special transport needed to take a child under 19 to or from school, where the transport is not provided by the local authority.[20] As with fares for visiting the sick, these payments are for 'additional requirements' but may cover either a single journey or the cost of regular journeys. The provision is somewhat anomalous, since there is no power to make such payments where neither of the parents is on strike.

Single Payments and Urgent Need Payments

Neither single payments nor urgent need payments can normally be made while the claimant or the claimant's wife or husband is on strike.[21] In certain cases, however, 'urgent need' payments can be made instead under the Trade Disputes Regulations. Some of these cases, where the payments are or may be made on a regular weekly basis during the strike, are mentioned above. Others, where the payments are comparable to the single payments and urgent need payments described in Chapters 7 and 8, are mentioned below. Apart from emergency relief, they are subject to the restrictions mentioned on page 238: there must be no other means by which the need can be met, and any resources the claimant may have are taken into account.

Emergency relief. Payments are made to strikers, including single strikers, to meet emergency needs after a disaster, on the same basis as to other people affected by a disaster (see pages 188–91), and subject to the same rules regarding recovery of the payments (see pages 186–8).[22]

Maternity needs. A payment can be made for the same items as under the Single Payments Regulations (see page 145), but only in the expected week of confinement or after the baby is born or adopted, and the strike must already have lasted at least eleven weeks (if the payment is made after the birth, the strike must have lasted eleven weeks up to the date of birth).[23]

Essential household equipment. For this purpose, essential equipment includes only cookers, space-heating equipment and fire-guards – and the item in question must be 'essential to the health or safety of the assessment unit'. A payment for a cooker or heating equipment can be made only where the existing equipment has broken down and is in need of repair. If it is beyond repair, or has not broken down but is in a dangerous state, there is, strictly speaking, no entitlement to a payment. Where immediate repairs are practicable, the payment must be of the amount needed to cover 'the reasonable cost of essential repairs', unless this is more than it would cost to replace the item or provide a substitute (e.g. a heater where central heating has broken down). If the equipment cannot be repaired immediately or it is cheaper to provide a replacement or substitute, the payment must cover the cost of a reconditioned item if available; otherwise a second-hand item. If neither a reconditioned nor a second-hand item 'of the minimum standard needed' is available, the weekly cost of buying the item on hire purchase is to be met instead.[24]

Returning to Work after a Trade Dispute

Supplementary benefit can be paid for up to fifteen days after a return to work,[25] just as it can after a period of unemployment or sickness (see page 267). Once the stoppage of work due to the trade dispute is over, section 8 no longer applies and the requirements of a person involved in the dispute can be taken into account in the normal way. This means that a single person, who cannot normally claim benefit during the strike, may become entitled when the strike ends. The right to benefit on a return to work after a trade dispute is, however, subject to three special rules:

(1) Any earnings received during the first fifteen days are to be taken into account in full, without deducting the usual £4 'disregard'. Moreover, any loan, advance of earnings or *ex gratia* payment *made or offered* by the employer during that period is also to be taken into

account in full.[26] The object of this rule is to ensure that, as far as possible, once the strike is over those involved in it look to the employer rather than to the supplementary benefit scheme for any help they may need to tide them over until the next pay-day.

(2) The minimum benefit payable is £3 a week.[27] If the claimant would be entitled to less than this, no payment is made.

(3) Any supplementary benefit paid during the fifteen days after the return to work is recoverable, normally through the employer.[28] The procedure is explained below.

A monthly paid employee who returns to work near the beginning of the month and cannot get an advance from the employer may be in need of benefit for more than fifteen days. Any further payments must be made under the Urgent Cases Regulations and are recoverable in the same way as other such payments (see page 193).

Recovery of post-dispute payments

The adjudication officer, on awarding benefit during the first fifteen days after the end of the dispute, must inform the claimant in writing of the amount of benefit payable, the fact that it is recoverable, and the claimant's 'protected earnings' figure. The protected earnings are calculated by taking the scale rates for the assessment unit (see Appendix 2); adding the weekly rent or, if no rent is payable, the 'housing requirements' (mortgage interest, etc. – see Chapter 4); adding another £8; and subtracting any child benefit. Rent, for this purpose, is the full amount of rent payable, without any deductions for rates, non-dependants, etc.[29]

Next, the social security office must serve a 'deduction notice' on the employer, showing the amount of benefit to be recovered (after deducting any amount that has already been repaid) and the claimant's protected earnings.[30] A deduction notice remains valid for up to twenty-six weeks.[31] The employer must proceed to make deductions from the claimant's earnings, starting not later than the first pay day that falls more than a month after the deduction notice was served on the employer. The amount to be deducted, where the earnings are paid weekly, is half the amount by which the net earnings (after all other lawful deductions) exceed the protected earnings – but no deduction is to be made in any week for which the earnings do not exceed the protected earnings by at least £1. Any bonus, commission or similar payment received between pay days is treated as part of the earnings payable on the following pay day. Where the earnings are paid

241

monthly, the protected earnings figure is multiplied by five and no deduction is to be made unless the net earnings for the month are at least £5 more than the protected earnings. Similarly, where earnings are paid daily, the protected earnings figure is divided by five and the £1 margin reduced to 20p.[32] Once the total amount deducted by the employer is equal to the amount shown on the deduction notice, the notice lapses and no further deductions are to be made.[33]

A deduction notice also lapses if the claimant leaves the employment of the employer on whom it was served,[34] but a new deduction notice may be served on the new employer, if any.[35] The claimant is required to inform the social security office within ten working days of leaving the employment and must also report the name and address of the new employer within ten working days of restarting work.[36] Failure to do so can lead to a fine of up to £200.[37]

If at any time recovery of benefit by means of a deduction notice is not practicable, the Department of Health and Social Security can use other means of recovering the money direct from the claimant, including legal action;[38] but this is unlikely to happen unless the claimant is deliberately avoiding repayment.

There is no right of appeal against a decision that benefit payments to a striker during the fifteen days after the end of the dispute are recoverable, nor against the actual process of recovery, whether by deduction from earnings or by other means. But there is a right of appeal against the adjudication officer's decision regarding the amount of 'protected earnings', if the claimant thinks it has been miscalculated.

REFERENCES

1. SB Act, s. 8(2).
2. Adjudication Regs. 69(1).
3. Housing Benefits Regs. 31(2)(a).
4. Social Security (No. 2) Act 1980, s. 6(1)(b).
5. Requirements Regs., schedule 3, para. 12.
6. Social Security (No. 2) Act 1980, s. 6(1)(b).
7. Trade Disputes Regs. 12.
8. Social Security (No. 2) Act 1980, s. 6(2) and (3).
9. Social Security (No. 2) Act 1980, s. 6(1)(a)(i) and s. 6(4).
10. Conditions of Entitlement Regs. 9(1)(b).
11. Resources Regs. 10(2)(e).
12. Resources Regs. 10(3).
13. Trade Disputes Regs. 3(3).
14. Requirements Regs. 12(2)(a) and (b) and schedule 4, paras. 1(2), 1(3) and 7.

15. Requirements Regs. 13(3) and (4) and schedule 4, para. 12.
16. Requirements Regs. 13(3) and (4) and schedule 4, para. 14(a), (d) and (e).
17. Trade Disputes Regs. 5.
18. Requirements Regs. 13(3) and (4) and schedule 4, para. 17.
19. Trade Disputes Regs. 9.
20. Trade Disputes Regs. 6.
21. Single Payments Regs. 6(1)(b); Social Security (No. 2) Act 1980, s. 6(1)(c).
22. Trade Disputes Regs. 4.
23. Trade Disputes Regs. 7.
24. Trade Disputes Regs. 8.
25. SB Act, s. 9(1).
26. Resources Regs. 10(6).
27. Claims and Payments Regs. 10(2).
28. SB Act, s. 9(2).
29. Trade Disputes Regs. 14.
30. Trade Disputes Regs. 15(1) and (2).
31. Trade Disputes Regs. 16(1)(d).
32. Trade Disputes Regs. 17.
33. Trade Disputes Regs. 16(1)(c).
34. Trade Disputes Regs. 16(1)(b).
35. Trade Disputes Regs. 20(1).
36. Trade Disputes Regs. 23.
37. SB Act, s. 24.
38. Trade Disputes Regs. 21.

Chapter 14

Some Special Cases

This chapter deals with the supplementary benefit entitlement of people in a variety of situations to which the normal rules of the scheme do not apply: hospital patients, those receiving residential care in other types of accommodation, homeless people, prisoners, full-time students, and people going or coming from abroad (including the help available to immigrants who want to return to their country of origin).

Hospital Patients

The supplementary benefit entitlement of hospital patients depends on their family circumstances and how long they have been in hospital.

Married patients

If a husband or wife (or one member of an unmarried couple living as husband and wife) is admitted to hospital, payment of supplementary benefit continues for the first eight weeks at the same rate as if they were both at home, with the following exceptions:

(a) A heating addition awarded because the patient was getting an attendance allowance will be withdrawn at the same time as the attendance allowance – usually after four weeks.

(b) The admission to hospital may give rise to a new additional requirement, either for domestic assistance for the partner remaining at home (see page 74) or – where the costs of visiting are high – for fares (see pages 80–82).

After eight weeks, if the patient is still in hospital, the couple's normal requirements are reduced by one-fifth of the basic retirement pension rate[1] – a reduction of £7.15 at November 1984 rates – to take account of the assumed reduction in the household's living expenses. If the patient is drawing a national insurance pension or other benefit as well as supplementary benefit, the insurance benefit is normally reduced by

244

the same amount, so that the amount of supplementary benefit needed to top up the insurance benefit remains the same as before. If the supplementary benefit includes additional requirements based on the patient's own needs – heating additions on grounds of ill health or disability, or additions for diet, laundry, baths, attendance needs or wear and tear of clothing – they are withdrawn at this stage.[2] The reduction of benefit may, however, result in a new or increased entitlement to an addition for the cost of visiting the patient (see page 81). A heating addition on the grounds that the patient is aged 65 or over continues until he or she has been in hospital for thirteen weeks[3] – but it will not be withdrawn then if the partner remaining at home is also over 65.

The period of eight weeks mentioned in the previous paragraph need not be continuous. If the patient is discharged and then re-admitted within 28 days, the periods in hospital are added together and, if benefit had already been reduced in the earlier period, the reduction will apply again immediately on re-admission.[4]

Apart from the adjustments already mentioned, the couple's supplementary benefit is not affected by the absence of one of them in hospital unless he or she remains there continuously for more than two years or, at an earlier stage, the adjudication officer decides that, in his opinion, the stay in hospital has become 'other than temporary'. From then on, the patient will no longer be regarded as a member of the household but will be treated in the same way as a single person without dependants (see below).[5] The requirements of the partner left at home will be assessed separately, due allowance being made for the cost of visiting the patient (see pages 80–81).

If a couple are *both* in hospital, and there are no dependent children, they are treated in the same way as two single persons in hospital (see below), their normal requirements being reduced at once to £7.15 each. If there are dependent children left at home or still regarded as members of the household, this reduction does not take place until the parents have both been in hospital for eight weeks, and the single householder scale rate is then allowed for the eldest or only child instead of the scale rate appropriate to the child's age.[6] Additional requirements are treated in the same way as for a couple of whom one is in hospital (see above), except that:

(a) if the children are not still at home, any heating addition based on the difficulty or expense of heating the accommodation or the fact that it is centrally heated is withdrawn after four weeks;[7] and

245

(b) if a fixed charge is made by the landlord for fuel, a heating addition may be payable, as explained on page 71.

Housing costs will continue to be met either by housing benefit or as part of the couple's requirements for supplementary benefit purposes as long as the children remain at home. If no member of the assessment unit is still living at home, the local authority is expected to continue paying housing benefit for up to a year if one of them is expected to return home,[8] while the supplementary benefit regulations provide for housing requirements to be met provided that the absence is unlikely to be for much more than a year and it is reasonable for the home to be retained.[9]

Single patients without children

The supplementary benefit entitlement of a single person (whether unmarried, separated, divorced or widowed) is reduced immediately on admission to hospital. Normal requirements are assessed at £7.15 a week – the standard allowance for personal expenses of a person in hospital or 'Part III' accommodation.[10] Housing needs are met, as explained above, for up to a year under the housing benefit scheme or for a little longer if they are included in the patient's requirements for supplementary benefit purposes (e.g. for an owner-occupier). A retainer for lodgings can be met, on a discretionary basis, as part of the supplementary benefit requirements;[11] the situation is reviewed after eight weeks to ensure that there is still a real prospect of the patient returning to the accommodation.[12]

Additional requirements based on the personal circumstances of the claimant – heating additions on grounds of ill health or disability, additions for diet, laundry, baths, domestic assistance, attendance needs or wear and tear of clothing, and the additions for age (over 80) and blindness – are withdrawn immediately.[13] Heating additions for accommodation which is difficult or expensive to heat or for central heating are withdrawn after four weeks in hospital[14] and heating additions on grounds of age after 13 weeks.[15] The special arrangements regarding heating additions where the landlord makes a fixed charge for fuel (see page 71) come into operation immediately. Other additional requirements – for hire purchase, furniture storage and clothing or footwear of non-standard sizes or fittings – are not affected, though an addition for clothing or footwear might be withdrawn on the grounds that no extra cost was incurred during the stay in hospital.

Single patients with children

If a single parent goes into hospital and the children are taken into the care of the local authority, the parent's supplementary benefit is reduced to the same level as that of a single patient without children. If the children remain dependent on her (or him), the reduction does not take place until the parent has been in hospital for eight weeks. The single householder scale rate is then allowed for the eldest child instead of the children's rate,[16] and any additional requirements for the parent's needs are withdrawn.[17] If the children have to leave home, a heating addition for accommodation which is difficult or expensive to heat or centrally heated is withdrawn after four weeks' absence.[18] The special arrangements where the landlord makes a fixed charged for fuel (see page 71) come into operation when the benefit is adjusted after eight weeks in hospital. Additions for hire purchase, furniture storage and special clothing or footwear continue.

There is some doubt as to the proper treatment of cases where a single parent is in hospital and a child is cared for by another family on supplementary benefit. Adjudication officers are told to treat the child as a member of the carers' family, on the basis of a provision in the Aggregation Regulations to the effect that a supplementary benefit claimant is to be treated as responsible for a child who is 'a member of the same household'.[19] The effect of doing so is that the carers' benefit is increased by the child's scale rate, while the parent's benefit is immediately reduced to £7.15 a week (unless there are other children still dependent on her or him). The Child Poverty Action Group has argued that the child should be treated as still being a member of the *parent's* household, as would normally be done during a period of temporary absence.[20] The parent's benefit would then be paid in full for the first eight weeks, after which the requirements of the eldest or only child would be assessed at the single householder rate. Advice on this matter can be obtained from the Citizens' Rights Office, 1 Macklin Street, London WC2B 5NH.

Children in hospital

If a child whose parents are entitled to supplementary benefit is admitted to hospital, their benefit continues unaltered for the first twelve weeks, unless either a heating addition has to be withdrawn because payment of attendance or mobility allowance ceases, or there is an additional requirement for the cost of hospital visiting (see pages

81–2). The same applies where a newborn baby remains in hospital for some time after the birth: the normal child's scale rate is allowed, as if the baby was already at home.

After twelve weeks, the child's requirements are assessed at £7.15 a week instead of the normal scale rate,[21] and any additional requirements related to the child's needs are withdrawn [22] (a heating addition for a child under five is withdrawn after thirteen weeks, unless there is another child under five in the family).[23] The parents may then be entitled to a new or increased allowance for the cost of visiting.

Mental hospital patients

Patients in hospitals for mentally ill and mentally subnormal people have the same entitlement to supplementary benefit as other hospital patients, apart from a residual group of patients admitted before 17 November 1975. They are not entitled to benefit [24] but the hospital authorities are responsible for providing them with money for their personal expenses, up to a maximum of £7.15 a week – the amount allowed for a single patient on supplementary benefit. These payments can be reduced or withheld if the hospital doctor considers that, because of the patient's condition, the money cannot be used for his or her personal comfort or enjoyment.

Long-term patients

If a patient who has been in hospital for at least a year is unable to deal with his or her own affairs and the benefit – normally £7.15 a week – is being paid to the hospital under the 'appointee' arrangements described on pages 208–9, it can be reduced or discontinued if the doctor certifies that it cannot all be used on the patient's behalf.[25] This prevents the accumulation of money in the patient's account from which he or she derives no benefit. Care should be taken, however, to ensure that the benefit is not reduced if there is any way in which it can be used to the patient's advantage, or if he or she is likely to be able to spend the money at some future time.

Patients on leave

Hospital patients sent home, or to stay with relatives or friends, for weekends or other short periods, whether as part of their treatment or to meet the hospital's convenience, are entitled to supplementary benefit calculated in the normal way for each day spent away from the hospital, including the day of departure and the day of return.

Homes for the Elderly

Local authorities in England and Wales provide accommodation under Part III of the National Assistance Act 1948, for 'persons who by reason of age, infirmity or any other circumstances are in need of care and attention which is not otherwise available to them'. [26] Such accommodation, generally known as 'Part III accommodation', can be provided either directly by the local authority or by arrangement with a voluntary body or a private home. For supplementary benefit purposes, what matters is that the local authority has accepted financial responsibility for providing the accommodation, whether in its own premises or not, and that the claimant's stay 'has become other than temporary'.[27] In Scotland, similar arrangements are made under the Social Work (Scotland) Act 1968.

The requirements of an elderly person living in 'residential accommodation' – i.e. in a local authority home or 'sponsored' by the local authority in a voluntary or private home registered under section 1 of the Residential Homes Act 1980 or section 61 of the Social Work (Scotland) Act 1968 – are assessed at a special rate, known as the 'Part III rate', which is the same as the basic retirement pension rate for a single person: £35.80 from November 1984. Of this sum, four-fifths (£28.65) is the minimum charge which the local authority has to make for the accommodation, and one-fifth (£7.15) is the amount the resident is allowed to keep for personal expenses. For a married couple in 'residential accommodation' the figures are doubled.[28]

The personal expenses allowance of £7.15 is lower than the allowance for personal expenses of a 'boarder' – £10.30 for those over 60 (see page 60). This is because it is assumed that the local authority will supply certain basic needs, including clothing and 'toilet requisites', for which a boarder in private accommodation would have to pay. It is important, therefore, that local authorities should make adequate arrangements for the provision of new clothing for residents in their homes. *(See page 64 for proposed changes.)*

A claimant in 'residential accommodation' to whom the Part III rate applies will not normally have any 'additional requirements' for heating, diet, etc., because these needs are covered by the charge made for the accommodation. Nor will he or she qualify for the additional allowances of 25p a week for a person over 80 or £1.25 for a blind person.[29] The heating additions on grounds of age for a person aged 65 or over will, however, continue for thirteen weeks after admission to the home (items (a) and (e) on pages 68–9).[30] Rent and other outgoings for the person's own home can be met for a time, in the same way as for a hospital patient, if there is a possibility of returning to it – but not for more than a year under the housing benefit scheme or about fifteen months in the case of an owner-occupier. The costs of a home which is being put up for sale can be met for up to a year (see pages 95 and 106). If the rent is still being paid and includes a charge for fuel, for which a deduction is made in the rent rebate or allowance calculation, an addition is made to the supplementary benefit payments to make good this deduction (see page 71). Other continuing commitments for hire purchase and furniture storage can also be met by additions to the supplementary benefit in appropriate cases (see pages 79–80).

Single payments can be made to people in 'residential accommodation' for some, but not all, of the items mentioned in Chapter 7: maternity needs (unlikely to arise in homes for the elderly), funeral expenses, house repairs and unpredictable housing costs, travelling expenses, needs arising from a past underpayment (see page 143), and payments under the 'safety net' regulation which are 'the only means by which serious damage or serious risk to the health or safety of (the claimant) may be prevented' (see pages 177–9).[31] Urgent need payments can be made for only one purpose: travelling expenses to visit a critically ill relative (see page 196).[32]

The arrangements described above apply to all elderly people in local authority homes and to those in voluntary and private homes who are sponsored by the local authority. Residents in voluntary or private homes for whom the local authority has *not* accepted financial responsibility – whether because they are not 'in need of care and attention which is not otherwise available to them' or for some other reason – are treated as 'boarders' and their normal requirements are assessed under the rules explained on pages 59–63 (*but note the proposed new rules summarized on page 64*). This means that the charge made by the home for board and lodging is met in full provided that it is not more than £16.15 a week above the 'local limit' for residential homes (see page 61); and if it is more than this the excess not covered by any disregarded income can be met for up to thirteen weeks to allow time to find alternative accommodation, provided that the claimant moved in more than a year ago and could afford the charge at the time (see pages 63–4). If the charge cannot be met in full, any payments from charitable sources or relatives (other than the claimant's husband or wife) to cover the excess charge will be ignored.[33]

The usual personal expenses allowance for a boarder, £10.30 (but see page 64), applies to old people in voluntary and private homes who are not sponsored by the local authority. Housing and additional requirements are met on the same basis as for 'Part III' residents, to enable the claimant's home and furniture to be retained on a temporary basis or to allow time for its sale. Heating additions, too, are payable in the same circumstances as for 'Part III' residents. But the ban on single payments and urgent need payments to people in 'residential accommodation' does not apply to unsponsored residents.

Other People Receiving Residential Care

The treatment of other people in residential accommodation depends, similarly, on whether the accommodation is provided by the local authority, either directly or by accepting financial responsibility for it. If it is, and the claimant's stay has become, in the adjudication officer's opinion, 'other than temporary', the claimant's normal requirements will be assessed at the 'Part III' rate.[34] If not, he or she will be assessed as a 'boarder', unless the living arrangements justify treatment as a householder or joint householder.

The powers and duties of local authorities to provide residential accommodation under section 21 of the National Assistance Act 1948, for persons in need of care and attention not otherwise available to them, extend not only to elderly people but also to those in need of care and attention because of 'infirmity or other circumstances'. Disabled people living in local authority homes, or sponsored by the local authority in voluntary or private homes, are therefore assessed at the Part III rate – £35.80, of which £7.15 is for their personal expenses. The rules regarding additional requirements and single payments are the same as for elderly people in Part III residential accommodation (see above).

If the local authority has power to accept financial responsibility but has declined to do so, a claimant in a voluntary or private home is treated as a boarder, the board and lodging charge being met in full subject to the usual maximum (see pages 60–63 – *but note the proposed new rules summarized on page 64*). The 'local limit' for residential homes, fixed as explained on page 63, applies to accommodation of a type provided by registered homes, even if it is not in fact registered.[35] In all these cases a charge of up to £16.15 above the local limit can be met in full on the grounds that the person is 'infirm by reason of physical or mental disability' (see page 61).

The same arrangements apply to accommodation provided for people who are or have been suffering from mental disorder, or for expectant and nursing mothers. If the home is provided by the local authority, or the person is sponsored by the local authority, the Part III rate applies. If not, the person is treated as a boarder, with the same entitlement to any additional requirements or single payments as any other boarder, and a board and lodging charge of up to £16.15 above the local limit is met in full.

The same rules apply also to patients in private nursing homes, except that a patient sent to a nursing home under the National Health Service is treated as a hospital patient for supplementary benefit purposes. Where a person in a private nursing home is treated as a boarder, any part of the board and lodging charge which is for medical requirements will be excluded in deciding how much of the charge can be met by supplementary benefit; but normal day-to-day nursing of an elderly or infirm patient is not regarded as 'medical'.[36]

A claimant living in a centre for the rehabilitation of alcoholics or drug addicts is treated as a boarder, subject to the ordinary board and lodging limit (see page 61), even if the accommodation is registered and part of the fees are paid by the local authority.[37] A mental patient boarded out by the local authority in a private household is also assessed as a boarder, not as a Part III resident.

Homeless People

Homeless families provided with accommodation by the local authority have their requirements assessed for supplementary benefit purposes in the same way as other people in similar accommodation. If they are placed in bed-and-breakfast accommodation, the board and lodging charge is allowed up to the usual limits, together with allowances for meals that are not provided and for personal expenses (see pages 59–64). If the board and lodging charge is too high to be met in full, the balance should be paid by the local authority.

The requirements of a homeless person who has literally nowhere to stay are assessed on the basis of the allowances for meals not included in a board and lodging charge – a total of £4.20 a day (£29.40 a week) for breakfast and midday and evening meals.[38] But the means of obtaining accommodation (and the fares to get to it – see page 174) can also be provided in any of the following ways:

(a) A payment can be made for board and lodging – but more usually a voucher is issued for this purpose, rather than cash, for use at a named address, though the claimant is told that he or she is not obliged to go there and can choose any other reasonable accommodation (see page 201).

(b) An urgent need payment can be made to enable the claimant to pay a deposit for accommodation (see pages 197–8) or, if rented accommodation has been found, single payments can be made for a deposit and rent in advance (see page 157).

(c) The claimant can be referred to a resettlement unit, run by the DHSS to provide people 'without a settled way of life' with temporary accommodation 'with a view to influencing them to lead a more settled life'.[39] While there, the claimant is entitled, after the first two days, to an allowance for personal expenses of £7.15 a week, in addition to the charge for board and lodging.[40]

Fuller information on the rights of homeless people can be found in *Housing and Supplementary Benefits: a rights guide for single homeless people, boarders and hostel residents* (£2.80 from CHAR, 5–15 Cromer Street, London WCIH 8BR).

Members of Religious Orders

A member of a religious order who is fully maintained by the order has no entitlement to supplementary benefit. The only exceptions are for housing costs for the person's home if he or she is likely to return to it within about fifteen months or needs time to sell it (see page 95).[41] If a member ceases to be fully maintained by the order, he or she is entitled to claim supplementary benefit under the normal rules.

Prisoners

Supplementary benefit can be paid to a prisoner while on remand or in custody awaiting trial or sentence, but only in respect of housing requirements for which provision is made in the supplementary benefit regulations[42] (the local authority should continue paying housing benefit for the rent and rates during periods of absence of up to a year, including periods spent in prison).[43] Apart from this, a prisoner has no requirements, for supplementary benefit purposes, while in legal custody and therefore cannot receive supplementary benefit.[44] If a prisoner qualifies for supplementary benefit on discharge, however, a single payment can be made for debts accrued during the time in prison for housing requirements covered by supplementary benefit (e.g. mortgage interest) or storage of essential furniture, subject to the following conditions:

(a) The period of detention was less than a year.

(b) *Either* the ex-prisoner is chronically sick, physically or mentally disabled or over pension age, *or*, if the debt is for housing requirements, the accommodation has been or will be occupied by the ex-prisoner's wife, husband or children.

(c) Nobody else would have been treated as responsible for the housing requirements, for supplementary benefit purposes, while the debt was accruing.

(d) The accommodation or furniture would be lost if the payment were not made.

If a single payment is made, it must be either the amount of the debt or what would have been the claimant's housing requirements for the period in question, whichever is less, after deducting any capital (including the first £500 which would normally be disregarded).[45]

A prisoner's wife can claim supplementary benefit to meet her needs or those of her children, if any, while the husband is in prison. If there are dependent children (including a child over 16 still at school) she is treated as a single parent and half of her earnings between £4 and £20 is disregarded, in addition to the normal £4 disregard (see page 120). The husband remains liable for her maintenance and any resources of his that are available to her are taken into account. In the less usual situation where the wife is in prison, the husband has similar rights. The provisions regarding payment of travelling expenses for visiting a prisoner are explained on pages 175–6.

If a prisoner is allowed a short period of leave before discharge and spends it in the home of a person receiving supplementary benefit, that person can claim a single payment for the prisoner's requirements. If the person is the prisoner's wife (or husband), the single payment is the difference between her (or his) scale rate and the ordinary scale rate for a married couple; otherwise the single payment is based on the non-householder scale rate. In either case, it is calculated on a daily basis: one-seventh of the weekly rate for each day of leave.[46]

On discharge, a prisoner can claim supplementary benefit in the normal way. Any discharge grant is taken into account in full in calculating the first week's benefit.[47] A prisoner who does not receive a discharge grant should claim benefit immediately: the requirement to be available for work can be waived for the first seven days,[48] and benefit can therefore be paid at once (in the form of a voucher for board and lodging if he has no address to go to) to tide over the period until the first normal benefit pay-day.

A discharged prisoner may be entitled to single payments for expenses connected with finding and starting work (see pages 174 and 176) as well as to a payment for debts relating to housing or furniture storage as explained above.

Full-time Students

With rare exceptions, full-time students cannot claim supplementary benefit except during vacations. This is because the support of students is regarded as primarily the responsibility of the education authorities or the students' parents, not of the social security system. Different rules apply, however, depending on whether the student is under 19 or older.

Under 19

Young people attending full-time at school or a college of further education to complete their secondary education are treated as their parents' dependants. The parents receive child benefit for them and they cannot claim supplementary benefit in their own right except in the unusual circumstances explained on page 33. A full-time course, for this purpose, is one which takes up more than twelve hours a week, excluding meal breaks and unsupervised study.[49]

Young people who have left school and are doing a full-time advanced course (above GCE A-level) cannot claim supplementary benefit during term-time, except in the three cases mentioned below, because they cannot satisfy the condition of being available for employment (even if they are willing to give up the course and take any job that is offered, the regulations state that they are not to be treated as available).[50] Whether an advanced course is full-time does not depend on whether it occupies more than twelve hours a week but must be decided on the facts of the case. The Commissioners have held that it is not the number of hours the student is actually attending the course that counts but whether the course itself is full-time, and that a statement that it is full-time made by the educational establishment concerned should be accepted as conclusive unless there is substantial evidence to the contrary.[51]

The three cases in which a young person doing a full-time advanced course can claim supplementary benefit, other than during the vacations, are:

(a) A single parent.

(b) A student who, because of a disability, would be less likely than other students to obtain employment within a reasonable period.

(c) An unmarried couple living as husband and wife, where one partner is a student and the other either has a child of whom the student is not the other parent or has been unable to work for the last eight weeks because of illness or physical or mental disablement (the reason for this exception is that the student hardship scheme, for students whose dependants are not provided for in their main grant, does not apply to unmarried students).[52]

A student under 19 on an advanced course can claim supplementary benefit during the vacations in the same way as an older student.

Over 19

A full-time student aged 19 or over is treated as not available for employment during term-time, and therefore unable to claim supplementary benefit except on grounds of urgent need (see Chapter 8), whether the course is advanced or not, subject to the three exceptions (a), (b) and (c) mentioned above. The twelve-hours definition of a full-time course does not apply to students over 19. Whether a course, advanced or non-advanced, is full-time must be decided on the facts of the case and, in particular, whether it is regarded as full-time by the school or college concerned.

Although disqualified during term-time, a full-time student can claim supplementary benefit during the vacations, subject to being available for employment and not engaged in a programme of vacation studies (including practical work placements).[53] If a claim is made during the Christmas or Easter vacations, the student is assumed to have an income equivalent to the vacation element in the grant. In the case of a mandatory grant, this is the same as the supplementary benefit scale rate for a non-householder (£22.45 per week) plus the standard rent contribution for a non-householder (£3.30) – £25.75 a week in total.[54] In the case of a discretionary grant, unless it is for term-time maintenance only, or a specific amount is stated to be for the vacations, the total grant, less any allowance included for books, travelling expenses, etc., is assumed to be spread evenly over the whole period to which it relates, in order to arrive at the weekly income to be taken into account during the vacations.[55] The result, at least where a mandatory grant is in payment, is that a student living at his or her parents' home during the Christmas and Easter vacations, whose requirements are assessed at the non-householder rate, is not normally entitled to supplementary benefit. Entitlement is more likely to arise during the summer vacation, which is not usually covered by the grant.

If the grant is reduced because the student's parents are assumed to be contributing to his or her maintenance, the parental contributions are taken into account whether they are actually paid or not. There are, however, special rules for students who are married (or living with another person as husband and wife), single parents or, because of a disability, less likely than other students to find employment within a reasonable period. For these categories, unpaid parental contributions are not taken into account,[56] any additional grant made to a disabled student is ignored[57] and, in the case of a student who is disabled or has a child, the first £2 a week of the grant is ignored.[58]

A student, full-time or part-time, can claim housing benefit from the local authority, both during term-time and in the vacations. Certificated housing benefit is awarded in the normal way if the student is receiving supplementary benefit. If not, special rules apply to the calculation of standard housing benefit, to take account of the amount included for accommodation in the student's grant.[59] Supplementary benefit paid during the vacations cannot include anything for housing requirements in respect of the student's term-time accommodation from which he or she is for the time being absent;[60] nor can it include a retaining fee for term-time lodgings.

Part-time Students

A part-time student may be eligible for supplementary benefit, not as a student but as an unemployed person who, though studying part-time, is available for employment (or as a person who, for one of the reasons set out on pages 34–6, is not required to be available). As with full-time study, different rules apply to those under and over 19. The 21-hour rule, however, which enables those unemployed for three months or more to take part-time courses which might not otherwise be permitted, applies to both age groups and is therefore discussed separately below.

Under 19

A young person under 19 taking a non-advanced course – e.g. for GCE O- or A-levels – which involves not more than twelve hours a week of supervised study is not regarded as being in full-time education[61] and, subject to being available for employment, can claim supplementary benefit. The parents then cease to be entitled to child benefit for that child. The same applies to a person under 19 doing a part-time advanced course, except that the decision as to whether the course is part-time is based on the facts of the case and not on whether it involves more than twelve hours of supervised study.[62] Whether a part-time student is available for employment will depend in part on whether the course can reasonably be combined with employment and, if not, whether the student is prepared to give it up as soon as a suitable job becomes available.

Over 19

The same rules apply except that, as noted above, whether the course is regarded as part-time depends on the facts of the case and not on whether it involves more than twelve hours of study, even if the course is non-advanced.

The 21-hour rule

The normal rules are relaxed in the case of a person of any age who is required to be available for work and who, for the three months before starting a course, has been getting unemployment benefit (or supplementary benefit as an unemployed person) or sickness benefit or has been on a Youth Training Scheme course; or during a longer period not exceeding six months has spent at least three months in these situations and the rest of the time in full-time work or earning too much to claim benefit. Where these conditions are satisfied, the person is allowed to study for up to twenty-one hours a week, excluding meal breaks and unsupervised study, and still be treated as available for employment and therefore entitled to receive supplementary benefit – but only if he or she is prepared to give up the course immediately if a suitable job becomes available. The course can consist of academic study, non-advanced or advanced, or of practical training. In the case of a young person under 19 taking a non-advanced course, the 21-hour rule overrides the normal definition of a part-time course as involving not more than twelve hours of study. The three months' qualifying period, however, means that it is not possible to proceed directly from normal full-time education to a 21-hour course, since the three months cannot begin before the date when a school-leaver becomes eligible for supplementary benefit (see page 34). Thus a young person who leaves school in the summer and who would not be able to claim supplementary benefit until the beginning of September cannot start a course under the 21-hour rule until the beginning of December.[63] Meanwhile, however, he or she can follow a non-advanced course of study of up to twelve hours a week, or an advanced course which is accepted as 'part-time', provided that he or she remains available for employment.

Similarly a person aged 19 or over is free to follow a 'part-time' course, advanced or non-advanced, during the three months' qualifying period for starting a 21-hour course.

Going Abroad

Entitlement to supplementary benefit is limited by section 1(1) of the Supplementary Benefits Act to persons in Great Britain – which does not include Northern Ireland (where a similar scheme operates under separate legislation), the Isle of Man or the Channel Islands. There are, however, some cases in which a claimant already entitled to benefit, and who would have remained entitled if still in Great Britain, can continue to receive it for up to four weeks while temporarily out of the country and may also be entitled to a single payment for a debt accrued during the period of absence.

Any claimant can take advantage of this provision during the first four weeks of a visit to Northern Ireland, so long as all the other conditions of entitlement are satisfied. Claimants going to other countries can continue to receive benefit for up to four weeks if they are over pension age or are not required to be available for work (i.e. unemployed people of working age are excluded). If the reason for not having to be available is sickness, it must either have continued for six months before leaving Great Britain or, if not, the purpose of going abroad must be to get some form of treatment for the illness (it need not be medical treatment in the conventional sense); but in both these cases entitlement is not automatic – the Secretary of State must certify that payment of benefit is 'consistent with the proper administration of the Act'. If the claimant does not have to be available for work for some reason other than sickness, payment of benefit while abroad is dependent on that reason still existing: for instance, a single woman who is not required to register because she is caring for a disabled relative will qualify for benefit if she accompanies the relative on a visit abroad but not if she goes abroad without the relative. One category of claimants who, though not required to be available, cannot continue to receive benefit while abroad are strikers and others involved in a trade dispute. But as noted above, none of these restrictions applies if the claimant is visiting Northern Ireland.[64]

Provided that benefit was payable for at least part of the period of absence, and that the claimant again qualifies for benefit on returning to Great Britain after less than twenty-six weeks, a single payment can be made for a debt that has accrued for a 'continuing commitment' (see page 177).

Coming from Abroad

It is not a condition for claiming supplementary benefit that the claimant should be of British nationality or normally resident in Great Britain. This does not mean, however, that visitors from overseas who find themselves short of money can claim supplementary benefit in the same way as a person resident in Great Britain.

People allowed to remain in Great Britain as permanent residents do have the same benefit rights as if they had always lived in Britain, regardless of their country of origin. Like anybody else, they must be available for employment if under 60 and not prevented from working for other reasons. People from Northern Ireland or from the Irish Republic can also come to Great Britain and claim supplementary benefit without any special restrictions.

People from other EEC countries can come to Great Britain for a period to look for work and can claim supplementary benefit during that period subject to the normal condition of availability for employment. After they have received benefit for two weeks, however, a report is made to the Home Office,[65] which may result in their being asked to leave the country. Claiming unemployment benefit does not have this effect – only supplementary benefit.

Other visitors from EEC countries and people from some other parts of Europe – Iceland, Malta, Norway, Portugal, Sweden and Turkey – are not excluded from supplementary benefit, but their conditions of entry generally prevent them from satisfying the condition of availability for employment. If their circumstances are such that they would not be required to be available (see pages 34–6), they can get benefit. But, as with EEC nationals who are seeking work, they may be asked to leave the country as a result of claiming.

Other people from abroad who are admitted for a limited period on the understanding that they will not become a charge on public funds, or who have entered the country without permission, outstayed their leave to remain, or are subject to a deportation order, cannot claim supplementary benefit to meet normal living expenses [66] except by way of emergency relief after a disaster (see pages 188–91) or under regulation 21 of the Urgent Cases Regulations. Regulation 21 permits payments to people from abroad who are temporarily without money, or to a person who is awaiting a decision on an application to remain in the UK or on an appeal against refusal of permission, or is awaiting deportation, or is an illegal immigrant who has been allowed to stay (see pages 195–6). An urgent need payment can also be made, in a case to which regulation 21 applies, for travelling expenses to the point of departure from the United Kingdom (see page 197). People not covered by regulation 21, including those from EEC countries, who are without money for their journey home, may be entitled to an urgent need payment for travelling expenses within the UK on the grounds that they are 'stranded without the means to return home' (see page 196).

In the case of a married (or unmarried) couple where only one of them is entitled to benefit, because the other is present in the country without leave or with limited leave, benefit is calculated as for a single person.[67]

Repatriation of Immigrants

Under the Immigration Act 1971, people (other than British citizens) who have come to the United Kingdom from abroad with the right to settle permanently but want to resettle overseas can, in certain cases, be helped with the cost of travel for themselves and their families – but not to a European country. The scheme is discretionary and is administered by a voluntary body, International Social Service of Great Britain (ISS), which must satisfy itself that the proposed departure from the United Kingdom is likely to be in the best interests of the immigrant and any family concerned.

Single payments can be made for the same purpose under the supplementary benefits scheme to a person, receiving or entitled to supplementary benefit, who is a British citizen or wishes to return to a European country, including Malta or Cyprus. If the claimant wishes to go to a country other than the Republic of Ireland, the Isle of Man or the Channel Islands, the following conditions must be satisfied:

(a) The claimant has not been able to settle permanently in Great Britain and has no prospect of doing so.

(b) He or she *either* is not required to be available for work as a condition of receiving supplementary benefit, for reasons that are not merely temporary, *or* has no prospects of employment in Great Britain in the foreseeable future because of physical or mental disability, *or* is over 55.

(c) There is suitable accommodation and means of support in the new country for the claimant and those accompanying him or her.

(d) The claimant is able to travel and, if appropriate, suitable medical treatment will be available in the new country.

(e) The claimant will be accompanied by his wife (or her husband), if any, and by the children of either of them unless adequate arrangements have been made for their care and maintenance (if a child in the care of a local authority or whose other parent is not a member of the assessment unit is to accompany the claimant, the necessary approval must have been obtained).

(f) The Secretary of State is satisfied that if a payment is made there will be a net saving in expenditure on social security benefits within two years of the claimant's departure.

(g) The cost of the fare is not available to the claimant from any other source, including close friends, a sponsor, or the sale of any property owned by the claimant.

The amount of the single payment is the total cost, after deducting any capital resources of the claimant over £50, of the fares (by the cheapest available means), the return fare of an escort where necessary, any necessary documentation, and an allowance for incidental expenses during the journey based on the supplementary benefit scale rates. No payment is made for any excess baggage charge.[68]

If the claimant wants to go to the Irish Republic, the Isle of Man or the Channel Islands, conditions (c), (e) and (g) above must be satisfied, the claimant must have no immediate prospects of employment in Great Britain, and *either* the reason for the move is one of those listed on pages 157–8 (i.e. if the new home were in Great Britain a single payment for removal expenses would be made) *or* the claimant wants to rejoin a wife or husband where the couple are estranged and have at least one child living with one of them. The single fare by the cheapest available means will be paid, after deducting any capital resources over

£50. There is no provision for payment of an escort's fares if the claimant cannot travel alone, and no need to show that the move will result in a net saving in benefits.[69]

The conditions under which help with the cost of repatriation to countries outside Europe can be obtained through the discretionary I S S scheme, mentioned above, are less stringent in several respects:

(a) The person seeking help need not be out of work or entitled to supplementary benefit.

(b) Help may be given if the family's weekly income (subject to the usual 'disregards' – see pages 118–19) is not more than £20 above supplementary benefit level. The long-term scale rates are used for this purpose and the cost of maintaining children overseas is taken into account.

(c) Savings are not taken into account except to the extent that they exceed £500.

(d) It is not necessary to show that repatriation will entail a saving of public funds.

Fuller details of the I S S scheme can be obtained by writing to International Social Service of Great Britain, Cranmer House, 39 Brixton Road, London SW9 6DD. The scheme has never been extensively publicized, since it is intended only for those who decide as a matter of genuinely free choice that they wish to leave the United Kingdom. The Home Office has therefore laid down as a general principle that nobody in an official position should draw the attention of any individual to the existence of the scheme except in response to a specific inquiry.

REFERENCES

1. Requirements Regs., schedule 3, para. 2(*b*).
2. Requirements Regs. 12(4)(*b*) and 13(7)(*d*) and (*e*).
3. Requirements Regs. 12(2)(*c*)(ii).
4. Requirements Regs., schedule 3, para. 2.
5. Aggregation Regs. 2(3)(*b*).
6. Requirements Regs., schedule 3, para. 2(*a*).
7. Requirements Regs. 12(2)(*c*)(i).
8. Circular HB (82)2, para. 2.5.
9. Requirements Regs. 14(4)(*a*).
10. Requirements Regs., schedule 3, para. 2(*c*).
11. Requirements Regs. 10(4)(*b*).
12. *S Manual*, para. 3740.

13. Requirements Regs. 12(4)(*b*) and 13(7)(*c*), (*d*) and (*e*).
14. Requirements Regs. 12(2)(*c*)(i).
15. Requirements Regs. 12(2)(*c*)(ii).
16. Requirements Regs., schedule 3, para. 2(*c*).
17. Requirements Regs. 12(4)(*b*) and 13(7)(*c*), (*d*) and (*e*).
18. Requirements Regs. 12(2)(*c*)(i).
19. *S Manual*, para. 3749; Aggregation Regs. 3(2).
20. Janet Allbeson and John Douglas, *National Welfare Benefits Handbook*, 14th edition, p. 94.
21. Requirements Regs., schedule 3, para. 2(*d*).
22. Requirements Regs. 12(4)(*b*) and 13(7)(*c*), (*d*) and (*e*).
23. Requirements Regs. 12(2)(*c*)(ii).
24. Transitional Regs. 12.
25. Requirements Regs., schedule 3, para. 2(*e*).
26. National Assistance Act 1948, s. 21(1).
27. Requirements Regs. 10(5).
28. Requirements Regs., schedule 3, para. 1.
29. Requirements Regs. 12(4)(*b*) and 13(7)(*c*), (*d*) and (*e*).
30. Requirements Regs. 12(2)(*c*)(ii).
31. Single Payments Regs. 6(3).
32. Urgent Cases Regs. 6(1)(*c*).
33. Resources Regs. 11(4)(*j*)(ii).
34. Requirements Regs. 10(5).
35. Circular S/143, para. 10(1).
36. SB Act, s. 1(3); *S Manual*, para. 3588.
37. Requirements Regs. 10(5).
38. Requirements Regs., schedule 3, para. 4.
39. SB Act, s. 30 and schedule 5, para. 2(1).
40. Requirements Regs., schedule 3, para. 7.
41. Requirements Regs. 12(4)(*c*); 13(7)(*f*); 14(7)(*b*); and schedule 3, para. 8.
42. Requirements Regs. 14(7)(*d*).
43. Circular HB (82)2, para. 2.5.
44. Requirements Regs. 12(4)(*c*); 13(7)(*f*); 14(7)(*d*); and schedule 3, para. 9.
45. Single Payments Regs. 16.
46. Single Payments Regs. 29.
47. Resources Regs. 11(2)(*g*).
48. Conditions of Entitlement Regs. 6(*r*).
49. SB Act, s. 6(2) and (3); Conditions of Entitlement Regs. 10(1)(*a*).
50. Conditions of Entitlement Regs. 8(1)(*a*).
51. R(SB) 40/83 and R(SB) 41/83.
52. Conditions of Entitlement Regs. 8(1)(*a*).
53. Conditions of Entitlement Regs. 2(1) (definition of 'student').
54. Resources Regs. 4(12).
55. Resources Regs. 9(2)(*a*); R (SB) 19/84; *S Manual*, paras. 1661–3.
56. Resources Regs. 4(4).

57. Resources Regs. 11(4)(d)(i).
58. Resources Regs. 11(2)(l).
59. Housing Benefits Regs. 16(2)(e) and 16(4).
60. Requirements Regs. 14(4).
61. Conditions of Entitlement Regs. 10(1)(a).
62. R(SB) 40/83 and R(SB) 41/83.
63. Conditions of Entitlement Regs. 7(2).
64. Conditions of Entitlement Regs. 3.
65. *S Manual*, para. 3958.
66. Requirements Regs., schedule 3, para. 10(b).
67. Requirements Regs., schedule 3, para. 10(a).
68. Single Payments Regs. 25 (1) and (2).
69. Single Payments Regs. 25 (3) and (4).

Chapter 15

Supplementing Full-time Earnings

Supplementary benefit cannot normally be paid to a person who is in full-time work. The vast majority of people in full-time work would anyway not qualify for benefit, since their earnings, together with child benefit, are well above supplementary benefit level. But there remains a minority of workers who either do not earn enough to meet their requirements or need short-term help even though they would normally be able to manage on their earnings. In certain limited circumstances they can claim supplementary benefit, usually to tide them over an emergency or during a period of short-time work or the interval between starting a job and drawing the first week's wages. There is also a small category of claimants – self-employed disabled people – who can claim benefit on a regular basis. With this exception, supplementary benefit is not available as a regular weekly supplement to full-time earnings.

The effect of the full-time work disqualification is that a family may be living on an income well below the level of their requirements as set out in the supplementary benefit scale and yet be unable to claim supplementary benefit. They will, however, be entitled to other benefits. In this chapter, we shall first consider the limited circumstances in which the full-time work disqualification does not operate and supplementary benefit may therefore be payable. The remainder of the chapter describes briefly some of the other benefits available to people in full-time work.

Cases of Urgent Need

The circumstances in which and the purposes for which urgent need payments can be made are set out in Chapter 8. The full-time work disqualification does not apply to urgent need payments. Since such payments are available only where the need cannot readily be met from any other source, people in full-time work will rarely be entitled to them except in emergencies. Two types of cases in which urgent need payments are available should, however, be noted: where money is needed at the start of a new job and is not available under the normal fifteen-day rule, and where an employee has to take time off work without pay or with reduced pay (see pages 193–4). Urgent need payments to people in full-time work are normally recoverable.

Starting Work

The full-time work disqualification does not apply during the first fifteen days after the claimant becomes engaged in remunerative full-time work. Thus a person who has had a period off work, or in part-time work, can receive benefit for up to fifteen days in full-time work. But this does not apply if the person has merely changed jobs, with no interval between one full-time job and the next; nor during any part of the fifteen-day period covered by the last earnings from the previous job.[1] For example, a claimant who receives two weeks' pay on leaving a job is treated as being in full-time work for the next two weeks (see page 31); so if he starts another job after one week, he is not entitled to benefit for the first week of the new job.

The object of the 'first fifteen days' rule is to avoid hardship due to the fact that a person starting a new job normally has to wait at least a week for the first payment of wages. Where it is the custom of the trade to work 'a week in hand', the first week's wages are not paid until the end of the second week; hence the period of fifteen days specified in the regulations. Payment of benefit during this period is subject to the usual rules regarding the calculation of requirements and resources, the first £4 of earnings received in any week being disregarded (except after a trade dispute – see page 240). If no wages are payable in the first week, the employer may be willing to pay a 'sub' – an advance which will be recovered out of subsequent payments of wages. Claimants are not expected to ask for a 'sub' but if they receive one it is taken into account as earnings subject to the £4 disregard[2] (again there are different rules for those returning to work after a trade dispute – see pages 240–41).

The fifteen-day rule is designed to meet the needs of weekly paid workers. A claimant who starts work in a monthly paid job may need supplementary benefit for more than fifteen days. A person who goes straight from a weekly paid job to another which is monthly paid may also be in need of money during the first month. Urgent need payments can be made in such cases, though they are normally repayable (see page 193).

267

For the rules regarding recovery of benefit paid to strikers after return to work, see pages 241–2.

For details of single payments for expenses on starting a job, see page 176.

Irregular Hours

A claimant is treated as being in remunerative full-time work if the job involves an average of at least thirty hours' work per week – or thirty-five for a disabled person whose earning capacity is reduced by at least a quarter.[3] If the length of the working week fluctuates in a more or less consistent way, the average length is calculated over whatever seems a reasonable period. This can mean that a person is disqualified for benefit in a particular week when the number of hours worked is less than thirty; but it can also mean that benefit is payable for a week of thirty or more working hours if the average is less than thirty. The claimant's earnings are also averaged, so that the benefit payable does not have to be adjusted each week.[4]

Days Off Work

A person in a full-time job is treated as being in full-time employment when away from work without good cause or laid off during a recognized or customary holiday period. A person temporarily on short-time working is treated as in full-time work if working an average of thirty hours a week or more (thirty-five if disabled), but may be entitled to benefit if the average working week is less than this.[5] If the pattern of short-time working involves whole weeks off work, the claimant is not regarded as in full-time work during those weeks and they are ignored in calculating the length of the average working week.[6] The claimant's earnings, however, are averaged over both working and non-working weeks.[7]

Disabled Persons with Reduced Earning Power

As noted above, a disabled person with reduced earning power is not affected by the full-time work disqualification unless working at least thirty-five hours a week on average, whereas other claimants are disqualified if working thirty hours or more. In addition, a disabled person who is self-employed is not treated as in full-time work if his or her

268

earning power is substantially reduced compared with other people similarly occupied, regardless of the number of hours worked.[8]

Other Benefits for People in Full-time Work

Although, with the exceptions mentioned above, people in full-time work cannot receive supplementary benefit, they may be entitled to a number of other means-tested benefits. The details of these benefits are beyond the scope of this book. The best general source of information about them is the *National Welfare Benefits Handbook*, published annually by the Child Poverty Action Group (£3.50 including postage, from CPAG, 1 Macklin St, London WC2B 5NH). The main benefits are explained briefly below. Most of them are available to people on supplementary benefit as well as to other people with low incomes. The main exception is FIS (family income supplement) which is awarded *only* to people in full-time work.

Standard housing benefit

The way in which 'certificated' housing benefit meets all or most of the rent and rates of people on supplementary benefit is explained in Chapter 5. Other people can claim 'standard' housing benefit for the same purpose. The benefit comprises two elements: a rent rebate or allowance (rebate for council tenants, allowance for private tenants) and a rates rebate. The amount payable depends on the claimant's income, the size and composition of the household, and the amount of rent or rates. The benefit is normally awarded for up to twelve months if the claimant is over pension age or getting invalidity benefit, disablement pension or widow's pension and for up to seven months in other cases, including most people in full-time work;[9] but changes of circumstances during that period have to be reported and may result in immediate adjustment or withdrawal of the benefit.[10]

In some cases where the net income, after paying the rent and rates and taking into account the standard housing benefit, would be less than if the claimant were on supplementary benefit, a 'housing benefit supplement' is payable, bringing the net income up to supplementary benefit level (see pages 107–9). The supplement, however, is subject to the same conditions of entitlement as supplementary benefit itself, and is therefore not available to people in full-time work.

Family income supplement (FIS)

Family income supplement, generally known as FIS, is a benefit for families with at least one child under sixteen or still at school, where one of the parents is in full-time work.[11] The regulations define full-time work as meaning at least thirty hours a week, or at least twenty-four hours if the claimant is a single parent.[12] The supplement is half the amount by which the normal gross income of the claimant or couple falls short of a 'prescribed amount' which varies with the number of children: £90 for a family with one child and £10 for each additional child (November 1984 rates – the prescribed amounts are increased each November).[13] Income from most sources is taken into account in full in calculating the normal gross income, but child benefit, one-parent benefit, an education maintenance allowance (for a child over sixteen staying on at school), attendance allowance, mobility allowance, housing benefit and the first £4 of a war disablement pension are all ignored.[14] The maximum FIS payment is £23 a week for a family with one child, increased by £2 a week for each additional child.[15]

A claim for FIS must be made in writing, either on a form, FIS 1, obtainable from any post office or social security office, or in some other way acceptable to the DHSS,[16] and is dealt with at a central FIS office, not at the local social security office. But FIS appeals are heard by the local social security tribunal (see Chapter 16). FIS is normally awarded for a 52-week period, during which it continues at the same rate regardless of any change in income, family size or other circumstances of the family, and regardless of any increase in the 'prescribed amounts'.[17] It is therefore unwise to claim just before the prescribed amounts go up in November.

A successful claim for FIS brings automatic entitlement to the 'passport' benefits (see page 28): free prescriptions, free dental treatment, free glasses, free milk and vitamins for expectant mothers and children under five, free school meals and refunds of hospital fares. These entitlements also continue for the full 52-week period for which FIS is awarded.

Free prescriptions

People who are not entitled to free prescriptions under the supplementary benefit or FIS 'passport' can claim exemption on a number of other grounds. People over pension age, children under sixteen, women who are pregnant or have had a baby in the last twelve months, people suffering from certain chronic illnesses, and war pensioners needing prescriptions for their war disablement – all of these can claim exemption. Leaflet P 11, from a post office or social security office, shows how to claim. Finally, people on a low income – including those in full-time work – can claim free prescriptions by filling in the means-test form attached to leaflet P 11 and sending it to the local social security office. If entitled, they get an exemption certificate which lets them off prescription charges for several months. A low income, for this purpose, means an income below or only slightly above supplementary benefit level, after deducting rent, rates and mortgage payments (not just mortgage interest but the full amount, including capital repayments), life assurance premiums, and any of the 'additional requirements' mentioned in Chapter 3, and after disregarding the first £4 of earnings (or the first £4 each of a couple's earnings) and half a single parent's earnings between £4 and £20 a week. But, as with supplementary benefit, anyone with capital over £3,000 (excluding the first £1,500 of the surrender value of insurance policies) is not entitled. Leaflet P 11 gives some examples of income levels at which it is 'worth claiming'.

Dental treatment and glasses

The arrangements for exemption from charges for national health service dental treatment and glasses are similar to those for prescription charges. Some people are entitled under the supplementary benefit or F I S 'passport', or because they are already getting free milk (see below) or free prescriptions on grounds of low income. Others qualify automatically without a means test: young people under 18, or under 19 if still in full-time education (those over sixteen who have left school have to pay for dentures and bridges), and women who are pregnant or have had a baby in the last twelve months (for dental treatment only). And finally, people on a low income, including those in full-time work, can claim by filling in a means-test form supplied by the dentist or optician – or they can pay the charge and ask the social security office for a form (F 6) on which to claim a refund.

The rules about what is a 'low income' and about capital over £3,000 are almost exactly the same as for someone claiming free prescriptions. There is, however, an important difference. A person whose income is too high to qualify for free dental treatment or glasses may still be entitled to a reduction of the charge. The maximum charge they will have to pay is three times the excess of their weekly income over the

271

exemption limit. In the case of dental treatment, where the full charge can be well over £100, this means that someone in work, with earnings nearly £40 a week above supplementary benefit level, can claim a reduction in the charge. In a case where there are mortgage payments or life assurance premiums, the level of income up to which a reduction can be claimed is still higher. The procedure for claiming is exactly the same as for full exemption on grounds of low income.

From April 1985 there will be some changes in the arrangements for supplying NHS glasses free or at a reduced charge. Ask the optician or the social security office for details, or get leaflet G 11 from the post office.

Free milk and vitamins

The arrangements are again similar to those for prescription charges. Families on supplementary benefit or FIS should automatically receive tokens entitling them to a pint of milk a day for an expectant mother and each child under five and vitamin tablets (for a mother) or drops (for a child). Those who do not qualify under the supplementary benefit or FIS 'passport' can claim on grounds of low income, using the form attached to leaflet MV 11, obtainable from a post office or social security office. The income limits are a little higher than for free prescriptions, but the same capital limit applies. Anyone successfully claiming free milk should therefore be sent an exemption certificate for prescription charges. Similarly, anyone awarded free prescriptions on low-income grounds and who appears to be entitled to free milk and vitamins too is (or should be) asked if they wish to claim them.

Free school meals

Local authorities are obliged to provide school meals without charge to children whose parents are on supplementary benefit or FIS, though the 'meal' may be no more than a snack. They *may* also supply free meals to families with a low income but not on supplementary benefit or FIS. The education office should provide details of local arrangements regarding free meals and other education benefits, such as school uniform grants and maintenance allowances for over-16s staying on at school.

REFERENCES

1. Conditions of Entitlement Regs. 9(2)(*a*).
2. Resources Regs. 10(1)(*c*).
3. Conditions of Entitlement Regs. 9(1)(*a*).
4. Resources Regs. 9(2)(*d*).
5. Conditions of Entitlement Regs. 9(1)(*a*).
6. *S Manual*, para. 6425.
7. Resources Regs. 9(2)(*d*).
8. Conditions of Entitlement Regs. 9(2)(*b*).
9. Housing Benefits Regs. 26.
10. Housing Benefits Regs. 29–31.
11. Family Income Supplements Act 1970, s. 1.
12. Family Income Supplements (General) Regs. 1980, 5.
13. Family Income Supplements Act 1970, s. 2(1) and 3(1); Family Income Supplements (Computation) Regs. 1984, 2.
14. Family Income Supplements (General) Regs. 1980, 2(5).
15. Family Income Supplements Act 1970, s. 3(1); Family Income Supplements (Computation) Regs. 1984, 3.
16. Family Income Supplements (Claims and Payments) Regs. 1980, 2(1).
17. Family Income Supplements Act 1970, s. 6(3).

Chapter 16

Appeals

A claimant who is dissatisfied with a decision made by an adjudication officer about his or her entitlement to supplementary benefit can take a number of steps to get the decision altered. The adjudication officer can be asked to reconsider it. There is a right of appeal against the original decision, or any new decision the adjudication officer may make, to an independent tribunal. If that fails, there may be a further right of appeal to a Social Security Commissioner. The purpose of this chapter is to explain what happens at each of these stages in the appeal process.

Review by the Adjudication Officer

Before taking any formal steps to get a decision changed, it is important to understand exactly what the adjudication officer decided and why. As explained on pages 41–2, the claimant has a right to receive written notification of the decision, a brief notice of assessment if the decision was about entitlement (or non-entitlement) to weekly payments, and a statement of reasons if requested within 28 days. A fuller explanation of the assessment will also be supplied on form A 124 if requested.

If the decision looks wrong, the adjudication officer can be asked to reconsider it, or the claimant can appeal to a tribunal straight away, which will also mean that the case is reconsidered by an adjudication officer before it reaches the tribunal. It may save trouble and cause less resentment if the matter can be sorted out without an appeal. On the other hand, the case may be looked at more carefully if an appeal has already been lodged. Far more decisions are revised in the claimants' favour by an adjudication officer after an appeal has been lodged than by the appeal tribunals themselves.

A request for revision of the decision is likely to carry more weight if made through an organization which is knowledgeable on social security matters – e.g. a trade union, claimants' union, social work agency, advice bureau or the local branch of the Child Poverty Action Group –

or through an individual such as an MP, local councillor, clergyman or solicitor (if a question of law is involved, a local law centre is likely to be particularly helpful). Whether the request is made by the claimant himself or by somebody else, it is best to put it in writing – and keep a copy. If the matter is urgent, it may save time to telephone for an appointment at the local social security office (calling without an appointment is generally to be avoided if possible).

There are limits to the adjudication officer's power to 'review' a decision and substitute a different one. He can do so in three types of situation:

(a) *Change of circumstances.* If there has been a relevant change of circumstances since the decision was made, the decision can be reviewed to take account of the change – but, if a new decision results, it will take effect only from the date of the change of circumstances, and the original decision will stand for the period up to that date unless there are other grounds for altering it. The adjudication officer's power to review on a change of circumstances applies not only to his own decision or that of another adjudication officer but also to a decision made by an appeal tribunal or a Commissioner.

(b) *Wrong facts.* An adjudication officer can review a decision if satisfied that it was 'given in ignorance of, or was based on a mistake as to, some material fact'. This power, too, can be used to revise the decision of an appeal tribunal or a Commissioner; but in the case of a Commissioner's decision, there must be new evidence to justify the review.[1]

(c) *Error of law.* An adjudication officer can review a decision (but not a decision of an appeal tribunal or a Commissioner) on the ground that it was 'erroneous in point of law'.[2] The review can result from new arguments put forward by or on behalf of the claimant. It can also result from a Commissioner's decision in another case which shows that the regulations have been misinterpreted, possibly in large numbers of cases.

The power to review decisions cannot create rights going back more than a year. A decision about entitlement to a single payment will not be revised in the claimant's favour if the original claim was made more than 52 weeks before the request for a review (or the review itself if there was no request). Similarly, an increase in the weekly supplementary benefit, or payment of benefit previously refused altogether, cannot be backdated more than 52 weeks from the date of the request or of the review.[3]

Subject to the 52-week limit, a revised decision in the claimant's favour will normally lead to the payment of arrears; but there are some exceptions. If supplementary benefit entitlement was interrupted or ceased during the 52-week period, arrears are not paid for the period prior to the interruption if the underpayment was due to the claimant's failure to report a material fact or change of circumstances or the amount involved is £5 or less.[4]

If the adjudication officer cannot or will not make a new decision which is acceptable to the claimant, the next stage is to consider appealing to a tribunal. The procedure is explained on page 279.

The Tribunal

Until April 1984, the tribunals dealing with supplementary benefit appeals were separate from those dealing with national insurance and other social security appeals. The two systems were then amalgamated to form the present social security appeal tribunals, which deal with the whole range of social security benefits, including supplementary benefit and FIS (but not housing benefit – see page 109). Judge J. Byrt became the first President of Social Security Appeal Tribunals, with responsibility for appointment and training of tribunal members. In January 1985, the Lord Chancellor's office took over responsibility for the administration of the tribunal system from the Department of Health and Social Security. The old supplementary benefit tribunals were often criticized as being under the thumb of the DHSS. These changes should help to make the new tribunals genuinely independent.

Each large city in Great Britain has at least one social security appeal tribunal, but people living in small towns or rural areas may have to travel some distance to a tribunal hearing (travelling expenses are paid – see page 286). An appeal is normally heard by three members of the tribunal – the chairman and two others. The chairman is nominated by the President and is usually drawn from a panel of chairmen appointed by the Lord Chancellor (in Scotland by the Lord President of the Court of Session); or he may be one of a small number of full-time tribunal chairmen, also appointed by the Lord Chancellor. Very exceptionally the President may himself act as chairman of a tribunal. There has been a gradual move towards the appointment of lawyers as tribunal chairmen, and within a few years this will be the general rule. At present, chairmen with no legal qualification who were appointed before April 1984 are allowed to remain in office, though they are only allowed to hear supplementary benefit and FIS appeals, not national insurance appeals. As their appointments expire, they will be replaced by lawyers, and this process must be completed by April 1989 at the latest.[5]

There have also been changes in the way the other two members of the tribunal are selected. In the past, one of them was a 'work-people's representative' drawn from a panel whose names were put forward by the trades councils and the Scottish TUC. In future, both of them will be drawn from a single panel for each area consisting of 'persons appearing to the President to háve knowledge or experience of conditions in the area and to be representative of persons living or working in the area'. Before appointing people to the panel, the President must 'take into consideration any recommendations from such organizations or persons as he considers appropriate'.[6] Trades councils will therefore no doubt continue to play an important part in nominating panel members, but there will not automatically be a trade union representative on the tribunal.

The tribunal members, other than the chairmen, serve on a rota basis. So far as practicable, at least one member of the tribunal must be of the same sex as the claimant. Since the tribunal will usually hear appeals by claimants of both sexes at one sitting, and most chairmen are men, compliance with this rule normally means that one of the other members must be a woman. Subject to this requirement, however, the members are to be summoned in turn.[7] There should, therefore, be no question of 'awkward' members being passed over when their turn comes round, as was sometimes alleged to have happened in the past.

The duties of the President, some of which are delegated to seven 'regional chairmen', include arranging such meetings and training of tribunal chairmen and members as he considers appropriate, and ensuring that suitable 'works of reference relating to social security law' are available for their use.[8]

The Powers of the Tribunal

Anyone claiming or receiving supplementary benefit can appeal to the tribunal against any decision ('determination', to use the legal term) made by an adjudication officer regarding his claim. There is also a right of appeal against a decision that benefit has been overpaid and is recoverable (see page 45).[9] The vast majority of decisions made under the Supplementary Benefits Act and regulations can be the subject of an appeal – not only the amount of benefit, if any, to which a person is entitled, but also decisions on such questions as whether a claimant must be available for employment and whether payments should be made direct to the electricity board. Claims for single payments (see Chapter 7) are a particularly fruitful source of appeals. The only decisions against which there is no appeal to the tribunal are those made on behalf of the Secretary of State, not by an adjudication officer – for example, whether a single payment should be made to the supplier rather than to the claimant, whether emergency relief should continue for more than fourteen days, or whether a person is entitled to a payment for fares to the social security office. In addition to the right of appeal against an adjudication officer's decision, there is also a right of appeal against his refusal to review an earlier decision (see pages 274–5).[10] This is important where a claimant feels that a decision which may have been right when it was made should now be changed. It also provides a way of reopening a question when the time limit for an appeal has expired.

An adjudication officer can refer a claim, or a question arising in connection with a claim, to an appeal tribunal for decision instead of deciding it himself,[11] but this power, introduced in 1984, is likely to be used very rarely.

In deciding an appeal, the tribunal is free to make any decision that would have been within the powers of the adjudication officer.[12] As well as questions of fact, the tribunal may have to deal with both points of law and matters of judgement or discretion where, for example, the regulations leave it to the adjudication officer to decide what is 'reasonable'. The tribunal is bound by the law as laid down in the Acts and regulations or in decisions of the Commissioners or the courts; but it is not obliged to follow the guidance issued by the Chief Adjudication Officer in the *S Manual* (see page 25), which is addressed to adjudication officers, not to tribunals. On the contrary, the tribunal has a duty to apply its own judgement to the facts of the case, in the light of the provisions of the law, even if this results in a decision which is at variance with normal practice and may cause embarrassment or inconvenience to the Department of Health and Social Security.

How to Appeal

An appeal must be made in writing to a local social security or unemployment benefit office, normally within 28 days of the date when the decision was given to the claimant. If the claimant asks the adjudication officer for a statement of reasons for the decision within 28 days (see page 42), the 28 days for appealing run from the date when the statement of reasons was given.[13] Asking for a statement of reasons, therefore, does not involve any risk of being out of time for an appeal. If an appeal is outside the 28-day limit, the reasons for the delay should be explained fully. The appeal can still be heard if the chairman of the tribunal agrees that the time limit should be extended 'for special reasons'.[14]

A leaflet, *How to appeal* (NI 246), obtainable from the social security office, has a 'notice of appeal' form attached to it. At the top of the form are the words 'I wish to appeal to the Appeal Tribunal because . . .', followed by a large space in which to write the grounds of the appeal. At the bottom is a space to enter the name and address of anyone who is going to advise the claimant or speak for him or her at the appeal hearing, so that details of the appeal and the time and place of the hearing can be sent to that person as well as to the claimant. But there is no need to obtain the leaflet or to use an official form. A short letter to the manager of the local social security office will do just as well. It should state clearly what the appeal is about: e.g. 'I wish to appeal against the decision that I am not entitled to supplementary benefit' or 'I wish to appeal against the refusal of a single payment for an overcoat' or 'I wish to appeal against the amount of the payment awarded to me for the cost of my husband's funeral'. The grounds for making the appeal must be stated, briefly at least,[15] and the name and address of anyone to whom copies of the papers are to be sent should be given, as on the official form.

There is no need at that stage to give a more detailed explanation of the grounds of the appeal, and some people will prefer to do this at the hearing rather than attempt to put it in writing. However, there are some advantages in setting out the arguments in the notice of appeal, since it may increase the chances of a more favourable decision being made by the adjudication officer without the need for an appeal hearing. Besides, if the claimant has nobody to help in presenting the case at the hearing, it may be easier to put it in writing beforehand than to explain it orally in the presence of the tribunal. It is a matter of judgement and personal preference, therefore, whether to confine the notice of appeal to the bare essentials or to go into detail. Whichever is done, it is important that all the points in dispute should be mentioned, because the tribunal can only make a decision on questions which are the subject of the appeal. If other matters are raised in the course of the appeal hearing, the most that the tribunal can do is to suggest that they should be looked into after the hearing.

It often takes two months or more after the appeal is lodged before it comes before the tribunal. If serious hardship would be caused by such a delay, it is worth adding to the notice of appeal 'Will you please arrange for this appeal to be heard as soon as possible', together with a brief explanation of the reasons for the request. It should not be assumed that such a request will be complied with but, if the tribunal clerk is convinced that the urgency is genuine, he will generally try to fit the case in at an early hearing.

Before the Hearing

During the interval between the lodging of an appeal and the tribunal hearing, the disputed decision is re-examined to see whether there are grounds for reviewing it and substituting a new decision without recourse to the tribunal, either because it was based on a mistake as to law or fact or it was made in ignorance of a material fact (see page 275). This may involve a visit to the claimant if there are points which need clarification. If a new decision is made, covering all the points of the appeal, the claimant is told that the appeal will not be sent for hearing by the tribunal. If the amount of weekly benefit is involved, details are given of how it was calculated under both the original decision and the revised decision. The claimant is told that, if still dissatisfied, he or she has a fresh right of appeal against the new decision. The same procedure is followed if the new decision covers only some of the points mentioned in the appeal, but in that case the original appeal will still go forward to the tribunal for their decision on the remaining points.

At least ten days' notice of the hearing should be given. If less than ten days' notice has been given, the tribunal cannot hear the appeal without the claimant's consent.[16] The letter from the tribunal clerk giving the time and place of the hearing is accompanied by a form (AT 2) giving the following particulars:

(a) The decision against which the claimant is appealing.
(b) References to relevant provisions of the Acts and regulations

and relevant Commissioners' decisions, with a statement that they can be seen at the local social security office.

(c) The claimant's grounds of appeal, copied from the appeal form or letter.

(d) The adjudication officer's submission, consisting of a statement of the facts of the case and an explanation of the reasons for the decision.

Attached to form A T 2 are a 'statement of assessment' showing how the claimant's benefit is calculated (where this is relevant) and copies of other documents such as claim forms, reports and correspondence having a bearing on the appeal. Form A T 2 with the same attachments is supplied to each member of the tribunal.

It is advisable to work out in detail, as soon as possible after receiving form A T 2, the arguments to be presented to the tribunal. This not only ensures that important points are not overlooked; it also compels the claimant or his or her representative to think about the kinds of evidence needed to support their case. The form should be studied with care, the following points being particularly noted:

(a) Check that the adjudication officer's decision is correctly stated in the first section of the form (if the appeal is against more than one decision, each decision should be set out, normally on a separate form).

(b) If possible, check any references to the law, including Commissioners' decisions (telephone the social security office for an appointment to see the regulations and published decisions).

(c) Use the earlier chapters of this book to identify any other relevant regulations or Commissioners' decisions, which can also be looked up at the social security office (with the exception of unreported decisions – see page 27).

(d) Check the adjudication officer's submission for any factual errors or omissions. If there is any dispute as to the facts, consider what evidence can be produced to support the claimant's case.

The letter giving notice of the hearing is also accompanied by a tear-off form asking whether the claimant will be present or represented at the hearing. If the claimant does not intend to be present, the form asks why not and whether he or she could come on a different day. Postponement of the hearing to a more convenient day will usually be granted if there are good reasons why the claimant cannot attend, or if more time is needed to arrange for a representative to put the case to the tribunal. If the claimant cannot attend or be represented but wants a quick decision, it is advisable to attach a written statement to the form, setting out the facts and arguments in favour of the appeal and refuting, where possible, the arguments of the adjudication officer. This statement will be put before the tribunal at the hearing.

Help with Appeals

The appeal machinery has been kept relatively informal, since most claimants have little or no help in preparing their case and presenting it to the tribunal. Nobody should be afraid of appealing simply because they have nobody to help or advise them. The tribunals are used to dealing with claimants who have no expert knowledge and who are nervous and inarticulate. Indeed, the nervous and inarticulate claimant may well get a more sympathetic hearing.

Nevertheless, if expert advice and help are available, it generally pays to make use of them. The legal-aid scheme does not cover representation by a solicitor at a tribunal hearing, but it is possible to get legal advice and assistance before, after or even during the hearing either free or at low cost under the 'green form' scheme. Free advice and assistance up to the value of £50 (enough to pay for two hours' free advice) are available to anybody receiving supplementary benefit or FIS whose savings do not exceed certain limits. The maximum savings allowed are £765 for a single person, £965 for a person with one dependant, £1,085 with two dependants, plus £60 for each additional dependant (e.g. a man with a wife and three children could have savings of £1,205 and still get free advice and assistance from a solicitor). A person not receiving supplementary benefit or FIS but whose income and savings are small can also qualify for help but may have to pay at least part of the cost if his or her income is above a certain level. Fuller details of the scheme and a list of local solicitors who operate it can be obtained from a Citizens' Advice Bureau.

As the 'green form' scheme does not cover representation at the tribunal hearing, the claimant will usually have to present his or her case to the tribunal or get somebody other than a solicitor to do so. Some solicitors are, however, prepared to attend the hearing and speak on the claimant's behalf without charging for this service, especially if the case involves difficult legal questions. In particular, a number of law centres have been set up in London and other cities with the object of providing free legal services to people who would not normally go to a solicitor. These centres are manned by solicitors who specialize in social security, housing and other matters of concern to people with low incomes, and are therefore more likely than the average solicitor's office to be able to provide sound advice and practical help on such questions.

In most supplementary benefit appeals, the issues involved are only partly matters of law. Moreover, even where legal questions arise, many solicitors have less knowledge and experience of this branch of the law than people who, though not legally qualified, have taken a special interest in it. It may be best, therefore, to get advice and help from somebody with practical experience of how the social security system works and, if possible, experience of representing claimants at tribunal hearings. A representative does not have to be legally qualified and in practice most are not. The local Citizens Advice Bureau will usually know what are the best local sources of help of this kind and may even be able to provide such help. Many local authorities now employ welfare rights officers, usually attached to the social services department, who are generally well informed and may be able to help. Trade-union members may find that their union can help. Other sources of help may include a local advice centre, claimants' union or branch of the Child Poverty Action Group. Some of these bodies may be able to advise on whether there are grounds for an appeal, on the wording of the appeal and on the presentation of the case at the hearing, even if they cannot provide somebody to attend the hearing and represent the claimant.

The Tribunal Hearing

The tribunal must hold an oral hearing,[17] which is open to the public unless either the claimant asks for a private hearing or the chairman of the tribunal decides that intimate personal or financial circumstances may have to be disclosed (which will usually be the case) or that 'considerations of public security' are involved, in which case the hearing takes place in private.[18] At a private hearing, no member of the public, including the press, is admitted, with the exceptions noted below. Those allowed to attend a private hearing are:

(a) The members of the tribunal. If one of the three members is missing, the hearing can still go on provided that the chairman is present and that the claimant gives his or her consent.[19] In case of disagreement, when one member is missing, the chairman has a casting vote.[20]

(b) The tribunal clerk who, although appointed by the President to

283

serve the particular tribunal, is an official temporarily seconded by the Department of Health and Social Security for this purpose. The clerk is responsible for arranging tribunal hearings, distributing papers (including form A T 2), paying expenses, and notifying the claimant of the tribunal's decision.

(c) The claimant – but the hearing may, and frequently does, take place in the claimant's absence.[21]

(d) A person accompanying or representing the claimant. The claimant's representative may attend the hearing and speak on the claimant's behalf even if the claimant is not present.[22]

(e) Anyone who, in the chairman's opinion, is 'a person interested in the decision' (for example, the claimant's wife or husband, or a person with whom the claimant is alleged to be living as husband and wife).

(f) The adjudication officer or his representative, known as the 'presenting officer'.

(g) A person representing the Secretary of State. Any D H S S official could attend a hearing as the Secretary of State's representative, but this right is not usually exercised.

(h) The President and any full-time tribunal chairman.

(i) Anyone undergoing training as a tribunal chairman, member or clerk, or as an adjudication officer or an 'adjudicating medical practitioner' under the industrial injuries scheme.

(j) A member of the Council on Tribunals or the Scottish Committee of the Council.

(k) Anyone else – but only with the leave of the chairman and the consent of anyone in categories (c) to (g) who is actually present.[23]

People in categories (c) to (g) have the right not only to be present but to address the tribunal, to give evidence, to call witnesses and to put questions to any witness.[24] The claimant's representative, if any, has the same rights as the claimant.[25]

In most cases, the only people present at the hearing, apart from the claimant, are the tribunal members, the clerk and the presenting officer. In about half of all cases, the claimant is not present, and only a small minority of absent claimants send somebody to represent them. Yet the statistics show that claimants who attend are far more likely to succeed than those who do not, while representation seems to have an even more marked effect on the success rate than the presence of the claimant. In 1983, only 7 per cent of claimants who neither attended nor were represented won their appeals, while the success rate for those who attended alone was 21 per cent and for those accompanied and/or represented by 'social workers', whether they themselves attended the hearing or not, was as high as 47 per cent.

The precise way in which the hearing is to be conducted is left for the chairman to decide.[26] Both sides must have ample opportunity for speaking and putting questions to each other and to any witnesses. Each of the tribunal members should also have an opportunity of asking questions at each stage in the proceedings. The strict rules of evidence applied in court proceedings do not apply to tribunals, and evidence is not normally given on oath. Hearsay evidence can be admitted, provided that the tribunal conscientiously weighs up its value and that the other side has a fair opportunity of commenting on or contradicting it.[27] It 'should not normally prevail against evidence given orally to the tribunal by the person having first-hand knowledge of the matter'.[28] But a statement by the presenting officer unsupported by evidence is not a sufficient basis for a finding of fact by the tribunal.[29] It is open to the tribunal to consider evidence which was not available to the adjudication officer when the original decision was made,[30] or events which occurred after the decision but which have a bearing on the correctness of the decision.[31] If the subject of the appeal is a claim for a single payment, however, the tribunal must decide whether the need existed at the date of the claim;[32] the fact that it may have ceased to exist or have been satisfied by other means *after* the date of the claim is irrelevant, except perhaps as evidence that there was no real need at the date of the claim.

The tribunal can decide to adjourn the hearing at any time, either of its own accord or at the request of either of the parties.[33] An adjournment may be necessary, for example, if new evidence is presented and the other side needs time to consider it, or if the facts are in dispute and the tribunal feels that further evidence is required. From the claimant's point of view, the disadvantage of requesting an adjournment is that there will probably be a delay of several weeks before the resumed hearing. Moreover, the regulations require that, if one or more members of the tribunal at the resumed hearing were not present at the original hearing, there must be a complete rehearing of the case.[34] These facts should be borne in mind in considering whether an adjournment would be in the claimant's interests.

When the chairman is satisfied that all the relevant facts have been elicited, the claimant, anyone representing or accompanying the claimant, the presenting officer and any members of the public who are present are asked to withdraw. The clerk remains with the tribunal while they discuss the evidence and arrive at their decision (this stage of the proceedings is known as the tribunal's 'deliberations'). If the President, a full-time chairman or a member of the Council on Tribunals or its Scottish Committee is present, they have a right to remain during the deliberations. Anyone else who has been allowed to attend the hearing for training or other purposes can remain if the tribunal agrees and neither the claimant (or representative) nor the presenting officer objects.[35] The claimant and/or representative normally depart at this point and the claimant is informed of the tribunal's decision by post several days later. The tribunal may, but seldom does, ask the claimant to remain outside the room during the deliberations, to be told the result of the appeal immediately (a full notification of the decision is still sent through the post in due course). The claimant may also be asked to remain in case any points arise during the deliberations which the tribunal needs to pursue further in the presence of the parties.

One of the tribunal clerk's responsibilities is to pay the travelling expenses of the claimant and/or a person accompanying the claimant and any witnesses. If a person has to take time off work to attend an appeal hearing, compensation for loss of earnings is also paid, up to a limit of £21 a day and subsistence expenses can be paid if a lengthy absence from home (2½ hours or more) is involved. Payment is subject to the discretion of the Secretary of State and an unreasonable claim – for example, if the claimant were accompanied by a large number of friends who were not appearing as representatives or witnesses – would presumably not be met. Travelling expenses can, however, be paid even for representatives and witnesses who come from a considerable distance.[36] If the claimant's fares are likely to be more than £2 and he cannot wait until the hearing for a refund, the form sent to him with the notification of the time and place of the hearing explains how to request an advance payment. The expenses of representatives who are doing this as part of their paid work are not covered by these arrangements; they are expected to recover any expenses from their employers.

After the Hearing

The tribunal's decision must be sent to the claimant 'as soon as may be practicable',[37] which usually means a week or more after the hearing. The chairman of the tribunal is responsible for recording the decision, the reasons for it and the tribunal's findings on material questions of fact. If the decision was not unanimous, the reasons given by the dissenting member for his disagreement must be included in the chairman's record.[38] All these elements are included in the copy sent to the claimant. The local social security office is informed of the decision at the same time and should take any necessary action to implement it without delay. In rare cases where the adjudication officer applies for leave to appeal to a Commissioner on a point of law against the tribunal's decision, payment of benefit under that decision can be suspended until the application and (if the application succeeds) the appeal to the Commissioner has been decided.[39] The claimant may be able to claim urgent need payments during the period of suspension (see page 191).

If the claimant is dissatisfied with the tribunal's decision and wishes to pursue the matter further, several courses of action may be available. The first is to accept the tribunal's decision and wait until there is a relevant change of circumstances, when a new claim can be made, followed if necessary by a new appeal to the tribunal.

A second possibility of getting the tribunal's decision revised arises where the decision was 'given in ignorance of, or was based on a mistake as to, some material fact'. In these circumstances an adjudication officer can make a new decision in place of that of the tribunal (see page 275).

A third possible course of action is to apply for the tribunal's decision to be set aside so that the appeal can be heard again. The grounds on which this can be done are either that a document relating to the appeal was not received at the appropriate time by the claimant, the claimant's representative or the tribunal, or that the claimant or his or her representative was not present at the hearing. The application must be made in writing and must normally reach the tribunal clerk or the social security office within 28 days of the notification of the tribunal's decision. It is for the tribunal to decide whether, in fairness, the decision should be set aside, after considering any representations by the adjudication officer.[40] It is worth considering an application if, for example, the appeal papers were not sent to the claimant's representative, or relevant documents were not attached to form AT 2 when notice of the hearing was given, or if unforeseen circumstances prevented the claimant from being present or represented at the hearing.

Finally, if there are grounds for arguing that the tribunal's decision or the way in which it was arrived at or recorded is wrong in law, there is a further right of appeal to a Social Security Commissioner.[41]

Appeals to a Commissioner

Either the claimant or the adjudication officer may appeal to a Social Security Commissioner against the tribunal's decision,[42] but before they can do so they must be granted leave to appeal.[43] Application by the claimant for leave to appeal to a Commissioner can be made in any of the following ways:

(a) If the tribunal announces its decision at the end of the hearing, an application for leave to appeal can be made orally then and there to the tribunal chairman, whose decision will be sent with the tribunal's decision on the appeal.

(b) A written application to the tribunal chairman can be sent to the social security office within six weeks of the tribunal's decision being sent to the claimant.

(c) A written application to the Commissioner can be made within six weeks of a refusal of leave by the tribunal chairman being sent to the claimant or, if no application is made to the chairman, within three months of the tribunal's decision being sent; but these time limits can be extended by the Commissioner if there are 'special reasons', which should be stated in the application.[44]

A form to use for a written application under (b) or (c) can be obtained from the social security office. The point of law on which the tribunal is alleged to have erred must be stated on the form. Claimants should if possible get legal advice at this stage under the 'green form' scheme (see page 282).

The most obvious way in which the tribunal's decision may be wrong in law is that it is not in accordance with the provisions of the Act or the regulations, or is contrary to the principles laid down in previous decisions of the Commissioners or the courts. But a decision can also be wrong in law because of the way in which it was reached; for example, because there was no evidence to support it, or the tribunal hearing was not conducted fairly. Probably the most frequent error, however – though the move to legally qualified chairmen may make it less common in future – is failure to give adequate reasons for the tribunal's decision. It should be clear, from the record of the decision sent to the claimant, on what evidence and legal provisions the decision was based and why evidence in favour of the claimant's appeal was rejected. If the claimant is left in doubt as to how and why the tribunal decided as it did, this may be a sufficient ground for an appeal to a Commissioner.

If a written application is made to the tribunal chairman for leave to appeal to a Commissioner, the chairman will deal with the application without an oral hearing – or it can be dealt with by another tribunal chairman if this is necessary on practical grounds or to avoid delay.[45] If the application for leave is made to the Commissioner, he may hold an oral hearing and he must do so if requested by either party unless he is satisfied that the application can properly be decided without a hearing.[46] He may also decide to treat the application as if it were the actual appeal and deal with it in one stage instead of two, provided that both parties agree.[47] If this does not happen, the claimant has three months from the date when leave is given to make the appeal, on a form supplied for the purpose.[48] Again, the Commissioner may hold an oral hearing if asked to do so or if he considers it desirable, but he is not obliged to do so if he thinks the matter can be dealt with satisfactorily without a hearing.[49]

If the adjudication officer wishes to comment in writing on either an application to the Commissioner for leave to appeal or the appeal itself, he has four weeks to do so, and the claimant has another six weeks in which to make any written comments in reply. The Commissioner may also ask either side to submit written observations on any point before he decides the appeal, whether by an oral hearing or otherwise.[50]

If the Commissioner decides that the tribunal's decision was wrong in law, he can either substitute his own decision for that of the tribunal or send the appeal to be heard by another tribunal, with any directions for dealing with it.[51] If there are questions of fact to be resolved, the Commissioner has no option but to refer the case to another tribunal, since he cannot himself take evidence on such questions.

An oral hearing before the Commissioner is open to the public unless the Commissioner decides that intimate personal or financial circumstances may have to be disclosed or that considerations of public security are involved (unlike a tribunal hearing, the claimant has no right to insist on privacy).[52] Even if there is no public hearing, the Commissioner's decision may be published and, although claimants are not mentioned by name in published decisions, there is a possibility that they will be recognized from the details given of their circumstances. Commissioners' decisions, however, are not widely read and are rarely reported in the press.

Appealing to a Commissioner is a lengthy process. At best it will take several months to get a decision – and if the appeal succeeds, the most likely decision is that the case must be heard by another tribunal, which means another month or two of delay. Before deciding on an appeal to a Commissioner, therefore, it is usually worth considering the alternatives mentioned on page 287.

Appealing against a Commissioner's Decision

Anyone contemplating an appeal to the Appeal Court (or the Court of Session in Scotland) against a Commissioner's decision should first obtain legal advice. The appeal must be on a point of law and leave to appeal must be obtained either from the Commissioner or, if he refuses leave, from the Court.[53] Legal aid is available for an appeal to the Court.

REFERENCES

1. Social Security Act 1975, s. 104(1).
2. Social Security Act 1975, s. 104(1A); Adjudication Regs. 89(1).
3. Adjudication Regs. 87(1) and 89(2).
4. Adjudication Regs. 87(1)(c).
5. Adjudication Regs. 93.
6. Social Security Act 1975, s. 97(2A) and schedule 10, para. 1(2) and (2A).
7. Social Security Act 1975, schedule 10, para. 1(7) and (8).
8. Social Security Act 1975, schedule 10, para. 1D.
9. Adjudication Regs. 71(1).
10. Adjudication Regs., schedule 4, para. 7.
11. Adjudication Regs. 67(2)(b).
12. Adjudication Regs. 71(2).
13. Adjudication Regs., schedule 2, para. 4.
14. Adjudication Regs. 3(3).
15. Adjudication Regs. 3(4).
16. Adjudication Regs. 4(2).
17. Adjudication Regs. 18(1).
18. Adjudication Regs. 4(4).
19. Adjudication Regs. 18(2).
20. Adjudication Regs. 19(1).
21. Adjudication Regs. 4(3).
22. Adjudication Regs. 2(1)(b).
23. Adjudication Regs. 2(3), 4(5) and (6).
24. Adjudication Regs. 4(8).
25. Adjudication Regs. 2(1)(b).
26. Adjudication Regs. 2(1)(a).
27. Miller (T.A.) Ltd v. Minister of Housing and Local Government [1968] 1 W.L.R. 992; CSB 189/81; R(SB) 5/82.
28. CSB 531/83.
29. CSB 635/82.
30. R(SB) 9/81.
31. R(SB) 1/82.
32. R(SB) 26/83.

33. Adjudication Regs. 5(2).
34. Adjudication Regs. 18(3).
35. Adjudication Regs. 2(2).
36. Social Security Act 1975, schedule 10, para. 3(1)(b).
37. Adjudication Regs. 19(3).
38. Adjudication Regs. 19(2).
39. Determination of Questions Regs. 8(1).
40. Adjudication Regs. 10 and schedule 2, para. 11.
41. Social Security Act 1975, s. 101(1); Adjudication Regs. 65 and schedule 4, para. 2.
42. Adjudication Regs., schedule 4, para. 3.
43. Adjudication Regs., schedule 4, para. 2.
44. Adjudication Regs. 3(3); 20(1) and (3); 25(1).
45. Adjudication Regs. 20(4).
46. Adjudication Regs. 26(1) and (2).
47. Adjudication Regs. 25(4).
48. Social Security Act 1975, s. 101(5); Social Security Act 1980, s. 15(3).
49. Adjudication Regs. 26(1) and (2).
50. Adjudication Regs. 29.
51. Adjudication Regs. 27.
52. Adjudication Regs. 4(4).
53. Social Security Act 1980, s. 14(1) and (2).

Appendix 1

Examples of Supplementary Benefit Assessments

These examples illustrate some of the more common types of case. To understand the calculations, it may be necessary to refer to the sections of the guide in which particular points are explained in detail. The relevant page numbers are shown on the right-hand side. The amounts allowed for 'normal requirements' are shown in Appendix 2.

Example A

The A. family consists of Mr and Mrs A. and their three children – Harold (19) who has left school, Joan (15) and Eric (13). They live in a centrally heated council house, paying rent and rates (including water charges) of £16 a week. Mr A. is drawing sickness benefit of £44.05 a week. He and his wife have savings of £900, which are disregarded together with any income derived from them (see page 130).

			See page
Normal requirements			
Mr and Mrs A.		£45.55 ⎫	
Joan		14.35 ⎬	298
Eric		14.35 ⎭	
Additional requirements			
Central heating (five rooms)		4.20	69
Total requirements		78.45	
Resources			
Sickness benefit	£44.05		124
Child benefit (2 × £6.85)	13.70		123–4
		57.75	
Supplementary allowance		£20.70	
Housing benefit (certificated)			
Rent and rates		£16.00	99
Less deductions for non-dependant (Harold)		8.80	105
Rent and rate rebates		£7.20	

292

Example B

Mrs B. is a widow aged 45 with a daughter, Judith (17), at school, for whom she receives an education maintenance allowance of £7.50. She gets a widowed mother's allowance of £43.45 a week and is repaying a mortgage on her house at the rate of £18 a week, £12 of which represents interest. Her father pays her £6 a week so that she can keep up the capital repayments. Mrs B. works part-time, earning £18 per week net (after deducting £2 for fares to work and 60p for lunches – see page 120). She has been on supplementary benefit for more than a year and therefore qualifies for the long-term rate. She is diabetic and needs a special diet.

			See page
Normal requirements			
Mrs B.		£35.70 ⎱	298
Judith		17.30 ⎰	
Housing requirements			
Mortgage interest	£12.00		86
Water charges	1.50		91–2
Maintenance and insurance	1.80		91
	———	15.30	
Additional requirements			
Special diet	3.60		72
Less part of long-term rate available to meet additional requirements	1.00		66–7
	———	2.60	
		———	
		70.90	
Total requirements			
Resources			
Widowed mother's allowance	43.45		124
Child benefit	6.85		123–4
Earnings (£18 *less* £11 disregarded)	7.00		120
	———	57.30	
Supplementary allowance		£13.60	

Note: Both the education maintenance allowance and the allowance from Mrs B.'s father are disregarded. See page 118 (item 38) and page 128.

Housing benefit (certificated)		
Rate rebate (covering the whole of the rates)	£7.00	99

Example C

David C. (16) pays his parents £10 a week for board and lodging. He is unemployed but has not paid enough insurance contributions to qualify for unemployment benefit.

Normal requirements		*See page*
Non-householder rate	£17.30	58 and 298
Resources	Nil	
	———	
Supplementary allowance	£17.30	

Example D

Miss Mary D. (80) lives in a guest-house, paying £50 a week for full board and lodging. She has a non-contributory retirement pension of £21.50 a week and an allowance of £20 a week from her brother, part of which is intended to help with the board and lodging charge. The 'local limit' for board and lodging charges is £31, increased by £16.15 for a pensioner.

Normal requirements			*See page*
Board and lodging			
(maximum: £31 + £16.15)	£47.15		61
Personal expenses allowance	10.30		60
	———		
Total requirements	57.45		
Resources			
Retirement pension	£21.50		124
Allowance from brother (£20 less £4 disregard and £2.85 needed to cover the excess board and lodging charge)	13.15		128
	———		
		34.65	
		———	
Supplementary pension		£22.80	

Example E

Edward E. has been on strike for two weeks. His wife has a part-time job, earning £16.20 a week net. They have three children, aged 5, 7 and 8, and pay £15.96 rent and rates. Their home is centrally heated. The union provides strike pay of £10 a week.

			See page
Normal requirements (wife and children only)			
Mrs E.		£22.45	236
Children (3 × £9.60)		28.80	298
Total requirements		51.25	
Resources			
Wife's earnings (£16.20 *less* £4 disregarded)	£12.20		120
Child benefit (3 × £6.85)	20.55		123–4
		32.75	
		18.50	
Trade dispute reduction		16.00	236
Supplementary allowance		£2.50	

Note: Strike pay of up to £16 a week is disregarded (see page 237). No heating addition is allowed (see pages 237–8).

Housing benefit (certificated)		
Rent and rate rebates (covering the whole of the rent and rates, including water charges)	£15.96	100–101

Example F

Mark F. is a student sharing a flat with two friends. They live as one household and are jointly responsible for the rent of £36 a week, inclusive of rates, and the extra charge of £10 a week made by the landlord for heating and hot water. Mark spends £8.50 a week on fares to visit his father in hospital. He is looking for work in the summer vacation (see page 256) but not entitled to unemployment benefit.

		See page
Normal requirements		
Non-householder rate	£22.45	
One-third of £5.60 (difference between £22.45 for a non-householder and £28.05 for a householder)	1.87	56–7
	———	
	£24.32	
Additional requirements		
Hospital visiting	8.50	80–81
	———	
Total requirements	32.82	
	———	
Resources	Nil	
	———	
Supplementary allowance	£32.82	
	———	
Housing benefit (certificated)		
One-third of rent and rates	12.00	99
One-third of amount by which landlord's charge for heating and hot water exceeds £7 (i.e. one-third of £3)	1.00	101
	———	
Rent allowance and rate rebate	£13.00	

Example G (*Housing benefit supplement*)

Sally G. lives in a council flat with her two children, both under 5. Her ex-husband pays her £33 a week. On claiming supplementary benefit she was told her income was £1.60 more than her requirements, but she was given a housing benefit claim form. She claimed housing benefit, which covered the whole of her rent and rates except £4.80 a week.

			See page
Normal requirements			
Sally G.		£28.05 ⎫	298
Children (2 × £9.60)		19.20 ⎭	
Additional requirements			
Heating		2.10	68
		———	
Total requirements		49.35	
Resources			
Child benefit (2 × £6.85)	£13.70	⎫	123–4
One-parent benefit	4.25	⎬	
Maintenance from ex-husband	33.00	⎭	126
	———		
		50.95	
'Excess income'		1.60	
Net housing costs (not covered by housing benefit)		4.80	
		———	
Housing benefit supplement		£3.20	107–8

Supplementary Benefit Scales for 'Normal' Requirements

(from 26 November 1984)

	Ordinary weekly rate	Long-term weekly rate (see note 2)
Husband and wife	£45.55	£57.10
Single householder	28.05	35.70
Non-householder (living in someone else's household and not treated as a boarder):		
Aged 18 or over (see note 3)	22.45	28.55
Aged 16 or 17	17.30	21.90
Child:		
Aged 11–15	£14.35	
Under 11	9.60	

Notes

1. The amounts shown above are for 'normal' requirements only (see Chapter 2). Other amounts can be added for 'additional' requirements (Chapter 3) and housing requirements (Chapter 4) to arrive at the total weekly requirements of the 'assessment unit'.

2. The qualifying conditions for the long-term rates are explained on pages 53–4.

3. The housing requirements of a non-householder aged 21 or over are fixed at a standard amount of £3.30 (see page 59).

4. An automatic addition of 25p a week is allowed for a person aged 80 or over (see page 67).

5. A similar addition of £1.25 is allowed for a blind person aged 16 or over; and a blind non-householder is allowed the householder scale rate (see page 67).

6. The rules for calculating the requirements of boarders and people living in hospitals, homes for the elderly, etc., are explained on pages 59–64 and in Chapter 14.

7. The scale rates are increased annually. The rates shown above are likely to remain in force until 24 November 1985.

Appendix 3

Clothing Price Lists

These price lists, taken from schedule 2 of the Single Payments Regulations, are used in calculating single payments for clothing. The items listed are the only items of clothing for which single payments can be made, except under the 'safety net' provisions of regulation 30. (See pages 162–7.)

Part I. Men's Clothing

Anorak	£22.50
Cap	7.00
Cardigan	11.50
Dressing-gown	17.75
Overcoat	55.00
Pullover	10.00
Pyjamas	9.20
Raincoat	31.00
Shirt	8.50
Shoes	17.00
Slippers	6.00
Socks	1.50
Sports jacket	37.00
Suit	60.00
Trousers	16.00
Underpants:	
Briefs	1.75
Thermal (short)	4.50
Thermal (long)	5.00
Vest:	
Singlet	2.25
Thermal	5.00

Part II. Women's Clothing

Blouse	£9.00
Boots (ankle)	18.00
Brassière	5.00
Briefs	1.40
Cardigan	10.00
Corselette	16.25
Dress:	
Summer weight	15.00
Winter weight	18.50
Dressing-gown	15.00
Hat	5.50
Jumper	9.00
Knickers	2.60
Nightdress:	
Standard length	7.00
Full length	8.60
Overcoat	43.00
Pantie-girdle or open girdle	10.75
Petticoat	5.50
Pyjamas	10.00
Raincoat	31.00
Shoes	15.00
Skirt	11.50
Slippers	5.50
Stockings/tights	0.75
Trousers	13.00
Vest:	
Cotton	2.50
Thermal	2.75

Part III. Working Clothes

Boiler suit	£12.50
Boots	16.75
Donkey-jacket	20.00
Dungarees	11.50
Jeans	12.50
Overalls	10.50
Suit	60.00
Wellingtons	12.00

Part IV. Boys' Clothing

	Small	Large
Dressing-gown	£8.60	£12.00
Duffle-coat	17.00	23.00
Jacket/anorak	11.00	16.00
Overcoat	18.25	26.00
Pyjamas	4.90	8.00
Raincoat	13.50	21.00
Shirt	4.30	6.50
Shoes	8.90	12.50
Slippers	3.50	5.00
Socks	0.85	1.05
Sweater	5.00	7.50
Trousers:		
Long	6.80	10.00
Short	4.50	5.50
Underpants	1.25	1.25
Vest	1.45	1.45
Wellingtons	4.15	6.20

Part V. Girls' Clothing

	Small	Large
Blouse	4.70	8.30
Brassière	3.00	3.00
Briefs	1.10	1.10
Cardigan	5.00	8.00
Dress:		
Summer weight	5.50	13.00
Winter weight	7.50	15.00
Dressing-gown	8.60	13.00
Duffle-coat	17.00	23.00
Jacket/anorak	11.00	16.00
Jumper	4.90	7.50
Nightdress	5.00	7.30
Overcoat	17.25	25.00
Pantie-girdle or open girdle	10.75	10.75
Petticoat	2.15	3.05
Pyjamas	4.90	8.00
Raincoat	13.50	20.00

	Small	*Large*
Shoes	£8.90	£12.50
Skirt	5.90	9.40
Slippers	3.50	5.00
Socks	0.85	1.05
Stockings/tights	0.75	0.75
Trousers	6.50	10.00
Vest	1.40	1.40
Wellingtons	4.15	6.20

Part VI. Baby Clothing

Napkin	£1.15
One-piece stretch sleeping-suit	4.00
Plastic pants	0.90
Pram-suit	6.50
Vest	1.00
Wrap/shawl	5.40

Appendix 4

Bedclothes Price List

This list, in schedule 1 of the Single Payments Regulations, is used in calculating single payments for bedclothes (see page 156).

Blanket:
  Cot   £5.70
  Single   15.00
  Double   18.00
Pillow   4.70
Pillow-case   2.10
Eiderdown (terylene):
  Single   16.00
  Double   22.00
Sheet:
  Polyester and cotton mix – Single   7.00
                              Double   9.00
  Flannelette – Cot   3.65
              Single   7.00
              Double   9.00
  Nylon – Single   5.20
          Double   6.80

Regulations in force in November 1984

Full title and Statutory Instrument No.	Referred to in this book as
Supplementary Benefit (Requirements) Regulations 1983 (No. 1399)	Requirements Regulations
Supplementary Benefit (Resources) Regulations 1981 (No. 1527)	Resources Regulations
Supplementary Benefit (Aggregation) Regulations 1981 (No. 1524)	Aggregation Regulations
Supplementary Benefit (Single Payments) Regulations 1981 (No. 1528)	Single Payments Regulations
Supplementary Benefit (Urgent Cases) Regulations 1981 (No. 1529)	Urgent Cases Regulations
Supplementary Benefit (Duplication and Overpayment) Regulations 1980 (No. 1580)	Duplication and Overpayment Regulations
Supplementary Benefit (Trade Disputes and Recovery from Earnings) Regulations 1980 (No. 1641)	Trade Disputes Regulations
Supplementary Benefit (Conditions of Entitlement) Regulations 1981 (No. 1526)	Conditions of Entitlement Regulations
Supplementary Benefit (Determination of Questions) Regulations 1980 (No. 1643)	Determination of Questions Regulations
Supplementary Benefit (Claims and Payments) Regulations 1981 (No. 1525)	Claims and Payments Regulations

Full title and Statutory Instrument No.	*Referred to in this book as*
Supplementary Benefit (Transitional) Regulations 1980 (No. 984)	Transitional Regulations
Social Security (Adjudication) Regulations 1984 (No. 451)	Adjudication Regulations
Housing Benefits Regulations 1982 (No. 1124)	Housing Benefits Regulations

Note: Many of these regulations were amended at various times between 1980 and 1984. References to the regulations in this book take account of amendments which had come into operation by the end of November 1984.

Index

MORE ABOUT PENGUINS, PELICANS AND PUFFINS

For further information about books available from Penguins please write to Dept EP, Penguin Books Ltd, Harmondsworth, Middlesex UB7 0DA.

In the U.S.A.: For a complete list of books available from Penguins in the United States write to Dept DG, Penguin Books, 299 Murray Hill Parkway, East Rutherford, New Jersey 07073.

In Canada: For a complete list of books available from Penguins in Canada write to Penguin Books Canada Ltd, 2801 John Street, Markham, Ontario L3R 1B4.

In Australia: For a complete list of books available from Penguins in Australia write to the Marketing Department, Penguin Books Australia Ltd, P.O. Box 257, Ringwood, Victoria 3134.

In New Zealand: For a complete list of books available from Penguins in New Zealand write to the Marketing Department, Penguin Books (N.Z.) Ltd, Private Bag, Takapuna, Auckland 9.

In India: For a complete list of books available from Penguins in India write to Penguin Overseas Ltd, 706 Eros Apartments, 56 Nehru Place, New Delhi 110019.

Know Your Rights:
The Questions and the Answers

WOMEN'S RIGHTS IN THE WORKPLACE

Tess Gill and Larry Whitty

Women and training * Working part-time * Maternity rights *
Women and new technology * Paid work at home * Women and
employment law * Creches and child-care at work

Whether you're employed in an office, a factory or a school,
Women's Rights in the Workplace is designed to arm you with the
information – and the expertise and confidence – to get a better
deal at work. Containing full, up-to-date information on women's
jobs, pay and conditions, it is the essential handbook for all working women.

YOUR SOCIAL SECURITY

Fran Bennett

School-leavers and social security * Benefit and one-parent families * Retirement pensions * Family income supplement

In practical question and answer format, here at last is a handbook
to guide you through the maze of social security benefit regulations. Whether you are out of work, a single parent, retired, disabled or simply grossly underpaid, this book will give you the essential information to help you claim your rights from the State.

Other volumes in this new Penguin series *Know Your Rights: The
Questions and the Answers* cover marital rights and the rights of
ethnic minorities.

THE IMPOVERISHMENT OF BRITAIN

Peter Townsend

Since the early post-war years social conditions in Britain have deteriorated and poverty is increasing on a mass scale. This is the central argument of Peter Townsend's controversial book and is, he believes, the central problem of domestic politics.

The author begins by tracing the development of the problem – the growth of unemployment, the deprivation of racial minorities, unequal health provision and the erosion of public services. Next, he considers some of the major causes – the growth of multi-national corporations and international finance, Monetarism and anti-social planning of the economy, authoritarian management of the state and expanding arms expenditure.

From this powerful analysis, he draws out the kind of policies which are required to create a radically alternative Britain.

TOWARDS 2000

Raymond Williams

What sort of world will we have in 2000 AD?

Mass unemployment and nuclear war are two of the crises which may darken an uncertain future. Here, the radical thinker Raymond Williams, examines our current predicament and points the way forward. Taking his essay on Britain in the sixties as a starting point, Williams reassesses and extends the arguments of *The Long Revolution* (a book which set the guidelines for the socialist debate). In discussing the major changes within British society, he raises proposals for fresh political structures which take account of true equality and revitalized socialism.

'The nearest thing the British New Left has to a sage' – *Observer*

POLITICAL TRIALS IN BRITAIN

Peter Hain

Is law enforcement founded on political decisions?

Peter Hain examines this crucial issue, analysing overtly political cases involving official secrecy, conspiracy, public order, trade unions, Northern Ireland and race relations, and challenging the whole notion of the law as an impartial and technical instrument.

'A well-documented argument that discretionary power is exercised by the police, prosecuting authorities, magistrates and judges as a weapon to intimidate, discredit and exhaust those who "threaten the social and political status quo" ' – *The Times Literary Supplement*

'A valuable hunting ground for those who want to attack the alleged impartiality of the arms of the state' – *Tribune*

MORE ROUGH JUSTICE

Peter Hill and Martin Young
with Tom Sargant

Breaking all audience viewing records for television current affairs documentaries, *Rough Justice* has provoked a storm of public interest and outrage. Following the first series, four men convicted of murder were released from prison. In *More Rough Justice* (based on a further television series) the authors have reopened three further cases:

* A teenage boy is found dead with stab wounds; after hours of police questioning, his mother confesses to the murder
* A girl's body is found hidden in an oil tank; a worker at the plant who admitted that he knew her is convicted of murder
* A young woman is murdered *en route* to a railway station; even her family believe that the local train-spotter, now ten years into a life-sentence, is innocent

With the help of lawyers and forensic experts, Martin Young and Peter Hill set out to discover what really happened. Their findings – in an outstanding piece of investigative journalism and detective work – provide detailed and disturbing evidence to suggest that in all three cases there has been a serious miscarriage of justice.

A CHOICE OF PENGUINS

☐ **The English House Through Seven Centuries**
Olive Cook   £10.95

From Norman defensiveness and Tudor flourish to Georgian elegance and Victorian grandeur, this beautiful book records and describes the wealth of domestic architecture in Britain. With photographs by Edwin Smith.

☐ **The Daughters of Karl Marx**   £4.95

The letters of Jenny, Laura and Eleanor Marx: 'An enlightening introduction to the preoccupations, political and personal, of the Marx family' – Lionel Kochan. 'The tale they tell is riveting' – *Standard*

☐ **The First Day on the Somme**
Martin Middlebrook   £3.95

1 July 1916 was the blackest day of slaughter in the history of the British Army. 'The soldiers receive the best service a historian can provide: their story told in their own words' – *Guardian*

☐ **Lord Hervey's Memoirs**   £4.95

As an intimate of the Royal Court – and as a particularly witty and malicious raconteur – Lord Hervey was ideally equipped to write this sparkling account of royal personalities, politics and intrigues, 1727–37.

☐ **Some Lovely Islands Leslie Thomas**   £5.95

The islands off the coast of Britain, and their islanders, are celebrated in this delightful book by well-known novelist Leslie Thomas. With photographs by Peter Chèze-Brown.

☐ **Harold Nicolson: Diaries and Letters 1930–64**   £4.95

A selection of Nicolson's famous diaries and letters. 'A brilliant portrait of English society . . . a touching self-portrait of a highly intelligent and civilized man' – Kenneth Clark

A CHOICE OF PENGUINS

☐ *A Colder Eye* **Hugh Kenner** £4.95

A study of the modern Irish writers. 'Anyone interested in language, in theatre history, in, indeed, the great comic literature of Joyce, Beckett and O'Brien will find this a highly enjoyable read' – *Punch*

☐ *The Europeans* **Luigi Barzini** £2.95

Witty, stylish and provocative, this is a veteran journalist's-eye view of the past and present character of the British, French, Germans, Italians and Dutch. 'Fascinating . . . read it immediately' – *The New York Times*

☐ *In Search of Ancient Astronomies* **Ed. E. C. Krupp** £4.95

Forming an introduction to archaeo-astronomy, a series of new essays on the world's most spectacular ancient monuments, from Stonehenge to the pyramids. 'Outstanding . . . accessible even to the beginner' – Patrick Moore

☐ *Clinging to the Wreckage* **John Mortimer** £2.50

The bestselling autobiography by the creator of Rumpole and the playwright author of *A Voyage Round My Father*. 'Enchantingly witty . . . England would be a poor place without Mr Mortimer' – Auberon Waugh

☐ *Chips: The Diaries of Sir Henry Channon* £4.95

'Chips' Channon, M.P., knew everybody that was anybody. Here, from the abdication of Edward VIII to the coronation of Elizabeth II, he serves up history with an irresistible 'H.P.' sauce of gossip and glamour.

☐ *The Miracle of Dunkirk* **Walter Lord** £2.95

'This is contemporary history at its most readable' – *The New York Times*. 'It gives an effective new polish to the golden legend' – *The Times*

PENGUINS ON HEALTH, SPORT AND PHYSICAL FITNESS

☐ **The F-Plan Audrey Eyton** £1.95

The book that started the diet revolution of the decade, *The F-Plan* is, quite simply, a phenomenon! Here Britain's top diet expert, Audrey Eyton, provides the recipes, menus and remarkable health revelations – everything you need to know to make that slim, fit future realistically possible.

☐ **The F-Plan Calorie Counter and Fibre Chart**
Audrey Eyton £1.95

An indispensable companion to the F-Plan diet. High-fibre fresh, canned and packaged foods are listed, there's a separate chart for drinks, *plus* a wonderful new selection of effortless F-Plan meals.

☐ **The Arthritis Book**
Ephraim P. Engleman and Milton Silverman £2.50

Written for patients and their families, this is a clear, expert and up-to-date handbook on arthritis, containing information on the latest drugs and treatments, and advice on how to cope.

☐ **Vogue Natural Health and Beauty**
Bronwen Meredith £7.50

Health foods, yoga, spas, recipes, natural remedies and beauty preparations are all included in this superb, fully illustrated guide and companion to the bestselling *Vogue Body and Beauty Book*.

☐ **Alternative Medicine Andrew Stanway** £3.25

From Acupuncture and Alexander Technique to Macrobiotics, Radionics and Yoga, Dr Stanway provides an expert and objective guide to thirty-two therapies, for everyone interested in alternatives to conventional medicine.

☐ **The Runner's Handbook**
Bob Glover and Jack Shepherd £2.95

Supplementary exercises, injuries, women on the run, running shoes and clothing, training for competitions and lots more information is included in this internationally famous manual.

PENGUIN COOKERY BOOKS

☐ *Mediterranean Cookbook* **Arabella Boxer**   £2.50

A gastronomic grand tour of the region: 'The best book on Mediterranean cookery I have read since Elizabeth David' – *Sunday Express*

☐ *Josceline Dimbleby's Book of Puddings, Desserts and Savouries*   £1.75

By the *Sunday Telegraph*'s popular cookery columnist, a book 'full of the most delicious and novel ideas for every type of pudding, from the tasty, filling family variety to exotic pastry concoctions' – *Lady*

☐ *Penguin Cordon Bleu Cookery*   £2.50

Find the highest quality of European cooking with a French accent in this classic Penguin cookery book, prepared by Rosemary Hume and Muriel Downes, co-principals of the English Cordon Bleu School.

☐ *A Concise Encyclopedia of Gastronomy* **André Simon**   £7.50

Expertly edited, with wit and wisdom, this is the most comprehensive survey ever published, and a treasure-house of good food.

☐ *An Invitation to Indian Cooking* **Madhur Jaffrey**   £2.95

A witty, practical and irresistible handbook on Indian cooking by the presenter of the highly successful BBC television series.

☐ *The Chocolate Book* **Helge Rubinstein**   £2.95

Part cookery book, part social history, this sumptuous book offers an unbeatable selection of recipes – chocolate cakes, ice-creams, pies, truffles, drinks and savoury dishes galore.

PENGUIN CROSSWORD BOOKS